INTERVIEW POWER
Selling Yourself Face To Face

Tom Washington

Mount Vernon Press
Bellevue, Washington

Mount Vernon Press
1750 112th NE C-224
Bellevue, Washington 98004
(425) 454-6982

Important note: None of the advice in this book should be construed as constituting legal advice. If you feel a prospective employer has discriminated against you, you should contact the appropriate government agencies and a competent attorney to assess your rights and options under state and federal law.

The editor was Fran Mason (Seattle, Washington).
The cover design was by Charles Fuhrman (Forest Knolls, California). Charles died on May 17, 1995. He left behind many powerful book designs and many special friends.
The typesetting was by Steve Wozenski (Novato, California).
The illustrations and cartoons were drawn by Edith Allgood (Berkeley, California).

Cataloging-in-Publication Data:

Washington, Tom, 1949-
Interview power: selling yourself face to face
        274 p. cm.
ISBN 0-931213-15-0: $14.95
Includes bibliographical references and index
Bibliography: p.
1. Employment interviewing 2. Job hunting I. Title
HF5549.5.I6W37 2000
650.14—dc20

Dedicated to the ones I love

This work is dedicated to Tim, Dan, Molly, and Brian.

You four are much blessed with God-given talents. May you have the determination to fully develop those talents and the wisdom to fully use them. By using your talents and remaining true to your values you will guarantee your success in life. Create a vision for yourself and do all in your power to achieve it. May you continue to seek the One who loves you and watches over you.

Acknowledgments

Many people have shared in this endeavor who deserve a great deal of thanks. As always, my first thanks must go to my wife Lois. She keeps me on target and prevents me from dispensing what would otherwise be confusing advice. Her editing and sharp-eyed proofreading have saved me many times.

Charles Fuhrman has designed three book covers for me. He has a great sense of design and color and knows how to produce powerful covers. Charles died on May 17, 1995, shortly after completing the cover to *Interview Power*. He will be missed by many.

Fran Mason has done an excellent job of editing *Interview Power* and has strengthened its readability.

I want to thank those who spent a lot of time proofreading and catching those little errors that try to slip through. I want to thank Ian Buchanan, Don and Pauline Burns, Beau Hamilton, Gary Kanter, Barbara Robertson, Suzan Schneider, and Richard Wasser.

A hearty thanks to Bob Couture for his help at a critical time.

I want to express my appreciation to Howard Figler and Dick Knowdell for their friendship and their many contributions to the field of career development.

Tony Lee of the *National Business Employment Weekly* has provided me with many opportunities to express my ideas. He has played a key role in creating an outstanding forum for career and job specialists around the country to share their insights with the public.

I want to thank David Roy for his cheerful attitude and his constant encouragement. He has dedicated himself to empowering people to obtain the jobs they deserve.

CONTENTS

Chapter 1

WINNING AT INTERVIEWING

Elbert Hubbard, a nineteenth century writer, once wrote, "There's something rare, something finer far, something more scarce than ability. It's the ability to recognize ability." That quote summarizes the entire interviewing process. The interviewer's challenge is to recognize ability; your challenge is to sell yourself so thoroughly that the interviewer cannot possibly fail to recognize your ability.

This book is about learning how to sell yourself. While the typical job hunter gets sweaty palms just thinking about interviews, you can go into each interview with confidence, looking forward to the challenge that each interview presents. You'll know how to answer all of the difficult questions and how to overcome objections. Most importantly, you'll know how to get job offers.

You may be thinking, "I'm pretty good once I get face to face with the interviewer." I'll guarantee, however, that by studying this book you'll improve your interviewing ability by at least 20%, and probably closer to 50%. Many readers will double and triple their interviewing ability. Just a 10% improvement can make the difference between being the number one choice and the number two choice. Pause for a moment and consider how you would respond to questions like:

"Tell me about yourself."

"What are the major problems you have with coworkers?"

"What is your greatest weakness?"

"Give me an example of a time when you were unable to work out a disagreement with your boss."

"Why should I hire you?"

"What is the biggest mistake you ever made?"

"Describe the last time you were angry."

Those are tough questions, and to answer them you'll need to completely understand the psychology of interviewing. You need to know what is going on in the mind of the interviewer. You need to sense the person's hot buttons, and press them appropriately. Let's begin.

THE INTERVIEWING SCALE

It is useful to think of interviewing as a process in which your skills, attributes, and potential will be weighed on a balance scale against those of other candidates. At the end of the interviewing cycle, whoever has the most weight on his or her side of the scale will get the job offer. During an interview, weights are continually being added or subtracted from the scale, depending on the quality of your answers. By answering each question as effectively as possible, each of your answers will carry a little more weight than the answers of those who are less prepared than you. After the final interview there will be no doubt who should get the job.

The balance scale metaphor also demonstrates the importance of always using your best example and telling it vividly. Assume that you have a great example that would add five pounds to your side of the scale, but under the stress of the interview you're not able to recall it. Instead, you remember an example that's worth only three pounds. Repeatedly forgetting your best examples and substituting them with less impressive examples could easily cost you several pounds on your side of the scale. Unless your background has placed you head and shoulders above the competition, this failure to present your best examples may cost you the job offer.

INTERVIEWING PRINCIPLES

Effective interviewing is an art which can be learned, and the pay-offs can be tremendous. You'll work so hard to get each interview that it would be a shame to go into an interview unprepared. By knowing what to expect and by preparing for all of the difficult questions you'll encounter, you will greatly enhance your chance of receiving the job offer. The following fourteen principles provide you with an overview of things you should consider before going into an interview.

1. An interview is simply an opportunity for two people to meet and determine whether an employer-employee relationship will prove beneficial to both parties.

2. Interviewing is a two-way street. You're not begging for a job, you're an equal.

3. The employer is actually on your side. He or she has a need and has every reason to hope you are the right person to meet it. Keep the employer on your side through attentive listening, and by detecting the employer's real needs.

4. An objection is not a rejection, it is a request for more information. If the employer states, "You don't have as much experience as we normally want," he is not rejecting you. In fact, the person could be totally sold on you but for this one concern. Your task is to sell yourself and overcome that objection. You will do this by emphasizing your strengths, not by arguing.

5. Let the employer talk. You listen. The longer the employer talks at the beginning, the more you can learn about the organization. This will help you formulate positive responses.

6. Increase your chance for a second interview by dressing properly, being on time, listening intently, demonstrating potential and enthusiasm, appearing relaxed, providing brief, well thought-out responses, and asking a few intelligent questions.

7. Hiring decisions are based mostly on emotion. Do I like her? Will we get along? Will she accept criticism and be a good team worker? Being liked by the employer is just as important as having the qualifications.

8. Concentrate on giving examples of your accomplishments. Accomplishments demonstrate your potential. Stress how you can benefit the organization.

9. Be yourself, but also be your best. If you tend to be overly aggressive, consciously tone it down during the interview. If you have strong opinions on everything and like to express them, keep them to yourself. If you tend to be too quiet and reserved, try to be a little more outgoing and enthusiastic during the interview.

10. Use examples to back up any statements you make. Be prepared for questions like, "Are you good with details?" "Are you a hard worker?" "Can you handle difficult people?" You can begin your response with, "Yes, I am good with details. For example . . ."

11. Be able to explain any statements included in your resume, such as accomplishments or job duties. You can use your resume to predict many of the questions that will be asked. Practice describing your job duties in the most concise way possible.

12. Showing confidence in yourself will create a favorable impression. Such confidence can come only from truly knowing yourself and recognizing your own potential.

13. Send a thank-you note the evening of the interview. Some employers have never received a thank-you note, yet this simple courtesy frequently makes the difference between selection and rejection.

14. Relax and enjoy your interviews.

Chapter 2

KEY INTERVIEWING SKILLS

Active Listening

Active listening is one of the most critical interviewing skills you need to develop. Active listening can be defined as high-level listening in which your entire attention is focused on the person speaking—your body, face, and eyes all confirm you are listening. Through active listening you'll pick up the cues and clues that the interviewer is consciously and unconsciously giving you. If you are well prepared for the interview, you will be able to process the clues to determine the interviewer's needs and biases. This will enable you to respond appropriately to those needs or biases at an opportune time. Attentive listeners are highly regarded by employers.

Do not allow your mind to wander. Not only will you miss key information, but more than one interviewee has been embarrassed by not hearing a question and then having to ask that it be repeated.

To be an active listener you must truly want to hear everything the person says. When the interviewer pauses from time to time, don't jump in with a comment. Let the interviewer collect his thoughts, and then continue. Your willingness to allow the person to continue sends a positive message to the person, and will cause him to provide you with more information. After you ask a question it is particularly important to let the person know you are attentively listening to the response.

Do not be concerned if the interviewer does a lot of talking at the beginning of the interview. That's exactly what you want. You'll have plenty of opportunities to speak. In the meantime, listening carefully will give you an opportunity to learn valuable things about the person, the job, and the organization.

"Listen" with your body. Be relaxed, but don't slouch. You should always be looking at the speaker, but with a gentle look, never a stare. When people speak, they often look away from the listener for 5–20 seconds, but when the speaker's eyes return to you, your eyes should be gently looking at him or her. You should not be looking at your watch, looking out the window, or looking at objects in the office. Nod at appropriate times to signal you are really hearing what the person is saying.

As you listen, you should be taking in and interpreting everything. While listening, part of your brain is deciphering the information and deciding what to do with it. For example, employers are often cautious about mentioning serious problems that exist, yet will often allude to them in obscure ways. If you aren't listening actively, the words might go right past you, and an opportunity would be missed. The interviewer might indirectly indicate that the company is experiencing high turnover and, thus, is looking for evidence of strong company loyalty. By sensing the need, you could provide evidence that demonstrates you have the kind of loyalty the company desires.

You will approach each interview with your own agenda, looking for opportunities to sell those skills which you feel are important for the job. You must also be flexible. You may pick up clues from the interviewer that the skills you had planned to emphasize are not as important as some other skills you possess. Only an active listener can recognize the need for a change in strategy, and then be able to make the appropriate shift.

By concentrating on what the interviewer says, you'll be better able to use the information later in the interview. For example, the interviewer may have presented evidence that the position requires an ability to quickly gain the confidence of customers. A half hour may pass before you have the opportunity to cover that talent. Because you listened, you'll remember.

Do not assume that just because you have years of experience you are a good listener. Most of us have learned how to appear attentive with the appropriate nods, uh-huhs, and an occasional "I know what you mean." You undoubtedly can recognize fake listening, and you don't like it. A good listener makes the speaker feel that everything said is of great interest and that there is a desire to hear the whole story.

Real listening occurs when you hear and understand the words, you properly interpret the feelings behind the words, and the person feels he or she has been listened to.

Preparation

In interviewing there is no substitute for preparation and practice. Fortunately for you, most people spend little time preparing for interviews. They will get a good night's sleep, polish their shoes, take a shower, and hope for the best. Their attitude is, "Since I don't know what the interviewer will ask, I'll just give it my best shot."

But you can anticipate and prepare for the questions that will be asked in an interview. There are approximately 75 basic questions, all others being variations of these. Then there are the technical questions that can be asked of people in your field. These too can be predicted. Questions will also arise from information you've provided in your resume, particularly your accomplishments.

A complete discussion of the most commonly asked questions is covered in chapters 19 through 26. In each case, the principle behind answering the question is discussed, with an example often included.

To prepare your responses, simply jot down the points you want to make. Do not try to develop word-for-word responses. That would require memorization, which is not recommended—if you forget a point during an interview, you could become flustered and completely blow the response. Giving memorized answers can also make you seem mechanical. Instead of memorizing, you should practice your responses several times. This will help you feel confident and relaxed. Say your answers slightly differently each time to give them a ring of spontaneity.

Thorough preparation takes time. Preparing and practicing your responses to the 75 basic questions, the 5-8 technical questions you suspect could be asked, and the 8-10 questions likely to come off your resume, might require 15-25 hours. The effort spent, however, will pay big dividends.

Building Rapport

Building rapport quickly with your interviewer is a vital skill in the process of obtaining job offers. The main aspect of rapport is a mutual trust and respect. Begin by utilizing your best social skills. Use the person's name several times throughout the interview, but don't overdo it. Use the name of the company and department on several occasions. Speaking the interviewer's language, including jargon and technical terms, goes a long way in causing the person to feel that you are "one of us." In addition to a courteous and friendly manner, attentive listening is critical to building rapport.

Establishing rapport creates an openness and a freer exchange of ideas—always a positive result in an interview. When rapport is established, each party feels better about the other.

Be Yourself/Be Your Best

The material in this chapter will provide you with many techniques to help you perform successfully during an interview. When you're using techniques, however, there is a danger of becoming too mechanical in your responses. As you use these techniques, remember to **Be Yourself**. By acting natural, relaxed, and confident, you will do well. My advice is to also **Be Your Best**. It is important, for example, to show enthusiasm during an interview. However, you may not be a naturally enthusiastic person. During an interview, then, you must consciously turn up your enthusiasm a notch or two. You are still being you, but you are being the best you are capable of. You should not try to raise your level of enthusiasm four or five notches above what is natural for you. That would be asking too much and would be self-defeating.

Getting More Information About The Job

Interviewers generally spend several minutes at the beginning of an interview describing the job and its requirements. Too frequently, however, the information you have about the job is still sketchy when the interviewer suddenly asks a really tough question. Without knowledge of where the organization is headed or what challenges it's facing, providing an effective answer will be difficult.

Suppose the interviewer begins by asking about your strengths without providing you with much background information about the job or the organization. Since you have many strengths and want to emphasize the right ones, it is important to have more information. You could respond by stating, "I've got a lot to offer, but in order to cover just the right points, it would help a lot to know more about the position and what your needs are." This will cause the interviewer to realize that further information is needed. Even after the interviewer gives you more information, you can still ask two or three questions to further clarify the job requirements. Practice how you will respond when such difficult questions arise early in the interview. This will give you the confidence to request more information. The success of your interview may depend on it.

Let Others Speak For You

When you're answering questions in an interview, let what others have said illustrate positive things about you. For example, in response to a question you might say, "My boss felt some of my most valuable attributes were..." Granted, that person is not there to confirm what you've just said, but if you have successfully established your credibility, your statement will be accepted. You can also quote customers, vendors, and coworkers.

Learn To Talk About Yourself

During an interview you will spend 40–60% of the time talking—mostly about yourself. Much of that time will be spent describing experiences, but you will also be describing the type of person you are. The interviewer will ask questions such as, "Tell me about yourself," "How would you describe yourself?" or "What would your friends say about you?" The problem with this is that most people spend very little time throughout their lives talking about themselves. People spend a lot of time talking about what they do—the restaurants, plays, concerts, sports events, and vacation spots they've been to—but they rarely discuss the kind of person they are. No wonder interviewing is difficult for most people.

Think about it. When was the last time you discussed whether you are a pragmatist or an idealist, or whether you are compassionate, easy-going, flexible, or resourceful? Since you're not used to it, you may not be very good at it. It takes practice. For that reason I strongly suggest that you complete the personality skills exercise on page 69. After you write about yourself, find someone you can share your thoughts with. If you can't find someone, simply record your thoughts on your personality skills using a tape recorder. Just hearing yourself talk about yourself will help you feel more comfortable and will improve your effectiveness in interviews.

Ending The Interview

Develop a close for your interviews by practicing a summary of the benefits you offer. Although the points you will want to make in the summary will vary somewhat from job to job, many of your points will be used repeatedly in interviews. You should be able to predict your primary assets so you can create a list of those points for the close.

Since you will not always be given a specific opportunity to summarize, you should sense when the interview is drawing to a close. That will often occur as the interviewer asks if you have any questions. Go ahead and ask those questions, but as soon as the interviewer finishes answering your last question you could interject, "Perhaps this would be a good time to summarize my strengths for this position," or "Maybe I should just take a couple of minutes to pull it all together and tell you why I think I'm the person for this job."

Chapter 3

OVERCOMING OBJECTIONS

Performing well in interviews requires an ability to recognize the important difference between rejections and objections. Virtually everyone must overcome several objections during the interviewing process before a job offer is made. People who perceive an objection as a rejection, however, may become defensive or simply give up and assume all is lost. Thus, the failure to understand objections and differentiate them from rejection can cause interviewees to sabotage their own success in an interview.

An Objection Is Not A Rejection

An objection is not a rejection. It is simply a request for more information. An employer may be very impressed with you, yet still have concerns such as your lack of experience in a specific area, or your four jobs in the last six years. Often all the interviewer wants is reassurance that you learn quickly or are now seeking a stable job. If the objection is handled well, a job offer may very well be made to you.

Good interviewees, like good salespeople, must learn to anticipate objections. Since cost is a common objection salespeople face, an effective salesperson might open with, "This is not the least expensive lawnmower on the market. But a recent survey showed that the average lawnmower lasts eight years, while ours are averaging over twelve years of trouble-free service." This way the objection may be overcome before it is ever expressed. It is important to anticipate an objection because once an objection is stated, it is much more difficult to neutralize or overcome.

Predict The Objections You'll Face

The first step in overcoming objections is predicting what they will be and developing effective responses to them. Objections are any aspects of you that raise doubts about your ability to do the job well or fit in well in the organization. The biggest objection of all is: "You don't have enough experience." The following circumstances are likely to give rise to some types of objections: you were fired from your last job; you appear to be a job hopper; there is a major gap in your work history; you're changing careers; you don't have a college degree and you're applying for a position that normally requires one; you have three or more years of college education but never received a degree; you're over

50 years of age; or you have too little or too much experience. The list could go on. Objections can also arise if you lack a certain type of knowledge or experience the employer is looking for in an ideal candidate.

Sensing a potential objection is exactly what Pat did. Pat was interviewing for a job in which she would train clients to use an accounting software package which cost several thousand dollars. The concern, which was never spoken directly but which was implied, was whether Pat could learn the package quickly enough to meet the employer's needs. Pat looked for the earliest opportunity to address this objection. Before the objection was directly mentioned, Pat shared that she had learned a complex accounting software package very quickly at her current job. As a result, the invoice error rate had decreased by 80%. Pat never stated that because she had learned the one package so quickly she could learn theirs as well. She didn't need to. Since the employer had not stated the objection, Pat was subtle in the way she dealt with it. She did, however, let them know how she had managed to learn the package so quickly—she had taken the manual home with her and studied it on her own time. Pat recalled that as she told her story, she could sense that her future supervisor was gaining confidence in her. By recognizing an objection and then neutralizing it, Pat was offered the job.

Since you will probably lack some desired skill or knowledge, look for ways to sell the fact that you learn quickly.

The value of anticipating objections is further demonstrated by John. His story was told to me by the person who hired him. Very early in the interview, John used an opportunity to reveal something about himself while at the same time selling himself. He knew it would come out during the interview that he had spent a year in prison for assault. When he was invited to talk about himself, he described how he had taught an English course while he was in prison. John emphasized that what made him feel really good was making valuable use of his prison time. Because of his candidness and the realization that he had a strong work ethic, this potentially disastrous piece of information was turned into something positive. He was offered a material handler position with a Fortune 500 company and became a valued employee.

Don't Argue With Employers

When overcoming an objection, don't argue with the employer. If the employer states, "You really don't have enough experience in this field," a good response might be:

I realize there may be others with more years of experience, but I really feel the quality of my experience is the key. Because of the variety of things I've done, and the level of responsibility I was given, I think my five years are equivalent to most people with ten. There's no question in my mind that I can do an outstanding job for you.

Describe Related Experience

Another way to deal with the issue of not having enough experience is to describe all of your *related* experience. Related experience is similar to what the employer is looking for, but not exactly the same. Your challenge is to get the employer believing that your experience is close to what they need. The more successful you are at making the employer see this similarity, the more likely you are to overcome the objection and get the job offer.

A classic story told by John Crystal reveals the importance of recognizing related experience in order to overcome objections. In the mid–1970s, Bill was interviewing for a middle management position. During the interview he was told that the person who got the job, in addition to the many other management duties, would manage the company-owned cafeteria. Bill had never managed a cafeteria before, and neither had the other remaining candidate. In this position, the head cook and cafeteria manager would actually run the day-to-day operations, but Bill would be responsible for the budget and approving major decisions made by the staff. If Bill had been like most job seekers, he would have said, "Well, I've never run a cafeteria before, but I am an excellent manager and I learn quickly. I know I could do an excellent job." He could have said that, and it would not have been a bad answer, but he had a better idea. In a flash Bill recalled that while he was stationed in Vietnam during the mid-60s, he was responsible for transporting warm food from the mess hall to troops in the field by Jeep, truck, tank, or even helicopter. Bill realized that his experience was not exactly what the employer had in mind, but he recognized that it was *related* to what they were seeking, so he decided to make the most of this example.

Bill also realized that he faced an objection if he did not successfully get the employer to buy his story. So he told the story with flair and vividness. He got the job and was convinced that his story had tipped the balance in his favor. He didn't get the job because of his Vietnam experience. But when the employer had to decide between two very qualified people, Bill had demonstrated that he had related experience regarding cafeterias. That was enough to enable him to edge out his competitor. I also believe that by telling a vivid tale, full of strong visual images, Bill revealed many qualities that also helped sell him. I am sure that the executive hiring Bill realized that Bill cared so greatly about his customers—those soldiers out in the trenches—that he provided a service far beyond what was expected. The executive knew that Bill would do the same in the position he was being interviewed for. Bill was obviously the person for the job.

Clearly, Bill overcame a potential objection by selling his related experience. Pat overcame a potential objection by selling her ability to learn new systems quickly. Both succeeded in heading off an objection caused by their lack of particular experience. Sometimes, however, the employer will state that you lack some experience before you've had an opportunity to anticipate or deal with the objection. In that case, you should sell your related experience *and* your ability to learn quickly. Use a highly vivid story to demonstrate your willingness to do whatever is necessary to become proficient quickly.

Chapter 4

PROJECT ENTHUSIASM AND POTENTIAL

Enthusiasm and potential will land you more job offers than any other qualities. The two are inseparable.

EMPLOYERS DESIRE ENTHUSIASTIC PEOPLE

Employers seek enthusiastic people who really want to get involved in the job. You should demonstrate genuine enthusiasm—enthusiasm for yourself, enthusiasm for the job, enthusiasm for your future boss, and enthusiasm for the company.

Enthusiasm For Yourself

Enthusiasm for yourself will come through by showing self-confidence and your belief that you can do the job. When you're asked "What is your greatest strength?" you must be able to respond with enthusiasm. If you can't stir up enthusiasm about yourself with a question like that, you won't be able to do it at all.

It's hard to sound enthusiastic if you're overly nervous, since nervous people tend to either speak too rapidly or in a monotone.

Neither will present the right impression. That's why preparation is so important. Preparation gives you confidence and minimizes nervousness.

Enthusiasm For The Job

You'll demonstrate enthusiasm for the job by showing interest throughout the interview and by asking questions that reveal your genuine interest in the job. One of the best ways to demonstrate enthusiasm for the job is to tell the interviewer that you really want the job and that you know you can perform it well. When it comes across as genuine, you'll score many points with the interviewer.

Enthusiasm For Your Future Boss

You'll show enthusiasm for your prospective boss by listening intently to everything he says. Look for an opportunity to ask for his management style and philosophy (if he hasn't described it already) and then listen enthusiastically. Asking questions to further clarify his style and philosophy will show that you really are interested in everything he has to say. You could make small comments like, "I think that's really important," "I think the best managers share that philosophy," or "I don't think there are a lot of managers who really develop their staff, as you obviously do." At the end of the interview, perhaps as you're standing up to get ready to leave, you could say, "I would really like working for you." Whatever you say must be genuine. Any hint of apple polishing will actually cost you points.

Enthusiasm For The Organization

Let the interviewer know that you want to work for the organization. During the interview you could ask what she likes and dislikes about the organization. She will undoubtedly emphasize positives. Toward the end of the interview you could state what you like about the organization. This could be based on what the interviewer has stated, what you've learned from people who work for or have worked for the organization, plus what you've read about the organization. This is an excellent way to demonstrate that you've everything possible to learn about the organization.

Selling Your Enthusiasm

Summing up your enthusiasm at the end of an interview is very effective. You can virtually always discern when the interview is coming to a close. That's when you look for the opportunity to speak a concluding word. Even if the interview comes to an abrupt end and you haven't had an opportunity to give a summary of why you should be hired, you can do it even as the two of you are standing and about to shake hands as you part. You could simply stand there and say something like:

> I appreciate your taking time to talk with me today. I have to say that this is a job I would really like. It seems to make good use of my strengths and I would enjoy it a lot. It's the kind of job you can really sink your teeth into. And everything I've heard about DataSystems plus what you've told me today indicates that it's well managed and develops its people. I like that. And I can tell I would enjoy working for you.

A statement like this may not seem to be a big deal, but I can guarantee it will resonate in the mind of the hiring manager. There are a lot of intangibles that get considered as a hiring decision is pondered. Virtually all managers want to give the job to someone who really wants it. Even if one or two others are more qualified, if you clearly want the job, and the manager has concluded you would fit into the organization, she will look for ways to justify hiring you.

Suppose the field has been narrowed to two equally qualified people. The employer will ask many questions to determine who is the best choice. A common question is, "If we offered you the position, would you accept it?" Notice the difference in the following two responses.

| Sandra: | Yeah, I definitely would accept it. The job seems interesting. |

I'm excited about this job. I like the philosophy of management and the steady growth of the This job will utilize my strengths and I'm ready to get started.

ese two people, there is little question as

nthusiastic is to be genuinely enthusiastic idered your long- and short-term goals, u attain those goals, it will be easy to

Demonstrate Enthusiasm Throughout The Interview

Enthusiasm is not demonstrated in just one response to one question. It must be demonstrated throughout the interview. It starts with listening. Really listening to the interviewer shows respect as well as enthusiasm. You can also show enthusiasm by speaking positively about previous jobs or supervisors. Describe how you put all of your energy into a job and describe the results you've achieved.

I am convinced that enthusiasm has gotten more people jobs than any other single quality. But because of the stress of interviews, most people tend to speak in a monotone and appear unenthusiastic. Some reduce their level of enthusiasm even further because of the mistaken notion that they should play "hard to get." At the end of an interview, if you truly want the job, tell the interviewer so. Be enthusiastic. When it comes down to two people who are equally qualified, the person most enthusiastic about the job will almost always get the offer.

Perform An Enthusiasm Check

Because enthusiasm is so important I encourage people to perform an enthusiasm check about every ten minutes during an interview. If you are well prepared for the interview, you can use part of your thinking process to check your enthusiasm level even while you are in the midst of answering a question.

If you realize your enthusiasm has waned, you should not try to instantly raise it several notches; that might seem obvious and contrived. Instead, since enthusiasm usually drops as you get too relaxed, you can begin by merely sitting up straighter in your chair. Over a period of two or three minutes, you should then introduce more hand gestures, raise the level of your voice slightly, and add more feeling to what you say. When you are saying something particularly important, raise your voice slightly, speed up your words a bit, and put more emphasis on key words. As you practice interviewing with yourself or others, record yourself and notice your enthusiasm level. If you can tell it is low, the interviewer will detect it also. It's something you need to work on.

POTENTIAL EQUALS FUTURE WORTH

Your potential is your future worth to an organization. Demonstrating enthusiasm without demonstrating potential will seldom lead to a job offer. The two must go together. Your enthusiasm will give the employer confidence that you want the job and that you will work hard at it. But if you don't also demonstrate your potential, you will not receive an offer.

Although companies occasionally use elaborate personality tests to determine potential, past success is still the best predictor of future success. If you are a top salesperson at your present company and you are interviewing for a new sales position, your past success will give the sales manager the confidence that you will continue to sell well. If you've been fired from four sales positions because of poor results, you'll have your work cut out for you as you try to convince a sales manager that you really do have potential.

Demonstrate Potential Through Accomplishments

Potential is best demonstrated by telling the employer about your accomplishments. For example, consider Paula, who is returning to work after 20 years out of the job market. She is applying for Administrative Assistant with a small association that represents pharmacists. Membership in the association has dropped because pharmacists feel they have not been effectively represented. In walks Paula, with no paid work experience and only one year of college, to compete with college graduates who have experience working with associations. Even with this competition, Paula lands the job, thanks to her one-year term as president of the PTA. During that year, attendance at meetings increased 60% over the previous year, and fund-raising activities brought in twice as much money. Paula also organized a banquet that people are still talking about. And she was considered to be the primary lobbying force for new state legislation that benefited her school district. By sharing these accomplishments, she proved that she could help turn the pharmacists' association around. That's potential.

Selling Potential Can Overcome A Lack Of Experience

Selling potential can get you job offers when others have more direct experience. Tim, who has been the chief financial officer of three companies, states that among the 30 or more people he has hired, he has never hired the "most qualified" person. He is quick to say he always hires qualified people. In fact, candidates are not even interviewed unless they have demonstrated competence in all key areas. But after narrowing the field down to two or three, he usually finds himself drawn to the person who shows great drive and desire. That person has never been the one with the most direct experience. It seems that those with the most experience generally fail to fully demonstrate enthusiasm and potential.

An interesting thing occurs during an interview as you sell your enthusiasm and potential. It begins with the employer's decision to interview you. Perhaps out of the six who were invited for interviews, you were rated number six, merely because you lacked some experience that was desired which the other candidates had. As you learned about the job, you knew it would be a challenge for you, but you also knew you could do it, and you knew you would enjoy experiencing a steep learning curve. As a result, your enthusiasm came out spontaneously during your interviews. You also related some interesting stories which demonstrated your strong work ethic, your desire for growth, and your ability to successfully take on new challenges. You came across as a person who would fit in well with the team. Three others who had more experience did not demonstrate such qualities and did not get second interviews.

When you learned you were being invited back for a second interview, your desire for the job motivated you to do more research on the organization. You learned about some problems (or challenges) you felt you could really tackle and help solve. In the second interview, you maintained your high level of enthusiasm and you sold your potential by sharing experiences that demonstrated your ability to contribute in these problem areas. You weren't aware of it yet, but the employer began to actually picture you in the job. The employer began leaning toward choosing you. As the employer's preference for you became stronger, she realized that she actually liked you better than the other two candidates. She hesitated to hire you, however, because on paper you were not as strong as the other two. But then she began a justification process: Granted, she might have to spend more time training you, but at least you would be trained in her methods. The other two could come in tomorrow and handle the job from day one, but they might insist on using their old methods.

Your ability to sell both your potential and your ability to learn new processes quickly made the employer realize that even though the other two candidates could do the job better for the first several months, your drive and ambition would probably put you ahead of them after six months. Can you see how this process unfolds during two or three interviews? It accurately describes the thought process that occurs in the minds of employers.

Being able to demonstrate enthusiasm and potential is just as crucial to the experienced person as it is for the less-experienced person. If you are experienced, let your enthusiasm come through as you explain how much you enjoy your field or work. Demonstrate your potential by discussing recent, solid, work-related accomplishments. This will indicate to the employer that there are many future accomplishments yet to come.

Chapter 5

MASTER THE ART OF STORY TELLING

Aloof as they may seem, employers are actually begging you to get them excited. Show that you can make or save them money, solve their operational problems, or ease their workloads, and they'll be thrilled to hire you. Merely saying you can increase productivity or get staff members to work as a team isn't enough. You must support your claims with vivid examples. People remember best those things that are stored in their minds as pictures. In fact, the latest brain research reveals that memories are stored as 3-D pictures. That means if your words do not create any images or emotions in the minds of employers, those words will literally pass in one ear and out the other—there will be no impact or long-term memory.

Consider what happens when a person is asked to describe himself. He may declare that he is hard working, energetic, a true leader, and a person who successfully juggles multiple tasks. He may be trying to sell too many things at once and doesn't do a good job with any of them. If he doesn't back up any of the claims with examples, none of the points will be remembered after he leaves the interview.

Employers Will Remember You For Weeks

Using anecdotes to describe job skills is a highly effective interview technique. In less than three minutes, you can tell a powerful story that will make interviewers remember you favorably for days, weeks, or even months after the interview. Since employers know that the best predictor of future success is past success, tell stories which vividly describe your successes.

Stories Have Impact

Stories are important because they say so much about you in an evocative, concentrated way. Paul Green, founder of Behavioral Technology in Memphis, Tennessee, teaches corporations how to utilize behavior-based interviewing, a system of interviewing in which each question requires an example from the interviewee. Paul gives an excellent example of how telling stories in an interview can make a difference. While he was conducting an interview, he asked the candidate for an example that would demonstrate a strong commitment to completing tasks. The candidate described a time when he had had his appendix removed on a Thursday and was back in the office on Monday—to the dismay of everyone. His explanation was that work was piling up and he might as well do everything he could, even though he was unable to work a full day for the first week. The story provided strong evidence that he was a driven, hard-working person. The memory he created was that he was "the appendix guy." To this day, when Paul thinks about this person, all he has to say to himself is, "the appendix guy," and a flood of memories and emotions return. The beauty of stories is that they can evoke a recollection of many skills, qualities, abilities, and characteristics.

When telling stories, provide all of the key information. Describe the situation and the challenges you faced. Then describe your analysis and the recommendations you made. Next, describe what you did and the results you obtained. Look for interesting tidbits and details which, though not crucial for understanding what occurred, will provide a stronger visual image of what you did.

Ron Saves A Processing Plant

A client shared a story with me that included vivid details and tidbits; it is a story I'll never forget. Ron had worked for 25 years in the management of seafood-processing plants in Oregon, Washington, and Alaska. Because of his reputation for working effectively with unions, he was asked to take over a plant in the Caribbean which was experiencing serious labor unrest. Always one for a challenge, Ron took it on. One day, about a week after he arrived at the Caribbean plant, he found himself surrounded by ten workers. When they began accusing him of trying to destroy the union, he simply faced them down and reiterated the changes he felt needed to be made. When he finished speaking, he walked through the crowd and began heading back to his office. As he walked away, he knew that one of the leaders had pulled out a gun and had pointed it at his back. Although his heart was racing, he kept walking and did not turn around. He was sure that at any moment he was going to have a bullet in his back. He had never been more frightened in his life. When he got back to his office he realized he had been so scared he actually wet his pants. He said it with laughter, of course, and we both laughed together. I heard that story over ten years ago, yet I still recall it most vividly.

Whenever I recall this story, I have very strong memories of Ron. The story didn't end there. Ron showed the workers that he could not be intimidated and that he was a man of integrity. The workers began to end their work slowdown, and they began to have confidence that he would be fair with them. Within six months the unrest was a distant memory and the plant began making a profit again. I'm not suggesting that in an interview Ron should mention his incontinence, but I'm pointing out how this detail makes the story more striking. Similarly, by imprinting vivid images in the brains of employers, you will be better remembered and more highly regarded.

All Experiences Can Be Told Vividly

Software engineers and other technical people tell me that their projects simply don't translate into colorful stories like the one described above. I agree with them to some extent—few of us have such dramatic stories to tell. But anyone can still tell a vivid story by emphasizing the challenges faced and by graphically describing how the problems were overcome. It's the details of a story that create strong visual images and strong emotional memories.

TELLING EFFECTIVE STORIES

There are several techniques for effectively telling stories. These techniques work very well, and because few job candidates use them, they can really make you stand out.

A Nonwork Experience With A Work Experience

One technique is to combine a nonwork experience with a work-related experience. The nonwork-related experience may be especially vivid or have a particularly useful "hook" in it which will help the employer remember you. A hook is any word-picture or imagery that will help a person recall a story. While the hook need not be a critical point of the story, it may be. The nonwork experience might be selected simply because it is the best experience you have which demonstrates a certain skill. Combining the nonwork experience with a recent work experience can help create a vivid picture of you that communicates a lot about your skills and qualities. It can demonstrate that these skills and qualities are an integral part of your being, as you use the skills both on and off the job. A nonwork experience could come from volunteer work such as being an officer or chairperson in a professional association, it could be related to a hobby, or it could come from any type of experience that is not directly associated with a job. Let's look at an example where the question was, "What is your greatest strength?"

> My greatest strength is my ability to take on difficult projects. I guess I just like the challenge. And people know that if I take something on, I'm going to get it done right. I'm an officer of a ski club that loves to ski at Crystal Mountain, where you have great snow and a beautiful view of Mount Rainier. We skied there often enough that we wanted to have our own lodge there. The problem was we couldn't afford one. And if we raised the dues too high, we'd lose some of our members. After three weeks of discussing the deal, virtually everyone thought it was a dead issue. I wasn't ready to give up, though. I studied tax codes and every angle imaginable to finance the project. Eventually I came up with a way that our more affluent members could own shares in the $500,000 project and would receive a very secure return that would be tax free. Sixteen months later we had a beautiful lodge.

> Another experience happened recently. The president of my company wanted to create a totally new product. We had the engineering _____ bility, but we had no way to finance it. After trying numerous

avenues, with nothing working, I suggested trying a joint venture with a Japanese company. I had studied joint ventures that had failed as well as ones that had succeeded. When they failed it was usually because the Japanese firm would gain new technology without giving much back to the joint venture partner. I identified a Japanese firm that already had had two successful joint ventures—one with an American company and the other with a German company. They really seemed to understand the idea of win-win. I was given permission to pursue a joint venture with the firm and after nine months of negotiating, finalized a deal. One year into the joint venture, both parties are satisfied. We got the financing we needed and an open market in Japan, and our partner has obtained some very valuable technology they can use in the future.

A Distant Experience With A Recent Experience

Combining a distant experience (work-related or nonwork-related) with a recent experience can also enrich your images and stories. It demonstrates that you have mastered that skill over time. If, for example, you are selling your ability to organize events, a related story from 5-15 years ago, when told in conjunction with a recent story, would clearly demonstrate that you've had the ability to organize events for a long time.

Something you should know about me is that I'm really good at organizing events. During my senior year in college I organized a white water rafting trip for our co-ed dormitory. In the past the dorm usually had a picnic which turned into more of a beer bash. On the rafting trip no beer was permitted and people had a lot more fun. In the past maybe a quarter of the students would go to the picnic, but on this trip we had nearly half the students out there rafting. Because of the teamwork required, it really brought people closer together.

Just three months ago I coordinated our national sales convention. We brought in 80 sales reps from around the country and gave them a great experience. I selected the speakers and negotiated the contracts with them, worked with the hotel in all of the details, and put in some touches that made it really special. I brought in one speaker that no one had heard of, but he had a new slant on sales and did it with such humor that he had the sales force rolling the aisles. Several of the reps told me later they thought it was the best convention in the past ten years.

Show How You Overcame The Problem

When telling stories that demonstrate how you've solved a problem or overcome an obstacle, create before and after pictures that highlight your impact on the situation. Paint the before picture as bleak as you can. Make the employer feel how bad the situation was. If you were dealing with a quality control problem, you might describe how angry your customers were and describe how some threatened to stop buying from your company or how some actually did. Don't exaggerate, but give the employer the full sense of the problem. As you complete your story, describe how smooth or effective things became. Create the strongest contrast possible without exaggerating. Bruce shared this story about his experience with a mobile home manufacturer:

> Before I took over the parts department, it was taking a month from the time we received a dealer's order until the dealer actually got the part. Because of this we had two problems—most dealers simply obtained their parts from other sources, while those who did order from the factory got their kicks out of yelling at me and telling me to get the parts to them pronto. The problem was that no system had been established. Orders either got lost or they didn't get down to the shipping department for days. And no one even knew if the parts were in stock. When they weren't in stock, no one bothered to notify the person who had placed the order. After a month on the job, I decided things had to change.

> The first thing I did was create forms for recording orders, something which had never been done even though the manufacturing facility had been operating for four years. My predecessor either wrote things down on scraps of paper or tried to remember things in his head. He was really a smart guy, but he couldn't remember everything. I established a hookup with the warehouse so our two computer systems could talk to each other. This system told me immediately whether the parts were available.

> Next, I got the warehouse and the shipping-and-receiving managers together and we found ways to help each other rather than squabble over turf. Within four months we got our delivery times down from four weeks to five days. We haven't lost an order for at least two years. Now I'm not wasting time tracking down lost or late shipments. And my hearing is getting better since people don't yell over the phone anymore. The best thing is that parts sales to our dealers have increased from $12,000 per month to over $60,000. Our dealers are happy, so they don't need to go to other suppliers anymore.

Didn't you actually picture this person on the phone getting his ears burned? Did you imagine the orders getting written down on scraps and then getting misplaced? Could you visualize these three managers who were working at cross purposes? If so, the story was successful. But you were not merely left with a picture. You were left with a result. It wasn't just that Bruce didn't get yelled at anymore, but that sales increased dramatically. Employers get excited when you demonstrate that you can make money, save money, solve problems, or reduce the boss's daily stress and pressure. Bruce demonstrated through this one story that he could do all four. The final point he made was that he could make money. After all, sales increased from $12,000 per month to $60,000. That did some very nice things to the company's bottom line.

How To Tell A Story

A helpful way to prepare your stories is to remember the acronym SHARE, developed by Paul Green. Make sure that each of your stories contain each aspect of SHARE:

Situation	Describe the situation and provide some background information,
Hindrances	Describe the problems, challenges, or hindrances you faced.
Actions	Describe what actions you took.
Results	Describe the results you or your team achieved. Quantify when possible.
Evaluation	Close with a summary or an evaluation of the experience.

Situation: Begin by describing the situation as you entered it. If it existed before you became involved, describe all of the negatives. In other words, do all you can to show how difficult the situation was. Your intention will be to create a strong before-and-after contrast. If you simply took on a project, describe the goals and objectives that were set by you or your boss. Explain why you got involved and why the project or your involvement was necessary.

Hindrances: If you are describing a project that you oversaw, describe the problems or challenges in the most graphic terms possible. Describe what made things difficult. It could be that the customer was particularly angry or refused to listen to reason. It could be that the problem was long standing. Then describe your recommendations or the conclusions you came to.

Actions: Explain what you developed and implemented. Describe your analysis of the situation and whatever research you applied to it. Provide a fair amount of detail about your actions because this will reveal a great deal about how you work and operate.

Results: Paint a picture of what things were like after they improved. If it was a project, concentrate on describing those parts of the project which met or exceeded objectives. Complete the story by describing how your work benefited the company. Quantify results whenever possible.

Evaluation: As you end the story, remind the interviewer of the primary skills or strengths the story demonstrates. Then you can add another two or three skills as well. This could be done by stating: "So I really do believe that experience demonstrates my ability to manage projects effectively (the originally stated strength), as well as my ability to motivate employees and find solutions to really difficult problems." The interviewer will readily agree that motivating employees and solving problems was fully demonstrated. The interviewer will consciously or unconsciously recognize another half dozen skills as well.

Many questions neither invite nor demand a story. Questions such as "What did you like best about your supervisor?" or "What frustrates you about your current job?" do not invite examples. While one could use specific examples for these questions, typically a person would answer them in a very brief and straightforward manner. If you had indicated that your supervisor often did not keep his staff well informed, the interviewer might possibly ask for a specific example, but that is unlikely. There are other questions which would never require a story, such as asking what public figure you most admire.

Even though many questions do not invite stories, you need to be prepared so that when an opportunity to tell a story presents itself, you're ready with the best example possible. In fact, as soon as the question is asked, make an instant decision about whether an example is appropriate. If it clearly is not appropriate, you can immediately concentrate just on your answer. If the question does present an opportunity for a story, you may not immediately know which example to use. That's okay. The human brain has an amazing ability. Go ahead and start your answer, and while you're speaking, another part of your brain can be searching for a good example. Your goal, of course, is to come up with your best example.

Occasionally you may complete your answer and still not have an example to use. Assuming the interviewer has not demanded an example, you can simply conclude your answer. Since few interviewees use examples in their interviews, the interviewer will not be wondering why you did not share an example. Of course an example would have scored more points on that question, but you will not hurt yourself by not including an example.

Here is an example of a story told in an interview using the SHARE concept where the interviewer asked about Brenda's greatest asset:

I'd have to say it's my drive. I've been told by several people that they've never seen anyone with the drive and determination that I have. I do whatever it takes to make things happen.

Situation. During my second year as manager of a gift store, I had to figure out how to meet or exceed our sales quota for the holidays. I had hired what seemed to be the right number of temporary staff to support our permanent staff. I scheduled them in such a way that we would have sufficient staffing throughout November and December. When November came we were very busy, which led me to believe that either people were simply shopping early or this would be our best holiday season ever. Once December hit it was incredible. I needed to hire more help but was having trouble finding people. I was so busy I couldn't even find time for lunch. Eventually I managed to hire four college students who were looking for work on their break, and that still didn't give us enough help.

My staff was amazing! They worked very long hours. We couldn't get the shelves stocked fast enough and we were running two stocking crews instead of the normal one. I was working from the opening at nine until the closing at ten. And I came in on most of my days off. It was fun, though, because our sales gain was the biggest I had ever seen.

Hindrances. Six days before Christmas Eve one of my assistant managers did not show up for work. We were all worried because she was the "mom" of our crew. She was very dependable and always a big support to the team. A day later she called from Austin, Texas (1200 miles away) telling me that a family emergency had come up and she would not be coming back. I wanted to talk longer with her but the store was so busy all I could say was that I understood. This was going to be a major blow to the crew and I couldn't afford to have it affect their morale.

Actions. I panicked for about thirty seconds and then told myself I could not let this get us down now. I grabbed the schedule and made whatever adjustments I could, but I knew we were hurting. I asked my four assistant managers to hang in there with me and we would make it through. I ordered pizza and other goodies to keep everyone going for the next five days and told everyone they cou on Christmas Eve. That night we sang songs and pass canes to the long lines. We made it through the night ar had fun. By the time we closed everyone was tired, but that we had helped a lot of people.

Results. When I came in on the 26th I knew we had had great sales, but I didn't know how great. When I got the results a couple days later I realized that we had increased sales 62% over the previous year. We had by far the biggest increase in the region of 18 stores. We succeeded because everyone pulled together and because over the past two years we had added many loyal customers by having unique merchandise and by providing great customer service.

Evaluation. That experience showed me what you can do when you have a staff that cares and is trained well. I put a lot of effort into hiring people who want to work and are trainable, then I show them how to sell our products and how our customers like to be treated. It's incredible what you can do as a team. I also realized at that time what I was capable of. I had always worked hard and I knew I had a lot of energy, but I didn't know that I could stay that focused for that length of time.

Let's review the story and the impact it had on you. Brenda told the story to back up her claim that she had drive. Without a doubt you are convinced that she has drive. She also created some word pictures that will help you remember her. You probably felt that moment of panic when a key assistant manager quit just seven days before Christmas. Then you probably visualized the staff eating pizza. Then you saw them in jeans singing songs and passing out candy canes and being very friendly even though all were exhausted.

Notice how Brenda created her word pictures. She mentioned the holidays so you probably pictured people bundled up. She said they couldn't keep the shelves stocked so you probably visualized people quickly grabbing items right off the shelves. Brenda has told a very effective story, in large part because she used SHARE.

Results Sell You

To have the greatest impact on interviewers, include results in your stories whenever possible. It is always best if you can describe accomplishments in terms of dollars or percentages. One of my clients was able to tell employers that in the two years since she had taken over her territory, she had increased the sales of shoes by 54% and profits on her sales by 68%. The company had been marketing in that territory for 20 years. You can see how impressive this would be to an employer. Another client stated, "I developed a simplified computer program for a client which reduced the computer runtime by 40% and saved over $17,000 per year."

Dollar figures and percentages are so valuable that you should even estimate them when necessary. The computer programmer in the example above had to estimate the dollar savings. She knew the runtime was reduced by 35–45%, so she chose 40% as her figure. She knew how frequently the program was run, and she knew the cost of the computer time. Thus, the $17,000 figure was calculated using simple arithmetic.

While not all results can be quantified, many can. When I'm talking with people to gather information for their resumes, I'm frequently told, "There's really no way to estimate it, I just improved it." I will then ask questions from different angles and we invariably arrive at a figure we can use. You can do the same with your results.

Below are additional statements which effectively convey quantifiable results.

I developed a new production technique which increased productivity by 7%.

Through more effective recruiting techniques, I reduced terminations company-wide by 30% and turnover by 23%.

I edited a newsletter for an architectural association, with readership increasing 28% in one year.

I implemented a 12% cut in staffing through attrition which resulted in virtually no reduction in output.

I organized a citizen task force which successfully wrote a statewide initiative, adopted with a 69% favorable vote.

As chairperson for fund raising, I developed a strategy which increased funds raised by 26% while reducing promotional costs.

I set a record of 46 days without a system failure.

Which/Which Resulted In

Results are powerful. Everything you've done on a job has had a result. When the result is positive *and* significant, it is worth sharing in an interview. Train yourself to look for results. Remember, you don't need computer printouts to verify your results. Your own honest estimate is sufficient. If asked about it during an interview, just describe how you arrived at the figure and then go into more detail concerning how you accomplished it. Results sell you.

I've developed a simple technique which will help you identify your results. Take each of your key experiences and add the words *which*, or *which resulted in*. Then simply ask yourself what the result was. For example, "Wrote an office procedures manual" becomes,

"Wrote an office procedures manual *which* decreased training time and billing errors." After you've taken time to quantify the results and to explain it more accurately, it will become, "Wrote an office procedures manual which decreased training time of new employees by 25% and reduced billing errors over 30%."

The trick is to identify the result or results first and then seek to quantify them by using the hard data you have available or by estimating the result. Also, don't stop with just one result or benefit. Many of your best experiences have had several results, so take the time to identify them. Each different result will come in handy at different times in an interview.

Let's look at a project that produced multiple results.

In my position as lobbyist for the Detroit realtors' association, I was very active in building coalitions with the homebuilders, the Economic Development Council of Detroit, and other housing groups. As part of these coalitions, I was asked to co-chair an affordable housing committee. From the realtors' perspective, government regulations were a major problem. So I pulled together an all-inclusive committee, including representatives from General Motors, Housing Coalition of Detroit, and the Detroit Housing Authority, as well as county and state officials. We brought in local experts on a variety of topics and asked for recommendations for reducing or streamlining unnecessary government regulations. We came up with over 80 recommendations and presented it at a regional event sponsored by the mayor and county executive as well as the *Detroit Free Press*. It was publicly well-received, and because of the quality of the recommendations and the breadth of the coalition, over 30 key recommendations were adopted in the past year, with more to follow I'm sure. By streamlining permit and building processes, builders are saving about $600 per home.

Sam demonstrated numerous skills in this project as well as several results. Let's examine the results and quantify them if we can.

Brought together a coalition of groups that usually oppose one another.

Persuaded government organizations and agencies to remove unnecessary government regulations.

Reduced the cost of building a home by over $600 each.

Reduced the average time to obtain construction permits from 120 days to 75 days.

Developed strong relationships with government agencies by showing that we realtors didn't oppose everything they recommended, and worked with them to actually strengthen some regulations.

Developed allies that we never had before. (With many of these allies we knew that we wouldn't agree on certain issues, but we found that we could work with them on others).

This array of businesses and organizations learned the importance of really listening to what each group was saying and of taking the time to learn what was most important and critical to them.

Got the ear of the mayor, who previously would not listen to us.

I personally gained great visibility by being interviewed by three major newspapers and by the CBS and ABC local affiliates.

Received a $5,000 bonus from the realtors.

Everybody wins. More affordable housing units can be constructed so more new homebuyers can get that first home. The city and region win because the changes did not compromise the quality of the homes or their energy efficiency.

In the first year the percentage of new homes purchased by minorities increased from 28% of all homes to 38%, a 36% increase.

When we first started identifying Sam's results I quickly saw about four, but I had no idea we would come up with this many. In an interview Sam can decide which results to discuss. He would virtually always mention that the cost of building homes was reduced by $600. That may not seem like much, but it was accomplished exclusively by eliminating some unnecessary regulations. Part of the cost reduction came by reducing the time required to obtain building permits. When land has been purchased with loans, every day that a home has not been completed (and sold) adds cost in the form of interest. If the profit on a $95,000 starter home would be about $9,000, then $600 equals 6% of the total profit. That's substantial. It takes time to come up with results and to quantify them, sometimes an hour or more. You may have the data necessary to quantify the result, but the information may be spread among several different sources. Of course sometimes the numbers are readily available and have already been calculated.

This should be a reminder to you for the future. As you start a project or look for a way to improve a particular process, figure out how you will measure your success. First you have to determine what you hope to accomplish. Then you have to determine what the current status is. If you are going to improve training in hopes of reducing turnover and errors, then you need to know what the current turnover and error rate is. If those rates are not currently being measured, then you'll have to do it. This effort is worth it because you can obtain a great payoff: you can bring it to the attention of your boss through a memo. You don't have to ask your boss to respond. As long as your boss does not dispute your results, it means he or she accepts them. Of course your results could help you get a raise, a promotion, or a bonus. But you have to let the key people know what you've done. Don't let yourself be a well-kept secret.

Chapter 6

CALCULATING RESULTS

To make the most out of your results you need to know how to quantify them. One reason people rarely use statistics in their interviews is that they don't know how to calculate results, and then don't know how to use or describe them to their best effect. Usually all it takes is simple arithmetic and a little logic.

Suppose you know that an action you took improved something—sales, profits, productivity, turnover—but you don't have documentation to prove it. Assume that the matter is turnover. When you came into the department morale was down, and people were continually leaving out of frustration. When you came into the department there were sixteen people. During the year you were assistant supervisor you saw five people leave and one get fired, for a total of six. That represents 38% turnover.

With a turnover rate that high, productivity is bound to be low because people don't stay around long enough to really learn the job. In addition, the supervisor has to devote a lot of time to training new people and correcting their mistakes. Eventually your boss is fired and you are promoted into the position. According to your observation, your boss never adequately trained people, got angry at them when they made mistakes, and never supplied positive feedback. As a result, people quit out of frustration.

So when you became supervisor you worked closely with the core group. This took a lot of overtime on your part, but you made sure they knew what they were doing. You gave them strokes and they appreciated that. During your first year on the job four people quit, the next year two people quit, and the following year two people quit. Your turnover rate for the first year was 25% (4 divided by 16). The second and third years it was 12% (2 divided by 16). It appears that things have definitely stabilized.

Now you need to determine the percentage by which you reduced turnover, and what other benefits accrued as a result. The turnover rate has been reduced from 38% to 12%. Just an approximation will tell you that the reduction is almost two-thirds, or 67%. To get the actual figure you would subtract 12 from 38 to get 26. You would then divide 26 by 38 and get 68%. As valuable as reducing turnover is, that is still not the end result. Because your people are now better trained they make fewer mistakes, get more done in a day, and provide better customer service. So, next you would measure the quality, productivity, and customer service improvements. In an interview you might say, "I developed an effective training program which reduced turnover from 38% to 12%. As a result of the program, productivity increased over 14%, and we really improved the quality of customer service." Such a statement will have real impact on employers.

In the process of calculating results, the first step is to identify all the benefits of an action you took. Start with the assumption that if you can identify it, you can quantify it. Quantifying results may require some guesstimating, but you can do it.

EXAMPLES

Determining An Average Annual Increase

Often a person will bring about improvements over a period of several years. A good way to express this figure is to show the annual increase. Selling something would be a typical example. The following example shows how one client used an increase in sales to its best effect.

John increased sales in his territory over a five-year period. Sales the year prior to his coming to the territory were $200,000. His first year he increased sales to $240,000, then $275,000, then $300,000, then $310,000, and finally $350,000. His first year increase was 20% since his increase of $40,000 is 20% of $200,000.

Mathematically it is figured this way:
    $240,000 - 200,000 = $40,000
    40,000 ÷ 200,000 = .20 or 20%
The second year his increase was 14%:
    $275,000 - $240,000 = $35,000
    35,000 ÷ 240,000 = 14%
The third year the increase was 9%, the fourth 3% (a recession year), and the fifth 13%.

Over the five years he increased sales 75%. To get the average annual increase add the increases from each year and total them (20+14+9+3+13 = 59). Then divide by the five years to get the figure (59 ÷ 5 years = 11.8%) of an 11.8% average annual increase. For a resume it would be rounded off to 12%. In an interview it could be stated, "I increased sales an average of 12% per year." Although he increased sales a total of 75% you cannot divide 75 by 5 to get the average annual increase.

Once the figures have been determined, a decision has to be made as to the strongest way to present the information. Sometimes the best way is simply to present the raw figures. In this case it would be, "In five years I took sales in the territory from $200,000 to $350,000." If those figures did not have the impact he wanted he could say, "I took over a mature territory and increased sales 75% in five years," or "During a serious economic downturn in the region, I increased sales an average of 12% per year."

Simple Increases

Simple increases might be figured according to the following method: In 1997 advertising revenue for a magazine had been $256,000. By the end of 1999 it had increased to $318,000. The percent of increase is 24% (318,000 - 256,000 = 62,000; 62,000 ÷ 256,000 = .242 or rounded off to 24%)

A formula for calculating increases is: $\frac{b-a}{a}$ where a is the original number and b is the new number. Another way to write this formula is: b minus a, and that number divided by a.

In the above example it would be $256,000 -$318.000 divided by $318,000 = .242 or 24%.

Simple Decreases

Simple decreases can be figured and expressed similar to the example below: A manufacturing supervisor reduced rejects (parts which did not meet specifications and were therefore rejected by quality control) from a rate of 6% to 2%. People often miscalculate such figures and might report that they reduced rejects by 4%, simply subtracting 2 from 6 and getting 4. Going from 6% to 2% actually represents a 67% reduction in rejects, however. The proper way to calculate this is 6 - 2 = 4; 4 ÷ 6 = .6666 or 67%.

The formula for decreases is: $\frac{a-b}{a}$ where a is the original number and b is the new number. Another way to write this formula is a minus b and that number divided by a. In the above example it would be 6 – 2 divided by 6 = .66.

In another example, assume that the average daily absenteeism in a department has been reduced from 15 people per day to 7. Logic tells you that absenteeism was cut by a little more than half so you know it will be slightly above 50%. If you wanted more precision you would calculate it. Reducing something from 15 to 7 equals 53% (15 - 7 = 8; 8 ÷ 15 = .53).

Using the formula it would be: 15 - 7 divided by 15 = .53.

Large Increases

With large increases you must be careful when calculating percentages. Let's say production in a plant went from 10,000 units per year to 30,000 over a five-year period. It is easy to see that units tripled, so one would tend to say that production increased 300%. The problem is that it actually represents a 200% increase. Going from 10,000 to 20,000 was a 100% increase, and going from 20,000 to 30,000 was another 100%, for a total of 200%.

Guesstimating

Quantifying figures often requires guesstimating. Whenever you have computer printouts and company documents which specify your improvements, by all means use them. Such "hard numbers" are rarely available, however. Guesstimating is a very accepted interview practice. To be accepted you merely need to explain what you did and how you did it.

Chapter 7

SELLING YOURSELF THROUGH ACCOMPLISHMENTS

Using experiences and accomplishments to sell yourself in interviews is the most powerful interviewing skill you can develop. Providing actual examples from your life experience convinces interviewers that you possess the necessary skills and qualities for the job. The following exercise will enable you to identify your top skills and will provide you with the evidence to support whatever claims you make about yourself. Taking time to complete this exercise will better prepare you for interviews and will set you apart from your less industrious competitors.

RECALLING YOUR ACCOMPLISHMENTS

Knowing your accomplishments—and identifying the skills used to achieve them—is one of the most important tasks of an effective job search. Recalling these key experiences will increase your self-confidence and will enable you to feel comfortable selling yourself.

Accomplishments can be big or small, very impressive or rather simple. An accomplishment is anything that includes at least one of these four items. You:

Enjoyed doing it

Did it well

Gained satisfaction from it

Are proud of it

Many accomplishments include all four aspects, while some may include just one or two. Accomplishments often involve solving problems. With some accomplishments you may receive recognition or compliments from parents, friends, coworkers, customers, or supervisors, while at other times you may be the only one who knows what you did. Some accomplishments are achieved through great effort, while others come easily. Many of your accomplishments were enjoyable and fondly recalled.

Other experiences are genuine accomplishments, but they may be "bittersweet." It may be an accomplishment simply because you overcame many adversities. At the time you may have been extremely frustrated. Even thinking about the experience may bring back those feelings of frustration, anger, or hurt. It's okay to remember the negative parts, but concentrate as much as you can on the positive aspects of the experience. In other words, concentrate on the result. These seemingly negative experiences often produce great personal growth.

Accomplishments are best thought of as specific experiences. Most of your accomplishments should be things that occurred during a relatively short period of time. It could be something that occurred from start to finish in fifteen minutes or several hours. More typically accomplishments are experiences which occurred over days or weeks. Although some accomplishments may take place over years, those long-term accomplishments can be broken into sub-accomplish-ments. For example, graduating from college is certainly an accomplishment. Although you should list an accomplishment like that, step back and consider all of the smaller accomplishments that enabled you to achieve the larger accomplishment. In the case of graduating from college that would include the key papers you wrote and the projects you worked on. Those papers and projects should be listed as well.

Now review the following list of accomplishments. These experiences have been provided by many different people. Notice how some of the accomplishments are impressive, while others seem rather common and ordinary. That's to be expected. Note that most of the accomplishment statements also contain a result. As you list an accomplishment, the result helps you clarify what made it an accomplishment. Once you review the list you will then read three accomplishments in which 5-10 skills were identified. Then you'll find instructions for completing this exercise. Basically you'll be asked to identify 30 or more experiences that can be considered accomplishments, and then write about your top twelve experiences. Then you'll identify the skills you used in each accomplishment. This is a critical exercise that can pay big dividends.

Jobs

I received a $600 award from Boeing for suggesting a money-saving idea.

I became the first woman engineer in the firm.

I earned my way through college painting houses.

I figured out a faster method of estimating the cost of our printing jobs.

My advertising jingle is credited with increasing sales 15%.

My plan for flextime has really reduced absenteeism.

I made a sale to a firm that had refused to deal with us for 15 years.

I increased sales in my territory 39% in two years.

I added 24 customers to my paper route.

Wrote recommendations for a hazardous waste program that were adopted by the state.

I received three promotions in four years.

I became one of the youngest store managers ever in the chain.

I produced a videotaped training program for our tellers which cut training time of new tellers about 20% and significantly reduced the errors they made.

I developed and implemented a plan to purchase a fleet of trucks to handle our own deliveries. The plan cut our costs by 5% and provided more reliable service to our customers.

Was able to make history and literature interesting to bored kids.

Created the first performance measurements, charts, statistics, and graphs for most functions of the department.

Developed a form and formula for calculating return on investment on large-quantity purchases.

Won the first "innovative achievement in purchasing" award from corporate.

Appeared with Mickey Rooney in four commercials.

Leveraged a $200,000 promotion budget into $1 million in on-air value.

Sold out the Spokane Opera House ten times and attracted 56,000 skiers to the Warren Miller ski film.

Convinced Roseanne to appear in a great but offbeat, low-budget ad campaign, just as she was hitting the big time.

School

I learned Russian so I could read *War and Peace* in the original language.

I got a B in chemistry after failing the midterm exam.

I got an A in chemistry from the toughest prof.

I wrote an outstanding paper on the causes of World War II.

I was elected senior class vice president.

I was committee chairperson of the junior prom decorations committee. Some teachers thought they were the best decorations in years.

Hobbies/Activities

I planted a garden, fought the weeds, and got 15 bushels of vegetables.

I hitchhiked alone from Paris through France, Italy, Greece, Turkey, Iran, Afghanistan, Pakistan, and India.

I planned and built a 400-square-foot deck.

I won honorable mention in a county bakeoff for a unique potato salad.

I wrote 25 short stories between 1985 and 1995 and got two published.

Getting paid assignments to photograph people.

Bought and redecorated (elegantly but on a small budget) a small condominium.

Designed a new dress, combining several patterns.

Took lessons and became a good dancer. Have taught others.

Sports/Physical Activities

I learned to ski at age 44.

I got third place in a cross-country track meet.

I scored a game-winning basket.

I won first place in a kite-flying contest.

I climbed Mt. Rainier.

I competed in my first 10K race at age 36.

Although I hate swimming, I became a certified scuba diver.

Tried parachuting—once.

Took the first group of American skiers (35 people) to Russia in 1986 for a 14-day exchange with the Russian Olympic team.

Volunteer

As president of the PTA I increased membership 36%.

I was elected secretary of my local accounting association.

As chairman of fund raising, I raised more money than any other Bay Area Lions Club in 1979.

My team built a very effective irrigation system during my Peace Corps tour.

Personal

I raised three mischievous boys and trained them to become well-adjusted adults.

I planned and arranged a wonderful three-week vacation in Europe with a tight budget.

I quit smoking.

I administered CPR to a man and saved his life.

After reviewing this list, read the expanded accomplishments on the following pages and notice how we identified skills. The real purpose of this exercise is to identify as many skills as possible, and especially to identify all of your "hooks." A hook is a special skill, or a skill described in such a way that it hooks an interviewer. Hooks get remembered. Typically in interviews all you need to do is know your hooks, and be prepared to give an example or two to back each one up. Knowing how to identify your hooks, and then learning how to use them in interviews, will be among the most important parts of your work.

Able to bring consensus in areas that had been chaotic

Achieve the unachievable

Effectively get people to review a concept objectively

Get people to value consensus and to be willing to compromise

Effectively organize large educational seminars

Excellent at resolving disputes among diverse interest groups

Excellent at marketing programs and getting strong attendance

Excellent writer

Effectively organize committees

People enjoy and value the events organized

For three years, beginning in 1982, I held a volunteer office with the Rocky Mountain Ski Instructors Association. I was elected to this position by the association's 3,000 ski instructors to reorganize and simplify the current methodology used for teaching skiing.

This had never been accomplished because there were so many systems of teaching, and there was also a widespread misuse of terminology. Everyone was set in their ways and were unwilling to compromise. This became a critical issue because state licensing and certification was necessary for ski instructors to teach on U.S. Forest Service land at state ski areas. The Forest Service required a single system.

To accomplish this I organized several large educational seminars each year to educate both ski instructors and certification examiners on a simplified American teaching system. As many as 500 people attended these two-day events. I spent many hours in various levels of committee meetings disseminating information and resolving disputes among these diverse interest groups. As a result of these efforts, I was able to develop a unified ski teaching method and get it adopted by the Rocky Mountain Ski Instructors Association.

In this accomplishment the two hooks are "Able to bring consensus in areas that had been chaotic," and "Achieve the unachievable." All the other skills are valuable, but the two hooks will have the most impact.

In interviews don't try to quote your skills exactly as they appear with your accomplishments. Instead, describe a skill in a way that is consistent with the way you talk. For example, you might say, "I'm the person who can achieve consensus when everyone is strongly disagreeing. Somehow I just find a way. I listen to all the sides and then help each side understand the needs of the other. Eventually we reach agreement on even the toughest issues."

Gain the support and involvement of people who are naturally defensive and hesitant

Develop innovative methods and techniques

Effectively analyze profitability of products and services

Able to analyze a complete product line, take it apart, and put it back together with greater profitability

Develop highly effective computer generated reports

Gain the confidence and absolute trust of people

I led a research group in studying the profitability of installment lending at U.S. Bancorp. I analyzed gross yields, handling costs, and loan losses for the various types of loans. I developed a consistent and accepted method for measuring handling costs among the several loan categories. My analysis gained credibility with the senior lending managers. I worked with the installment lending department and obtained their help in the project. The analysis revealed that some types of loans had very high handling costs and were not profitable. My analysis helped initiate a move away from unprofitable loan categories. After discussions with a senior executive at the bank, I developed a computer report for easy monitoring of the rates, maturity, and size characteristics of new loans. This process helped ensure that we kept profitability high.

In this example the hook is increasing profitability of products as mentioned in the fourth skill. The person might state, "My strength is producing products with greater profit margins. I have the ability to analyze a complete product line, take it apart and put it back together with greater profitability."

Develop effective systems that increase sales and productivity

Persuasive

Develop sales incentives that really work

Leader—motivate staff

Conduct useful meetings

Able to instill a need for planning and organization into staff

Conduct motivating sales meetings

In 1985 I was promoted from agent to district manager for New York Life. For the first month I hardly knew what I was supposed to do because there were no procedures or systems in place. Then I attended a seminar on insurance management put on by the Kinder brothers. They taught that you needed a system for everything. I learned a lot.

When I returned to the office I began to write a recruiting and training system. It really helped new agents get off to a fast start, and those early successes increased their motivation and self-confidence. I developed good campaigns with wonderful awards to motivate the achievers on the

Always create a winning team

Get people believing in themselves

Give people the tools to help them succeed

staff. We had training meetings which were always great occasions. I spent a lot of time with my new people and really got them going. I made mistakes but I did enough things right that it started to show. In 1986 we finished number three in the region and number one in 1987.

Here again, all the skills are valuable, but the hook is the ability to develop systems that increase sales and productivity. Look for ways to phrase your skills so they become hooks.

Now read the instructions for completing this exercise. I trust you will take the time to write about your top twelve accomplishments and then identify skills within them. These twelve experiences will undoubtedly be used frequently in your interviews. They are your best experiences and each contains 5-15 key skills. Any time you want to sell one of the skills identified, you've got at least one excellent example.

The accomplishments you did not write about will also be used in interviews. If you have 20 or 30 that you did not write about, take up to two minutes with each one to identify the 2-3 key skills that jump out at you. Rehearse these experiences as well.

Before you begin identifying your accomplishments, be sure to read all of the instructions. There are important points throughout that you need to know and understand before you begin.

WRITING ABOUT ACCOMPLISHMENTS

1. Write a list of at least 30 experiences that you would consider to be accomplishments.

a) List the experiences as they pop into your mind. Don't filter them out, just list them. They do not need to be "knock your socks off" types of experiences. Try to list 40 or more, but list at least 30. Once you get started listing them, one accomplishment will trigger another. An accomplishment is anything you:

> Enjoyed doing
> Did well
> Gained satisfaction from
> Are proud of

b) Since people often share non-job-related experiences in interviews, do not feel limited to work experiences. Those with little work experience will of course emphasize experiences from school, hobbies, sports, or volunteer activities.

c) Include at least fifteen work-related accomplishments (assuming you have job experience), with at least four coming from your current or most recent job. If you're frustrated in your current job, it's easy to assume there haven't been accomplishments,but there have been. Sometimes it merely takes a little more effort to identify them.

d) You have dozens of accomplishments. Don't screen them out because they seem insignificant. Even these so called "insignificant" experiences can be used powerfully in an interview. These seemingly small experiences are often the perfect vehicle to demonstrate a particular skill or quality.

e) Don't try to complete your list in one sitting. Over two or three days, think of the experiences as you drive to work or take a walk. As you drive you might be able to jot thoughts down as you wait for a stop light. Or, as you arrive at your destination, take five minutes to madly list your experiences. Then you might need two or three sessions at home where you really concentrate on recalling experiences for 15-20 minutes at each session.

2. Write about your top experiences.

a) Determine your absolute top twelve lifetime accomplishments. One way is to decide which have had the greatest impact on your life. Another way is to ask yourself which ones will reveal the most skills. Or, which ones will have the greatest impact in interviews. As you begin to write, be sure to leave a three-inch margin on the left so you'll have room to identify skills.

b) Write 100-400 words on each experience. Begin by describing the situation. Give some background. What were the circumstances? What were the problems you faced? How did you analyze the situation? What occurred? What actions did you take? What were the results? Use the SHARE model: Situation, Hindrances, Actions, Results, Evaluation. Write as completely as you can and give enough details so any reader would have a good understanding of what you did. If the accomplishment is job related, avoid acronyms or any technical jargon.

c) Describe your role. Many accomplishments are achieved through a group effort. You can still claim it as a personal accomplishment; simply concentrate on what your role in it was.

d) Describe the result. Every experience, every project, has a result. To describe the result, think about what your goal was. Did you achieve it? One of the best ways to think about results is to consider what you did, and then add the words, "which resulted in." An example would be: "I trained all year for cross-country, which resulted in my placing sixth in the state—the highest finish ever for someone from my high school."

e) Quantify your accomplishments whenever possible. It may mean estimating, but that's fine. Did your accomplishment increase productivity at the office? If so, how much—10%, 40%, 65%? As a manager, did you decrease turnover? If so, how much? As a committee leader for a volunteer organization you may have increased membership, attendance at monthly meetings, or revenue on fund raisers. For more on results, read pages 32-40.

f) Write as fast as you can—after all, this is an experience you lived through. Memories will jump into your consciousness. One memory will lead to another as you recall what occurred in the accomplishment. Try to make your pen keep up with your brain or make your fingers race along the keyboard without worrying about typos. You can correct those later. Do not be concerned about spelling, grammar, sentence structure, or polished writing, just get your thoughts on paper. This is not a philosophy paper where every word must be perfect.

3. Identify skills.

a) Study the sample accomplishments on pages 46-48 to see how skills and qualities are identified. Skills are important, but personal qualities and characteristics are just as important. As a skill you might say, "produce highly effective marketing plans." As a quality you might say, "extremely reliable," "work well with people," "hard worker," or "able and willing to take on greater responsibility." In actuality, these characteristics *are* skills.

b) Identify skills and qualities using phrases. Again, study the examples. In almost all cases a phrase has more impact than a single word. "Persistent" is a good word, but it doesn't have the same impact as, "I never give up until the job is done right." "Organizing" doesn't have the same impact as "Effectively plan and organize projects and obtain high quality results." Use words like *excellent, effective, effectively*. Words like those remind you that you didn't just do it, but that you did it well.

c) Identify as many skills as you can, even if you feel the same skills were identified in other accomplishments. If a particular skill has been used in several accomplishments, that tells you a lot about yourself. Probably it is a skill that you are very good at and enjoy using. Having used the skill in several accomplishments also allows you to select the very best experience when you are about to mention that skill in an interview.

d) One way to identify skills is to pull them right out of your descriptions. Often you can take a phrase almost word for word out of your accomplishment.

e) Don't skip the obvious skills. Sometimes a skill is so obvious to a person that it doesn't seem valuable or important. Go ahead and quickly write it in.

f) Don't skip a skill just because you think everyone can do it. Even if it is a common skill, it should still be listed. Often, however, a person only believes everyone can do it. This happens because the person has been skilled at it for a long time, and cannot remember a time when he or she could not do it. Because of that, it's easy to assume that anyone can do it. Don't get caught in that trap.

g) With your remaining accomplishments devote up to two minutes for each and identify the two or three most obvious skills.

Study the previous examples of accomplishments to get ideas on how to write about accomplishments and how to identify skills.

Involve someone in the process of identifying skills. It could be a friend, relative, or spouse. It's good if you can find a person who is in the same situation, so you can go through this process together. Each of you will be able to give considerable insight to the other.

Have this person read one of your accomplishments. Then the two of you would discuss it as you provide more details. Have the person ask you questions to clarify anything which is unclear. This will help you tell more concise and clear stories during interviews. Telling the story out loud will help you recall the experience even better and will give you good practice for interviews. By discussing the experience with you, your helper will identify skills that would have been missed if that person had merely read what you wrote. People find it enjoyable to talk about their accomplishments and to receive positive feedback from someone they respect. As you speak, the person should write down any skills which come to mind. Then the person will give you feedback when you're through describing the experience. Rather than simply reading back what was written, the person should expand on it and describe what convinced him or her that you have that skill. It might go like this:

> I wrote "You stand up for what you believe and provide leadership for others." I think it took a lot of guts to stand up to management and request, or almost demand, that safety out in the plant get more attention. Once you took the stand others were willing to back you up. I think that's what leadership is all about.

Writing about your accomplishments will prove enjoyable and enriching. Invariably people report their self-confidence increases as they become more aware of the positive things they've done.

Take the time to recall your accomplishments and identify your skills. Follow the instructions carefully. They are based on feedback from hundreds of people and will make the task much easier. Don't try to do it in one sitting. Spread it out over several days. Have fun with this exercise.

If you would like professional assistance in identifying your accomplishments, turn to page 271 for more information.

Chapter 8

DEVELOP YOUR AGENDA

Developing an agenda for your interviews is one of the most important interviewing skills you can gain. If you will be competing against people with more direct experience than you, devoting time to developing your agenda is critical.

Your Agenda

Establishing an agenda is simply a process of determining in advance the stories and strengths you must sell in order to get the job offer. Very few job seekers, however, take the time to develop their own agenda. This is a major mistake. By having a plan—an agenda—you can take advantage of all opportunities that present themselves during an interview. By identifying the strengths and experiences that will best sell you, prioritizing them, and determining the questions that would enable you to describe them, you will rarely fail to take full advantage of each question. The questions that are most useful are open-ended questions such as, "Tell me about yourself," "What is your greatest strength?" and "Why should I hire you?" Open-ended simply means it is a question that gives you wide latitude in answering it.

When asked such open-ended questions, you will have the opportunity to cover points from your agenda. If you've prioritized your stories and strengths, you can cover the most important ones first. It's important to sell these points as early in the interview as possible since you may not get another chance to do so later on.

There are several ways to make your key points. One way is to have a resume filled with results and benefits, causing the employer to ask about your results. A second is to jump at every opportunity. If you are asked one of the open-ended questions, such as describing your top strengths, you should be ready to bring out those strengths that will add the most weight to your side of the scale. Your analysis of the job description will enable you to do that.

A third way is to answer the question and include an example. Then, as you finish the story, state the specific strength you were emphasizing, and then add another strength. For example, if the interviewer had asked an interviewee whether she was a good team player, she would first describe what makes her a good team player and then back it up with an example. Once she finished telling the story she would state:

> I think that experience demonstrates that I am a very good team player. I believe it also demonstrates that I'm a person who comes up with unique marketing ideas. On that project I listened to all of the ideas of the team and utilized the best ideas from everyone. When we met a couple of days later, I had incorporated those ideas and mixed them with some unique ideas of my own. The group really liked it and that's what we went to management with. The product that came out of those marketing meetings has been one of our most successful products of the last five years.

Notice what the person did. She answered the question regarding being an excellent team player and provided a very good story to back it up. She then reminded the interviewer of what she had sold to him—proof that she was an excellent team player. This is important because sometimes interviewers actually forget the question they had asked you. When that happens, no matter how effective your answer is, you won't get maximum points. So develop a habit of restating the strength you've just discussed in your answer. Having restated the strength, it was then appropriate for her to mention from her agenda, at least one other strength that the experience demonstrated. It can be as simple as saying, "So I am a very good team player, and I think that experience also demonstrates that I develop effective marketing ideas."

The reason this technique works is that as soon as you mention the other skills that were being demonstrated in the example, the interviewer will instantly agree. This technique requires practice, so when you're rehearsing, be sure to add those additional skills. You'll get weight added to your side of the scale every time. If you have a friend act as your interviewer, be sure to practice it then also.

The Steps To Developing An Agenda

Below are the four steps needed to develop your agenda and to ensure that you fully sell yourself.

1) Identify Your Accomplishments And Skills

Identify your top 30-50 accomplishments (see pages 41-45). Remember that an accomplishment is any experience that you enjoyed, did well, or got satisfaction from. Pick twelve key accomplishments and write 100-400 words describing each experience. Identify 5-15 skills in each one. (See pages 46-52 for examples of describing experiences and identifying skills.)

After writing about your top twelve accomplishments, spend a couple of minutes with each remaining accomplishment and identify the 2-4 skills that jump out at you. The key here is to be quick and not get bogged down by spending more than two minutes with any of these remaining accomplishments. It might look like this:

Skills Used	*Accomplishment*
Work effectively with computer programmers	Worked closely with a programmer to develop
Find more efficient ways to do things	a computer program that
Make things happen/take initiative	allowed for automatic
Work hard for my customers	reorders for a customer, a 38-store chain.

By doing this, you will now have 30-50 stories to share in interviews. You will then be able to choose which story would best suit a particular question.

2) Identify Your Most Important Strengths

Identify and list the strengths, skills, an[d] have that will virtually always be desirable f you'll be applying for. It can help to clip out w to determine what employers are typically yourself to the ads. Ask yourself what perso 69-70), transferable skills (see pages 252-25 content skills (see pages 258-264) are important for success in your field. Prioritize these strengths. This will enable you to bring your top strengths into the interview at the earliest point possible.

Review your 30-50 accomplishments and determine which ones used the skills you most want to sell. The table on page 58 shows how this can be done. If you don't have a good example for a particular skill from your list of 30-50, take a couple of minutes to recall the experience in which you best demonstrated that skill. Then write it down.

3) Practice Your Stories

Practice describing all of the accomplishments you think you might use in interviews. Practice so that for each accomplishment you have a one-minute, a two-minute, and a three-minute version. With your longer version you can add details that reveal more about the experience and more about you as a person. With a one-minute version you have to work hard to determine the most critical points. It takes effort to remove all but the most important points from a story. Use the two- or three-minute version when you believe it will best sell you and if the interviewer appears to have an adequate attention span.

4) Match Your Strengths And Stories With 40 Key Questions

Examine the following 40 questions which are all covered in detail in chapters 19-26. Determine which strengths and stories you would likely mention when asked those questions. In that way you'll always mention your key strengths at the earliest opportunity.

Review the following questions. They come from the list of 101 toughest and most frequently asked questions. These are the most open-ended questions and the ones most likely to give you an opportunity to present the points you want to make.

1. Tell me about yourself.
2. What is your greatest strength?
3. What can you offer us that someone else can't?
4. What are your three most important career accomplishments?
5. How would you describe yourself?
6. Why should I hire you?
7. Describe your biggest crisis in your life (or career).
8. What is unique about you?
26. What do you think determines a person's progress with a good company?
27. Who has exercised the greatest influence over you?
28. What have you done to increase your personal development?

36. What was the most useful criticism you ever received?
37. What is the biggest change you've made in your life in the past ten years?
39. Can you work well under stress?
40. Are you a team player?
43. What are the things that motivate you?
45. What have you done that shows initiative?
46. What personal qualities are important for success in this field?
48. Are you willing to take calculated risks?
49. Can you establish effective methods and procedures?
51. We need someone who is resourceful.
52. What has been your biggest challenge?
53. Describe a team project where you are proud of the team's result as well as of your personal contribution.
54. Describe a difficult decision you've made and the process you went through to reach that decision.
55. Give me three qualities that are really helping you get ahead and three qualities that you must work on if you are going to achieve your career goals.
59. Why do you want to get into this field?
61. How long will it take before you make a positive contribution to our organization?
62. What do you like most about this position?
63. Tell me about your duties at your present job.
64. What is the most important aspect of your job?
67. What is the most difficult situation you ever faced?
69. What jobs have you enjoyed most? Why?
70. What duties have you enjoyed most?
74. Why would you like to work for us?
80. What kind of recommendations will you get from previous employers?
84. How has your supervisor helped you grow?
85. What did your supervisor rate you highest on during your last review?
89. Can you supervise people?
93. How would your subordinates describe you as a supervisor?
95. How have you improved as a supervisor over the years?

Once you've completed all four steps, you'll be rea(
interviews. Take the time to put all of these pieces toget
take time—5-15 hours is typical—but the quality of yo
bring about better results than you've ever experience(

A   Troubleshot delivery/quality issues with Quantel
B   Business/marketing plan for food service to airlines
C   Created spreadsheet templates and macros
D   Completed XYZ project three months ahead of schedule
E   United Way loaned executive
F   Worked with graphics group and got corporate award
G   Wind tunnel project
H   Business plan for first voice recognition product
I   Taught marketing course for new employees
J   Plan to reduce inventory

	A	B	C	D	E	F	G	H	I	J
Effective under stress	x	x		x			x	x		
Reliable	x	x	x	x	x	x	x	x	x	x
Take initiative	x		x	x	x				x	x
Create effective programs				x					x	
Plan projects well		x		x	x	x	x	x		
Excellent writer		x					x	x		
Make effective presentations		x			x	x			x	x
Effective facilitator				x	x			x		
Excellent team player		x		x	x	x	x			
Work well alone	x									
Work hard			x	x			x			
Excellent time management/ productive/efficient	x	x	x	x	x	x	x	x	x	x
Create useful reports from spreadsheets and databases		x	x				x			
Excellent trainer									x	
Develop staff well/staff often promoted				x			x			
Produce effective business/ marketing plans		x						x		x
Consistently solve customer problems	x			x		x				
Thoroughly understand sales and distribution channels for software								x		

Skills/Accomplishments Table

Chapter 9

SELL YOURSELF

Knowing how to sell yourself is the key to successful interviewing. Understanding the psychology of interviewing and knowing what is motivating your interviewer will play a major role in selling yourself more effectively. Building credibility and projecting a winning personality are the first steps.

The Ultimate Question

The ultimate question in any interview is "Why should I hire you?" No matter what questions are asked ("What are your strengths?" "Do you work well as part of a team?" or "Can you supervise people well?"), they are all ultimately asking "Why should I hire you?" Every time you say something, it is to give the interviewer more reasons to hire you, adding so much weight to your side of the scale that there is no question who should get the job.

Ten Key Things Employers Look For

Tom Jackson points out in *Interview Express* that every employer wants to know ten basic things about you: 1. What results will you achieve? 2. How soon will you become productive? 3. How much supervision will you need? 4. Do you generate more value than cost?

5. Can you become a high performer? 6. Will you fit into the culture? 7. Will you be fun to work with? 8. Are you responsible? 9. Can you manage your own development? and 10. Will you stay? One could add to the list, but these are the key issues that every employer wants the answer to. Every supervisor who has hired five or more people has been disappointed by at least one of those choices. So there is anxiety on the part of the supervisor that perhaps another mistake will be made. Your challenge is to assure the interviewer that there is no risk in hiring you because you can do the job. Throughout the interview you should share examples and answer questions in such a way that the interviewer knows you have these qualities at a high level. While you may be lacking some of the technical or specialized skills which are desirable, you'll have a good shot at landing the position if you can convince the person you have these qualities.

Let's look at these points one by one.

1. What results will you achieve?

Employers want results-oriented people. Therefore, you must describe past results and demonstrate that the results you have achieved in the past are typical of the results you will have in the future. Granted, the challenges you will face in the future will be different, but the employer will be satisfied if you can demonstrate that you seek challenges and consistently obtain positive results.

2. How soon will you become productive?

Employers want quick learners who have a knack for understanding what is expected and are willing to do whatever is necessary to get up to speed as rapidly as possible.

3. How much supervision will you need?

Your supervisor will expect you to be cooperative and accept advice and direction. But your supervisor also wants to give you assignments and know that they will be done on time and at high quality. Your supervisor may want periodic updates from you and he will want you to bring any major problems to his attention, but primarily he just wants the assignment done at high quality, with little intervention from him. Describe how past supervisors have entrusted heavy responsibility to you.

4. Do you generate more value than you cost?

The supervisor is looking for evidence that you are cost conscious and that you perform at a high level. Some people utilize excellent time management and prioritize well; as a result their value exceeds their cost. Throughout the interview look for opportunities to show that you bring real value to any job and any organization.

5. Can you become a high performer?

The employer is assessing your potential throughout the interview. The supervisor certainly wants to determine if you can handle the immediate job tasks, but also wants to determine how far you may go in the organization. Potential is sold by demonstrating a willingness to go beyond the norm, to learn quickly, and to work effectively with others.

6. Will you fit into the culture?

Every organization has its own culture. People with certain personalities will flourish in it while others may die slow lingering deaths. The corporate culture in some organizations rewards workaholism, while in others a social consciousness is emphasized. Knowing what the corporate culture is, and knowing in what types of environments you flourish, will help you sell yourself more effectively.

7. Will you be fun to work with?

The employer is not looking for the life of the party, or the person with a thousand jokes. Instead, employers want people who work well with others, are cooperative, considerate, and friendly, and who are enjoyable to be around. The grouch, the negativist, and the cynic are not sought after.

8. Are you responsible?

People who constantly seek more responsibility and can be trusted with it are highly desired. They take responsibility for their actions and do not attempt to blame their mistakes on others. They often volunteer for assignments and are willing to take on some of the "dirt work" because it will help them grow professionally.

9. Can you manage your own development?

While there is a place for training and mentoring, managers seek staff who will take responsibility for their own professional development. Show that you seek out opportunities and then go for it.

10. Will you stay?

If you have a stable work history, emphasize that you seek out high-quality organizations (such as the one you are then interviewing with) so you can grow and develop with them for many years. If your work history is checkered, look for opportunities to emphasize that what you want is stability and that you feel this organization will offer it.

Employers will also be looking for two other qualities:

Communication skills: While interviewing you the employer will be visualizing you dealing with customers, and key people from other departments. Without strong communication skills, the employer will not have confidence you can do the job.

Chemistry: The employer will be sensing whether the two of you can work well together. The employer will not be looking for a clone, but must have someone who is compatible. Demonstrate that you can get along with almost anyone. Sell your flexibility and adaptability. Throughout the interview keep in mind what it is that employers really want—and give it to them.

EXCITE AN EMPLOYER

Knowing the qualities employers look for (the above ten points) is very helpful as you prepare your interviewing strategy, determine which skills to sell, and decide which experiences you'll share. But we can take this concept one step further. You can actually get an employer excited about you by demonstrating that you can do any or all of the following: 1) **make** money for the organization; 2) **save** money for the organization; 3) **solve** problems the employer is facing; and 4) **reduce** the level of stress and pressure the employer is under.

If you succeed, you will actually cause the employer to visualize you already on the job. Your potential will become more important than any particular technical skill that you possess or lack. You will be judged by a different standard from your competitors. For example, before you convinced the employer that you could make money for her company or department, she was judging you to a large extent by how many of the required technical skills you possessed and how many years of experience you had in the field. Now a new element has been introduced. In fact, the roles are reversed as your competitors begin to be judged by whether they can make money for the organization. Their problem is that they have not been consciously selling the fact they can make money, save money, solve problems, or reduce the stress and pressure on the boss.

If you have been a good employee in the past and have a good work ethic, you have in fact made money for your organization, saved money, solved problems, and reduced the stress and pressure of your boss. I want to help you see how and when that has happened. Your competitors have also done so, but if they don't get the idea across, it won't show up as weight on their side of the scale.

Let's look at the specifics of how you can excite an employer.

Make Money For The Organization

When we think of making money for an organization, the emphasis is on increasing revenue. Ask yourself in what ways you have increased revenue for your past employers. An engineer who has personally designed successful products, or has consistently been part of teams that have developed successful products, has made money for an organization. People in marketing, advertising, and public relations will find obvious ways that they have made money for the organization.

There are several ways you can generate revenue for an organization.

Sales: If you were in sales and added new accounts, increased sales with existing accounts, or increased your market share, that is an obvious form of making money. If you are in inside sales and through solid product knowledge cause customers to purchase additional products that they might typically purchase elsewhere, you've made money for your organization.

Improve quality: If you can identify and implement ways to improve the products your organization sells, improve the service your organization delivers, or improve any internal processes, you will have generated more revenue. A shipping person who found a way to cut the average delivery time from three days to two days will have helped gain new customers and will have preserved existing customers.

Provide outstanding customer service: The 1990s were the decade of the customer. Good companies have always cared about their customers, but beginning in the late 1980s, it became a passion as organizations looked for every way to gain a competitive advantage. Organizations realized that providing great service to customers did not cost more money; it merely required hiring the type of people who were willing to deliver it. Companies that deliver great service hold on to existing customers even when they are not so competitive on price, and they gain new customers through referrals. Show that you truly care about your customers and you'll have an employer who is willing to pay a premium to get you to join their firm. Look for opportunities to share how you provide great service to customers. It should be an example where you went above and beyond the call of duty. The result might be that a customer has remained loyal for many years despite strong efforts of competitors to gain a foothold, or it might be a person who has continued to use your organization's services after moving to another company. If you know that your company has received referrals at least in part due to your efforts, mention that as well. If you have received verbal thanks from customers, quote them during an interview. If you have letters of thanks, either quote them or show them to the employer.

Save Money For The Organization

Saving money is just another form of making money. Employers love people who can save them money. Every dollar saved goes directly to improving the bottom line. If you came up with an idea that saved $10,000, that is equivalent to increasing sales $100,000 (assuming a 10% profit margin). Except for very large organizations, increasing sales $100,000 is not an easy thing to do. When it comes to saving money, nothing is insignificant. If you found a way to cut two hours a month on the production of a particular report, that's 24 hours saved per year. If everyone sought ways to save money, American corporations would be more productive, would be more competitive internationally, and would be able to provide you and your coworkers with raises.

Increase productivity: A client operated a very expensive piece of machining equipment at Boeing. His machine, along with the 20 others just like his, frequently experienced downtime. He began to experiment by replacing a two-dollar part about every eight weeks. His downtime was reduced significantly. Eventually all of the machine operators used his technique. He received an award of $4,000 for saving $40,000 per year with his idea.

Cut costs: Wise managers rely on their entire staff to identify ways to cut costs. Some organizations even form committees to identify new ways. Such a group at a local hospital recommended obtaining all of their disposable items from one source. By purchasing from one source they obtained a better discount, and the supplier agreed to stock each department on a daily basis. As a result the nurses devote more time to patient care and the supplier has a guaranteed revenue base. Making the system work required over 200 staff hours of discussion and planning, but it will pay for itself in less than six months.

Show that you are the type of person who is always looking for ways to cut costs. If you found ways to cut heating or energy costs, reduce overtime, cut the number of units that failed to meet specs, or any of hundreds of other ways to cut costs, share it with the interviewer.

Motivate others: Some people just have that ability to motivate others. Good supervisors have the ability. They hire good people and then provide them with the tools they need to do the job. They encourage them, reward them, praise them, and give them more responsibility. The staff in turn works harder and smarter and is always looking for better ways to do things. If you're that type of supervisor, describe situations where your ability to motivate people made a difference. Perhaps it was a really tough assignment where morale declined, but you encouraged and motivated them to give their best effort and they delivered a top quality product on schedule.

Some nonsupervisors also have this ability. Through their own high energy and willingness to take on even the grungiest tasks, they lead by example and cause others to put forth their very best effort. Look for experiences where you were the spark plug and share it vividly during the interview.

Managers love motivators. Not everyone has the ability, so if you are one who does, sell that fact throughout the interview.

Solve Problems

No organization has a shortage of problems or challenges. Even the most progressive and advanced organizations have problems and challenges because things change so rapidly. The system that was implemented three years ago and worked so well may be obsolete.

Some people just have the reputation of being problem solvers. They have the ability to identify problems early, when they are often easier and less expensive to solve. Others have the uncanny ability to put out fires. They develop such a reputation that even when they lack appropriate experience, they are still given major projects. Some are effective because even when they lack the expertise, they know how to assemble the experts and get the job done. They are known as doers.

Managers do not like problems. When their departments have problems, *their* bosses want to know when they'll be fixed. They don't care about the reasons and they don't want to hear excuses. They just want it fixed. You will make the life of your boss much easier if you are a problem solver.

The ability to put out fires is certainly a great skill to have, but to be a problem solver can also involve smaller problems as well. A problem solver can be one who knows instinctively what to do in a crisis situation. Karen was overseeing a fundraising auction and had hired a high-priced auctioneer. Just as things were about to begin, the hotel's sound system went dead. The egotistical auctioneer was ready to walk out, saying he would not participate without an adequate sound system. His solution was to reschedule the whole event. With more than 200 well-heeled people in attendance, that was not an option. Karen had the auctioneer sit tight for a few minutes as she discussed the situation with the hotel. Their only solution was to use a portable sound system. While the auctioneer balked at such an inadequate solution, he agreed to try it. As the setup was taking place, Karen entertained the troops and supplied them with more wine. Despite the less-than-perfect sound system, everyone had a good time and the auction set a new record for fundraising. Karen now has the confidence that she can handle virtually any crisis.

Effectively use technology: Some people know how and when to introduce technology. If a manual system works well, they won't seek to install a computerized system. When the old system doesn't measure up, however, they know how to estimate costs, bring in the experts, and make sure that the technology is installed on schedule and within budget. Whether the technology is a computer, a sophisticated communications system, or state-of-the-art manufacturing facilities, the person who can introduce technology effectively is highly regarded.

Being innovative: The innovative person sees ways to do things that simply do not occur to others. Some engineers, computer programmers, architects, and surgeons are known for their innovativeness. They are always looking for better ways to do things, often by making use of the latest technology. Others, however, are innovative because they come up with great solutions by using simple methods and low technology. If you are an innovative person, recall two or three experiences where you took a different path and made it work.

Reduce The Stress And Pressure On Your Boss

Every boss faces stress and pressure from various directions. Demonstrating that you can reduce the stress and pressure your prospective boss is facing will make you a highly desirable person. Start by selling your reliability, responsibility, and resourcefulness. By having confidence that responsibilities can be delegated to someone of your caliber, your prospective boss will actually visualize a life with less pressure.

Suppose your prospective boss attends a weekly two-hour meeting because he lacks confidence in any of his staff members to adequately represent the department. The boss feels his time could be better spent on other projects, but decisions are made at this committee meeting which sometimes have a major impact on the department.

During the interview you strike the employer as someone who can argue a strong case, and stand up to attacks from other departments. It quickly becomes obvious that several key responsibilities could be turned over to you. Suddenly this employer is feeling a great deal of weight rising from his shoulders. Maybe he could leave work an hour earlier a couple of nights a week. Perhaps he'll have time to work on that project that will establish his reputation in the company. It feels good to have some of the pressure off. "So what if she doesn't have experience with Excel. She's got so many other things going for her," he says to himself as he actually begins visualizing her acting on his behalf at that committee meeting.

CREDIBILITY

To interview effectively, you must convey your credibility. You accomplish this by showing that you are truthful, sincere, and genuine. Your truthfulness comes through by your not exaggerating your role in any of your accomplishments. It's hard to explain how, but many people can sense intuitively when someone is exaggerating. Your sincerity comes through by truly meaning what you say. Most employers will quickly see through a less than sincere, "I really like your tie," or some other comment that you might make. Genuineness comes through by showing that what you see is what you get. A genuine person does not put on airs or a false front. Of course you are trying to be your best, but you are not trying to appear to be something you are not. The great benefit of credibility is that once it's established, whatever you say from that point on tends to be believed. In fact, what you say will be believed unless you give the employer a reason to doubt you.

That's why you should do nothing to jeopardize your credibility. Consider, for example, how you might answer the question, "What is your biggest weakness?" Job hunting books written in the 1970s frequently recommended that you work out your answer so that your weakness really comes across as a strength. One recommended answer ran something like this, "I'd have to say that my greatest weakness is that I work too hard. My wife complains that I'm not around enough, and I guess sometimes I work my people too hard too." The employer was supposed to think, "Well, isn't it nice that if this guy is going to have a weakness it would be something like this." The problem is that the answer is so planned and contrived that it sounds insincere and thus lacks credibility.

Once you lose your credibility, everything you said before and everything you say after will come under greater scrutiny and there will always be an element of doubt about you. This is not the way to start a relationship. So do everything possible to establish credibility, and then do nothing to lose it.

PROJECT AND SELL A WINNING PERSONALITY

On a conscious and subconscious level, employers will be evaluating your personality and asking, "Do I like this person and will we work well together?" When considering two people with equal qualifications, the one with the most pleasing personality will always be hired. A job is similar to marriage in that the two of you may "live" together for many years. Work will be a lot more enjoyable if you like and respect each other.

In order to adequately sell yourself, you need to know your personality skills. Such skills include being appreciative, cooperative, energetic, loyal, mature, tactful, and emotionally stable. Employers highly value such qualities. Even someone seeking a CEO position must sell personality skills.

Your Actions Speak Loudly

During an interview you won't just rattle off claims of such characteristics as enthusiastic, energetic, tactful, or self-confident—you will demonstrate each one. In just twenty minutes, a perceptive interviewer can accurately assess you in each area—both by what you *say* and by what you *are*. The famous saying, "Your actions speak so loudly, I can't hear what you're saying," is especially applicable to the ways in which employers assess a job applicant's personality during an interview.

Imagine you are interviewing with a company that just fired an employee because he was uncooperative. You might be asked, "In this organization cooperation and teamwork are absolutely essential. Are you a cooperative person?" You might respond:

> Yes, I am very cooperative. When we were developing prototypes, I would have to coordinate the project with people from four or five different departments. We always got the project completed on time. None of us got our way on everything. We worked out our differences and we felt good about the results.

This example, which would be expanded upon in an actual interview, clearly illustrates that this is a cooperative, team-oriented person.

Reveal Positive Attributes

Your goal during the interview is to reveal as many positive attributes as possible. While your competitors are busy merely *describing* their technical strengths, you will be selling your personality skills as well as your technical skills.

Hiring Decisions Are Made On Emotion And Justified With Logic

There is a saying that sales are made on emotion and justified with logic. When you go to buy something, you start by liking it at an emotional level; you then look for ways to justify spending the money on the purchase. This process can be so subtle that few are even aware that it's taking place.

Hiring decisions are very similar. Your challenge is to get the employer to like you and to begin leaning your way. You do this by projecting enthusiasm, potential, and a winning personality. The employer has an emotional reaction— she begins to like you and feel comfortable with you. She senses your potential. Once you have hooked the employer emotionally, she will find a way to justify hiring you.

USING PERSONALITY SKILLS IN INTERVIEWING

Personality skills are skills that have become part of your personality. They are part of who you are. The tactful person does not wake up in the morning wondering if she should be tactful that day. Instead, when a situation arises which requires tact, the person spontaneously becomes tactful. Personality skills develop early in life and can be continually refined through experience.

Employers want evidence that a candidate is already strong in the personality skills deemed critical for a particular job. This is because it is difficult to improve people's personality skills through training. If you've never used a computer before, you can attend a two-day introductory course and begin navigating around with some confidence. It is extremely difficult, however, to send a tactless person to a one-week tactfulness workshop and expect the person to improve significantly.

You start the process by selling your personality skills. To identify and become more acquainted with your personality skills, rate yourself on the following 44 key skills. Rate yourself on a scale of 1–10, where 10 is excellent and 1 is poor. Be sure to give yourself a range—not all 8s, 9s and 10s. Avoid over-analyzing here—go through the list as quickly as you can.

For more information on personality skills visit www.cmr-mvp.com. You will find useful descriptio and sample statements for selling those skills in an int

Accepting	Goal-oriented
Appreciative	Growth-oriented
Assertive	Honesty/Integrity
Cheerful	Inquisitive
Compassionate	Insightful
Considerate	Loyal
Cooperative	Mature
Decision-making	Motivated
Decisive	Open-minded
Diplomatic	Optimistic
Discreet	Patient
Drive	Persistent
Easy-going	Reliable
Effective Under Stress	Resourceful
Efficient/Productive	Responsible
Emotionally Stable	Risk-taking
Energetic/Stamina	Self-confident
Enthusiastic	Sense of Humor
Flexible	Sincere
Forgiving	Sound Judgment
Friendly/Nice	Tactful
Generous	Thorough

Writing about your personality skills will prepare you for interviews. So once you've rated yourself on all these skills, pick out your top ten personality skills and write a short paragraph on each one describing how you are that way. This is a quick exercise; you're not trying for polished writing. Using your own shorthand, list an example for each skill. The example should illustrate your ability to use that skill at a high level. Your descriptions might read something like this:

Although some may say I seldom get excited, I do have a high degree of <u>enthusiasm</u> in many areas. It is not a gushy enthusiasm, but a strong, deep enthusiasm that comes from conviction. Example: Motivating the team on the Baxter project.

I am very <u>efficient</u>. This quality has been my worst enemy where I am now working. A difficult, demanding job appears so easy because I am efficient. No one fully recognizes my worth. Example: Cut the time it took to get month-end reports out from 8 days to 3 days.

I was <u>diplomatic</u> when I had to discuss accounting irregularities with the client's accountants. Example: Especially on the XYZ account, when we suspected fraud.

THE UNIVERSALLY DESIRED PERSONALITY SKILLS

Although all of the personality skills are valued by employers, only some of them are universally desired. For example, you can't even imagine an employer not wanting someone who is reliable. The universally desired personality skills are cooperative, effective under stress, efficient/productive, energetic, enthusiastic, reliable, responsible, and resourceful. Concentrate on these when you sell yourself in interviews, in addition to others that you rate yourself high in.

BEING WELL LIKED

Whenever a new person is being added to a department, there is always the question of whether the person will fit in. The employer has worked hard to create an effective team and now a new person is about to join the department. It is like a cook who has developed a delicious soup but now is considering adding a new ingredient. The new ingredient may provide just the right flavor or may completely spoil it. Of course the wrong decision with a soup is not nearly as serious as hiring the wrong person. The concern is whether the person will work effectively with the team *and* with the boss.

In an interview you will want to sell the fact that you have been well liked by colleagues and bosses in the past, but that is not enough. You must indicate the reasons you are well liked. That requires selling the skills that make one well liked: being appreciative, cheerful, considerate, cooperative, discreet, emotionally stable, friendly, loyal, optimistic, sincere, and tactful. You might indicate that you are the type who can get along with just about everyone, and then explain why. You would then describe some of your personality skills, using an example or two to verify you really do possess those qualities.

In interviews do not feel limited to using these specific words. Each of the words has synonyms which may be more appropriate or feel more natural for you. Sometimes a phrase will work better. Instead of saying you are joyful you might say, "I'm basically a person who enjoys life and people seem to like working with me." Or, instead of saying "I'm basically a very friendly person," you might say, "I'm the type of person who gets along with just about everyone." You could continue with:

> I like people and I try to find something good in everyone. I'm the only person who gets along with one particular coworker. She can be difficult, but she and I get along. I just ignore her idiosyncrasies. I'm cooperative and many colleagues ask me to join their task forces.

Selling Personality Skills And Transferable Skills

Once you've identified and described your personality skills, it's important to consider how you might best sell these skills. There are four primary ways: 1) State the skill and then give an example to back it up; 2) State the skill and describe how you use it; 3) While selling a skill using a specific experience, describe the experience so vividly that some of your other personality skills are clearly evidenced; and 4) *Be* it. That is, demonstrate that you possess the skill.

State the skill and give an example: During an interview you might be asked to describe your strengths. You could respond by saying:

> I'd have to say that one of my strengths is my ability to work effectively under stress. A good example would be when I was working on the Otis account. Out of nowhere our client told us that they needed a new ad campaign for a product that was not doing well. We had only two weeks to develop a campaign that would normally have been a two-month project. My staff and I practically lived at the office, but we got the campaign out. It was a very successful campaign for the customer.

If warranted, you could expand on this by taking two or three minutes to explain the details of the project.

State the skill and describe how you use it: Sometimes providing an example is not possible or not appropriate. Instead of giving an example you might say:

> I have a reputation for being reliable. People at work know that if a tough project has to get out on schedule, it should be given to me. When I agree to take on a project, my boss knows it's as good as done. I'll get it done no matter what.

In this instance a specific example was not used, but the person did everything possible to prove she is extremely reliable.

Describe an experience so vividly that other skills are evident: You may have indicated that one of your strengths is your flexibility and then offered an example which clearly illustrates your flexibility, but reveals other positive traits as well. When you describe your experiences vividly, even a halfway perceptive person will pick up other positive qualities without your having to label them. Of course you can also choose to state what some of those skills are.

Be it: Don't just say it, show it. For instance, you can demonstrate your energy level through the way you walk and talk, your body language, facial expressions, and your voice inflection. I can sense a person's energy level within the first minute we are together. Cheerfulness, insightfulness, joyfulness, open-mindedness, optimism, self-confidence, enthusiasm, sense of humor, and sincerity are all traits that can be demonstrated. Identify which skills you intend to demonstrate and determine how you will do so.

Practice: Practice telling your stories. Only by doing so can you really hone them down to their most important points. Describe the experiences so vividly that the interviewer forms a mental image. Mental images can last for weeks or months in an employer's mind; mere words may last five minutes.

Sell Exposure

If you know you lack certain skills or experience, look for ways to sell your exposure. In an interview your order of priority is: 1) Sell the experience you have that is identical or nearly identical to what is being sought; 2) Sell your related or similar experience; and 3) Sell exposure. Exposure means you have observed that task or skill being done by others, you worked closely with people who used that skill, or you assisted someone performing that skill on one or more occasions. People don't get hired *because* of their exposure to certain skills, but exposure can tip the balance scale just enough to make the difference. When all you have to sell is exposure to a skill, do not apologize. Rather, move straight ahead and make the most out of what you have to offer.

Let's assume that a person, who is currently a shipping and receiving manager for a medium-sized company, is interviewing for a management position with a smaller company in which he would be required to function in a variety of roles. Halfway through the interview he is asked, "Have you ever handled inside sales?" His response might be:

> As head of shipping and receiving, I had contact with the inside salespeople every day. By getting out rush orders for them, I saved their bacon a lot of times. Frequently, when customers had a question about a part and the inside salespeople were busy, the call would come to me. I know a lot of parts were sold because I was able to answer their questions.

This is selling exposure.

Notice there were no apologies and no saying, "Well, no, I've never really done it, but I have observed it." The person unabashedly and convincingly described his *exposure* to inside sales without giving any apologies or excuses regarding his lack of direct sales experience. He comes across as confident and aware.

Sell Yourself At Every Opportunity

The primary principle in interviewing is to always go for it. When the job you are interviewing for is fully described, and it seems to be less than what you really want, go for the offer anyway. People often consciously or unconsciously sabotage their own efforts, and as a result, don't get asked back for a second interview. My belief is that you never know whether you want the job until an offer is made, money is on the

Charlie

"... Well, *that's* out ... they want someone with at least two years' experience hosing down pigs on hot days ..."

*Had Charlie emphasized his transferable skills,
he might have gotten the job.*

table, benefits have been covered, and you have had a chance to negotiate in the things you want in, and to negotiate out the things you want out. People have negotiated for amazing things—and gotten them—but only because they had sold themselves so well that the employers were willing to do almost anything to bring them on board.

Sabotaging your efforts means that, somehow, you have failed to do your best. Consciously or unconsciously, your answers are not as sharp, or not as well thought out, or the zip in your voice is missing. The interviewer picks up on these cues.

I realize there are times when you immediately know the job is not for you. If this happens, resist the temptation to tune out. Perhaps the interviewer will also realize *this* job is not the right one for you and will offer you a *different* job instead.

You might indicate at the end of the interview that the job is not a good match. If you are highly interested in the company, however, or would especially like to work for this person, say so. There may be nothing else available right now, but the perfect job could materialize during the next six months, and you might be the primo candidate. If the person is impressed, he may refer you to someone else in the company who could use your talents. There is always the possibility that the job could be changed to suit you better. None of these positive things can happen if you stop selling yourself or fail to respond as best you can.

Power Words

Power words strengthen both resumes and interviews. Learn to use these action verbs in your speaking. Describe how you "decreased" absenteeism or "generated" new revenue. Look for ways to use these key words to add punch to your descriptions about yourself: I built a team of motivated staff and introduced new procedures that increased productivity.

Built	Initiated
Created	Introduced
Decreased	Organized
Designed	Pioneered
Enhanced	Saved
Established	Sold
Generated	Solved
Implemented	Transformed
Improved	Won
Increased	

SKILL-BENEFIT STATEMENTS

When you mention a skill, plan to turn it into a skill-benefit statement. Adding a benefit after mentioning a skill will double or triple its impact.

Salespeople are taught to emphasize benefits. If a salesperson merely mentions features (the same as skills for an interviewee) a sale will rarely take place. The customer wants to know how he or she will benefit if the product is purchased. It is the salesperson's responsibility to adequately explain the benefits of the product. It is your responsibility to sell the benefits that the employer will derive from the use of your skills. A customer needs the help of an honest and knowledgeable salesperson, just as an employer relies on the interviewee to make the strongest case possible for why his or her services should be purchased. Benefits are the key.

Review the following statements and notice the impact. These statements may have come in response to numerous questions including telling about yourself and describing your strengths.

> I establish rapport well with people. This has enabled me to gain a lot of new accounts. People trust me so they give me a small order and within a short time I usually have the bulk of their business.

> I really hear people. This enables me to mediate between groups having problems because they know I truly understand both sides.

> I'm an excellent problem solver. Everywhere I've worked I've taken on problems no one else could fix. I always find a way to fix a problem.

> I'm an excellent trainer. That means I can assess your training needs and in a short time have a program in place that ensures people are getting the right training.

What each person has done is state a skill, followed by a statement either indicating how it has helped past employers, or how it could help the prospective employer. Indicating how a skill has helped past employers clearly indicates how it will help a future employer.

In order to create skill-benefit statements, you must list the key skills you want to sell. List the skills first, then work on adding the benefit portion. You'll probably need to create three drafts of each skill-benefit statement until it is ready for use in an interview. When it is honed it will have the greatest impact.

CREATE YOUR TWO-MINUTE SELL

Every job seeker should develop a two-minute sell. At job fairs, in telephone screening interviews, during on-site screening interviews, or when talking to someone at a professional association meeting, your two-minute sell will open doors for you. A two-minute sell is simply a prepared spiel that quickly covers all of the key things that employers and others should know about you. If you have already identified 30-40 accomplishments and written about your top twelve, your two-minute sell will take 1-2 hours to develop and rehearse. Your competitors, who try to create a two-minute sell without having examined their accomplishments, will not be very effective.

Identify 4-6 Key Points You Want An Employer To Know About You

These points might include:
- Your education, degree(s), major
- Why you're interested in the position or the type of work
- Why you're attracted to the organization
- A summary of your work/volunteer experience with emphasis on successes
- A brief description of your current or most recent position
- A brief description of the job you've held that is most similar to the one you're interviewing for
- Two or three major strengths with one key example that demonstrates all of them
- Contributions you've made in jobs, in internships, or in voluntary roles
- Quantifiable results
- Awards
- Paraphrasing letters of appreciation from internal and external customers
- A paraphrased description of job reviews, mentioning only positives
- A summary of a project that demonstrates key skills

List the points you want to make. Do not write it word for Then begin practicing. Hone it until you can give it in less. Ask yourself—is it interesting? Will it hold the a interviewer? Is it well organized? Have I instilled a visu person's mind? Have I sold key personal qualities? Ha them I have the necessary technical skills?

Chapter 10

THE SEVENTEEN TYPES OF INTERVIEWS

There are seventeen basic types of interviews: telephone screening interviews, screening interviews, interviews with headhunters and employment agency counselors, second and third interviews, nondirected interviews, conversational interviews, panel interviews, group interviews, series interviews, behavior-based interviews, lunch interviews, simulation interviews, situation interviews, on-site interviews, campus interviews, stress interviews, and job fair interviews.

TELEPHONE SCREENING INTERVIEWS

Telephone interviews are always screening interviews. In five minutes the interviewer can often gather all the information necessary to determine whether a full interview is warranted. When local employers call, the telephone interview is usually quite short, typically no more than ten minutes. In recent years, however, some companies will spend up to an hour on a telephone screening interview. Ask in advance how long your interview will last.

Employers calling from out of state are likely to talk to you for half an hour. Those they choose to interview in person will be flown in, so everything possible must be done to determine that the person is a solid candidate.

While the process may seem unfair, in that it may screen you out before you've had a chance to demonstrate your worth, the telephone screening interview is heavily used. So determine to sell yourself. Make the interviewer want to meet you. Let your enthusiasm sparkle. Sell your expertise, your related experience, and your potential. Tell the person you are interested in the position and would like an interview.

Most telephone screening interviews are prearranged, but sometimes you'll be caught by surprise. For that reason, don't hesitate to tell the person that you'd like a few minutes to get yourself ready. Then offer to call the person back within five or ten minutes. Immediately reread the data you've accumulated on that employer. Then get mentally prepared to sell yourself.

To help you in telephone screening interviews, set out notes on your desk by the phone so you can refer to them. These should just be key words to remind you of accomplishments, skills, or major points you want to make.

When you are asked whether you have any questions, you know the interview is drawing to a close. Ask a question or two to clarify the duties and after getting the answer, close with, "It sounds like a very interesting position and one where I could definitely contribute. I guess my only other question is when can I meet with you?"

SCREENING INTERVIEWS

If the company is large enough to have a human resources department, the first interview will often be conducted by a personnel specialist, recruiter, or interviewer. These people interview frequently and often have extensive training in interviewing techniques. Their interviews will generally be planned in advance, and applicants will typically be asked the same questions. The screening interview is generally short; its purpose is to eliminate those applicants who are obviously not qualified. The problem is that the screener seldom has a full understanding of what the job entails. This can be particularly frustrating for applicants who have lots of potential but not much direct experience, since they are usually screened out after the screening interview. There are numerous things you can do, however, to make it past the screening stage.

It helps to understand the motivation of the screener. A screener will never be criticized for screening out someone who has potential but lacks the desired background. If someone slips through who a manager feels was completely unqualified, the screener is going to hear about it. That screener will not take such a chance a second time. With this in mind, your challenge is to show that you meet or exceed the minimum qualifications. Your only goal is to be passed on to the hiring manager.

A screening interview will consist primarily of probing questions designed to determine your technical competence. The screener may even have a checklist which will be gone through quickly to determine how much experience you have in each area. Questions will also be asked to reveal inconsistencies. These screeners will also be the ones most likely to check out your references. While the emphasis is on technical competence, they will also screen out those whose personalities clearly would not fit in the corporate culture. Don't be concerned if the screener seems rather impersonal—you may be the twentieth person interviewed that day. Simply do everything you can to gain the screener's seal of approval.

INTERVIEWS WITH HEADHUNTERS AND EMPLOYMENT AGENCY COUNSELORS

Whether it is a telephone or face-to-face interview with a headhunter, or a face-to-face interview with an employment agency counselor, you've got to sell yourself. Once the decision has been made to refer you to the client for an interview, the headhunter will help you land the position, but until then it is strictly sell, sell, sell.

Most interviews with headhunters will be by telephone since they will often be calling from out of town. Even if they are local, they will seldom bring you in for an interview until they are convinced you are a strong candidate. Many will do all their interviewing with you by phone. Accept that fact and then use the telephone to market yourself. The interview should be treated very much like any telephone interview.

Headhunters often call people asking for leads on qualified candidates. They will describe a position and then ask if you know anyone who would be a good fit. If the job seems interesting, respond by saying, "Well, it sounds like a job designed for me. Tell me more about it." If you don't want to commit so early, simply ask for more information. Then if you're still interested, sell yourself. In many cases you were the person the headhunter wanted anyway, but they often use this indirect way to get you to listen to their proposal.

Interviews with employment agency counselors will generally be face to face since that is the way they prefer to operate. View this type of interview as a screening interview. Your main goal is to demonstrate that you more than meet the minimum qualifications and that you have a great deal of potential.

SECOND AND THIRD INTERVIEWS

Obviously, being invited back for a second or third interview is a positive sign. If your first interview was with someone from human resources, and the person you will now meet with is your prospective boss, the interviewing process is really just beginning. If you are meeting for the second or third time with your prospective boss, a job offer may be coming, so preparation for salary negotiations is crucial.

If this is the first meeting with your prospective boss, prepare to sell yourself. Learn everything possible about the person and the position. During your interview with the human resources representative, you should have received a good overview of the position, but if not, you can call the HR person back to clarify some points. Be sure you know the name and title of the person you will interview with and the department. Write down questions about the position that you would like to have clarified.

If this will be a second or third interview with the same person, you should go into the interview with an agenda. You should identify the points you want to make in much the same way you should for a first interview. The difference is that you know much more about the position and the organization than you did at the first interview. You know what points you sold in the first interview, so you can prepare to sell additional skills in the next interview. You also know that there were areas in your experience that were not as strong as the employer desired. During this upcoming interview, you must do your best to sell whatever exposure you have in those areas.

By getting a second interview, you are already a finalist. Usually no more than four candidates are brought back for second interviews. A third interview usually means you are the number one choice and the interviewer is using one more opportunity to observe you and to see if anything about you might yet disqualify you. It could also mean that you are one of two finalists who are being brought back for a third interview. Continue to sell your strengths.

NONDIRECTED INTERVIEWS

Nondirected interviews are generally conducted by untrained interviewers who are simply asking a series of questions without specific goals in mind—hence they are nondirected. To do well in these interviews, remember that while you do not control the direction of the interview, you do control the content. Even if the interviewer seems unfocused, you should be very focused. You should enter the interview with your own agenda, making sure you share the experiences that will sell you. Interviewers have been known to run out of questions during this type of interview. If this happens, you might take some degree of control by saying, "Perhaps I should share with you some of my strengths that should prove helpful in this position." If the interviewer indicates a willingness for you to share this information, take it from there.

CONVERSATIONAL INTERVIEWS

Conversational interviews are interviews that just seem to flow, as a normal conversation would. Questions come as a result of what you've just previously said. You're often asked to elaborate on a previous point or experience. It appears that there is no prepared list of questions.

Conversational interviews come from two types of interviewers—trained and untrained. The trained conversational interviewer knows what he or she wants to accomplish and will find ways to take the conversation in the direction that will yield the necessary information about you. The untrained conversational interviewer has no plan and will probably not gain much insight from a directionless interview. With an untrained conversational interviewer you may need to give the conversation direction by offering to cover certain areas that the interviewer should probably know about. Most of the points covered here refer to an experienced conversational interviewer.

The conversational interviewer believes that rapport is crucial to a successful interview. The interviewer wants you to feel comfortable and will go out of his way for you not to feel pressure. The interview quickly takes the tone of two friends chatting and enjoying themselves. It often feels as if the interviewer is simply trying to get to know you better.

With an experienced conversational interviewer the goal is to get you feeling so comfortable that eventually you reveal things about yourself that you would not likely have shared in a structured interview. The conversational interviewer wants to get to know you as a person and uses conversation to get you out of the façade so many interviewees try to present. This interviewer wants the real you. Throughout the interview the conversational interviewer is trying to determine whether you'll fit in the organization.

The danger in this type of interview is becoming too relaxed. An experienced conversational interviewer has a plan and knows the type of information he or she seeks. Keep in mind that you are continually being evaluated. The interviewer has an agenda, knows the information he or she wants, and has determined that the conversational style works best.

Remember, you also should have your own agenda and you should never forget that each time you open your mouth it is to sell yourself. Use the conversation to bring in examples whenever possible. You can say, "What you just said reminds me of a time when…"

PANEL INTERVIEWS

In the panel interview, two or more people interview you simultaneously, usually taking turns asking questions. Sometimes the questions have been determined in advance. In other panel interviews you may be interviewed by five individuals who have their own separate agendas. In a panel interview you'll often find that the only person really listening to your answer to a question is the person who asked it. Your primary goal is to make *each* member feel totally involved in the interview *and* totally involved with each of your responses. You can do this by resisting the tendency to make eye contact only with the questioner. Keep each person involved by looking at each one and making each one feel important and attended to.

Government agencies frequently use the panel interview to narrow a field of candidates down to three. The department head then makes a final selection from among those three.

John Caple, author of *The Ultimate Interview*, suggests that during a panel interview, you identify the person who is most in sync with you. That person will be nodding in agreement, smiling, even laughing at times, and will be listening intently. Once you have that person on your side, do your best to draw in another person and make that person an ally as well. Don't be concerned about the relative power of these allies, they can often sway an entire group to be favorable toward you.

With panel interviews it is particularly important to be succinct. With long answers you will lose the attention of several panel members.

Do not be bothered if most panel members sit there with expressionless faces. This is typical. If you find one or two who are clearly involved, make the most of it, but don't be surprised if they show little enthusiasm. Just continue selling yourself and maintaining your high energy level throughout.

GROUP INTERVIEWS

In a group interview, you will find yourself amongst a group of candidates who are all vying for the same position. Although there will generally be a clearly identifiable person who is in charge of the process, there may also be other company employees in your midst who are pretending to be candidates. You won't know who they are, but they'll be closely observing what you say and how you behave. In some group processes the observers may be watching you from behind a one-way glass. In the group interview, the observers are trying to determine how you interact with people. They may divide the candidates into groups and give them a task to work on. They will then observe who the natural leaders are and which people actively participate in the group process. Generally, the candidates who offer the least to the group receive lower ratings. One question some airlines have used when interviewing flight attendants was, "Why would you make a better flight attendant than the person to your right?" The best way to answer that question, or questions like it, is not to put the other person down, but to emphasize your own strengths.

SERIES INTERVIEWS

The series interview consists of consecutive interviews with two or more people in the organization. Four or five interviews in one day is common. Typically, the interviewers have not met to determine who should ask certain questions or even to discuss the goal of the interview. After the interviews are completed, all of the interviewers will meet to discuss each person interviewed. While you certainly want to sell yourself to each person, the person who counts most is the hiring manager. Be sure you know in advance who that person is. It is rare to be interviewed by fewer than two people for anything other than entry-level positions.

You need to muster lots of energy to go through a series interview. It can be grueling to meet with four people over a three- to six-hour period. There is a tendency to forget what you said to whom. You may find yourself wondering, "Have I already shared that accomplishment with this person?" Except for one or two significant experiences that you might share with each interviewer, try to share a variety of stories and examples.

Before the interviewing begins, find out from the person arranging the interviews who you will be meeting with, and how much time to set aside. This is particularly important if the interviews will require that you take time off from work.

The most torturous interview I have ever heard of was told to me by a client. He flew in for his interview on Wednesday, and beginning Thursday morning, he interviewed with ten partners in a law firm over an eight-hour period. That evening he attended a party at the home of one of the partners and was in the spotlight throughout the party. He got back to his hotel room after midnight. At 7 a.m., he hopped a flight to another city where he began the interviewing process all over again with six partners at the home office of the law firm. Except for his five hours of sleep, this person was either on the hot seat (during the interviews) or on stage (during lunch and at the party) for 20 hours. He survived the experience, however, and is currently with that firm.

BEHAVIOR-BASED INTERVIEWS

Behavior-based interviewing consists of asking questions which enable the interviewer to know how you have actually reacted or behaved in certain types of situations. Research has confirmed that employers can more accurately determine those who will succeed on the job by identifying actual past behavior. Behavior-based interviewing is based on the concept that future behavior is best predicted by past behavior, and that future success is best predicted by past success. In *Get Hired*, Paul Green, who has popularized behavior-based interviewing, states, "Once we become adults, we tend to resist change. We develop habits, both good and bad, that are hard to break without concentrated effort. We also lose some awareness of these habits, so that when asked to describe how we behaved in a past situation, we tend to give a reasonably accurate picture of what we did. We may not even be aware that certain of these actions do not reflect well on us."

About 150,000 managers are being converted to this style of interviewing each year, and entire companies, Hewlett-Packard and AT&T among them, train all of their managers in the techniques.

While standard interviews consist of questions like, "Tell me about your last job," or "Why did you leave your last job?" behavior-based questions include:

Tell me about a time when you worked under an extremely tight deadline.

Tell me about a situation where you were particularly proud of the creativity you demonstrated.

Describe a situation where you had to deal with a difficult customer or coworker.

What makes behavior-based interviews unique is that each question must be answered with a specific example.

The behavior-based interview is one of the toughest types of interviews you will face, but if you are prepared, it can be the most enjoyable and challenging. Behavior-based interviews are usually conducted by people who have received extensive training in interviewing techniques. Every question is asked with a specific purpose and has been selected with great care. Managers prepare for the interviewing process by first analyzing the job and its requirements. During the analysis stage, the manager determines which technical skills and personal qualities are most needed to do the job.

Avoid Sketchy Responses

The person who does best in behavior-based interviews is the one who has taken the time to recall dozens of past experiences, and is prepared to share them in a vivid yet concise manner. Practitioners of behavior-based interviewing report to me that most interviewees provide responses which are simply too general and sketchy. For example, a typical response to a question like, "Tell me about a time when you responded well to a high-stress situation," would be:

> Well, as you know, I work for Alaska Airlines, and we are constantly under pressure to meet the needs of customers who have lost their luggage or missed a connecting flight. You just can't survive here if you can't handle stress well. I think I do my best work under stress.

The response of the behavior-based interviewer to such an answer would be to push for specifics by saying something like, "I appreciate your overview, but what I'd like is for you to give me a specific example when you were under a lot of stress and you really rose to the occasion." The behavior-based interviewer is like a bulldog who won't give up until the question has been properly answered. Those who are prepared to share specific examples really shine in these situations.

Be Prepared For Positive And Negative Questions

The behavior-based interviewer will typically have a list of 8–12 personal qualities and 5–10 technical skills which are deemed crucial to success on the job. Questions will have been selected to reveal that you have or don't have the required skills, knowledge, or experience. Because many of the questions will be difficult to answer, the interviewer will often encourage you to take as much time as you need to think of an example.

Another unique aspect of behavior-based interviewing is that you will be asked to describe situations in which you were not successful. In traditional interviews you might be asked one such question, but in a behavior-based interview, a positive question will often be followed by a negative question. For example, a line of questioning may begin, "Tell me about a time when you faced a difficult interpersonal conflict with a boss or coworker and you were able to improve the situation." That question may be followed with, "No one is able to overcome all interpersonal conflicts. Describe a situation where no matter what you did, you just weren't able to resolve the conflict."

In the language of behavior-based interviewing, this is a request for "disconfirming" or "contrary" evidence. The behavior-based interviewer wants to see all sides of you. If the behavior-based interviewer is feeling very positive about you, that person will intentionally ask you a question that will cause you to reveal a less positive side of you. You can see that this second question is particularly difficult. First, it may be difficult to even think of such an example. Second, you may have reservations about sharing the example that comes to mind because it may show you in a bad light. Remember, everyone will be asked the same or similar negative questions; no one will be allowed to dodge such questions. In this case the interviewer is using the question to determine whether you deal with conflict in a mature way, or whether you allow your emotions and insecurities to get in the way.

Be Prepared To Describe Each Job In Detail

Another type of behavior-based interviewing places great emphasis on having you give extensive information about each job you've held. When using this style, the interviewer will ask for particular information about each position. The information requested typically includes: job title, duties, major challenges you faced and how you handled them, most and least enjoyable aspects of the job, your greatest accomplishments, and your significant mistakes or disappointments. You will also be asked to describe each of your supervisors, including their strengths and weaknesses. Finally, you will for leaving. Then you will be asked focused q learning ability, analysis skills, judgment, inno munications skills, management style, and ma ingly, this type of interview can last as long a especially when interviewing for a managemen

Preparation Is The Key, So Recall Dozens Of Experiences

As in any interview, preparation is the key to selling yourself effectively in a behavior-based interview. That preparation consists of recalling 30–40 accomplishments and expanding on 8–15 of your top accomplishments. In addition, jot down notes to help you recall dozens of other experiences. Usually a phrase of five to ten words is sufficient. So in addition to a list of 30–40 accomplishments, you should list an additional 40–50 "experiences." These experiences will simply be things that happened to you that somehow stand out in your memory. Some will meet the definition of an accomplishment (something you did well, enjoyed doing, or got satisfaction from), but others will not. Some may even be negative experiences. This is important because behavior-based interviewers often ask for negative things about you. In behavior-based interviews, you must quickly recall several experiences, select the most appropriate one, and then describe it effectively.

In behavior-based interviews, you will always be given adequate time to think of an example. So once an example comes to mind, take five to ten seconds to quickly walk yourself through the experience to determine what the ramifications of using it will be. Those extra seconds could save you from sharing an inappropriate story.

Preparing for behavior-based interviews can take several hours, as you can see. The behavior-based interviewer wants you to be well prepared and wants to hear the very best example you have for each question. The better your responses, the better the interviewer can predict your success on the job. Since most people are not prepared to tell vivid stories which demonstrate specific strengths, you can set yourself apart by your preparation. Practitioners of behavior-based interviewing indicate that the typical interviewee requires five or six questions before they truly grasp what the interviewer wants. Your preparation will enable you to shine with the very first question.

EAKFAST/LUNCH/DINNER INTERVIEWS

rviews at restaurants may occur early in the interview process, you they are used when making a final decision. It represents to se rtunity to observe your social graces. The meal may also vour ability at conversation and to see how comfortable h settings. The interviewer may be using the occasion notability and your astuteness at interacting with senior managers. If you have already had two or more interviews with this person, and you notice that the interviewer is simply carrying on a conversation and is not asking typical interview questions, it is obvious that you are a finalist. The interviewer is seeking to observe another side of you. Accept this and do not work overly hard at mentioning personal strengths, but continue to show that your personality will fit in well with the organization.

Restaurant interviews tend to be more relaxed than other interviews, but they also require you to be more alert. There is a tendency to let down your guard during such an interview. While it is important to come across as genuine and willing to reveal yourself, you must also remember that even in this informal interview you are being judged, and therefore must take some care in what you reveal.

If the restaurant interview takes place early in the interview process, before you've had a chance to adequately sell yourself, you'll face special challenges. Because of the relaxed nature of a lunch interview (which it usually will be), it is all too easy to simply chat and talk about topics that may be interesting, but do not help you sell yourself. You must be sure to take the opportunity to sell yourself whenever possible.

Avoid finger food (other than sandwiches) and potentially messy food such as spaghetti. Eat while the host is speaking so you can talk later. Order something priced the same as your host's choice or slightly less. If unsure of the appropriate price range, ask your host what he or she recommends, since the person has undoubtedly dined there before. That will give you a clue as to the price range to look at. You can also casually ask what your host is going to have. Your host will always pick up the check. Merely thank the person for a delicious meal.

Do not order alcohol unless the host insists or orders for you. If you do drink, nurse it throughout the meal even if your host orders one or two more. If encouraged to order another, tactfully decline with a statement such as, "It's very good, but really, this is fine." If there is a bottle at the table and the waiter tries to pour another glass for you, merely put your hand over the glass and say no thank you. If your host pours another glass, accept it, but barely touch it throughout the rest of the meal. Remember, you're being observed and you must be at your best.

A former supervisor of mine was taken to lunch by four executives. During the lunch they regaled each other with some off-color jokes. Sam chose not to get involved and only smiled politely as the others were laughing. Wise for him. If he had joined in with some stories of his own, he would not have been hired. It was all a test, and he passed.

SIMULATION INTERVIEWS

In simulation interviews you are asked to demonstrate abilities by performing tasks or by taking on a role such as dealing with a difficult customer. For an office position you might be given a hundred folders and asked to alphabetize them. To test prioritization abilities you might be given ten tasks and be required to determine the best order in which to do the tasks. Relatively few interviews use simulation throughout. Far more frequent is an interview with one or two simulations. While most interviews contain no simulations, it is important to understand them and to have a sense of what to do in a simulation.

During an interview you might be given a situation with an angry customer, with the interviewer taking on the role of the customer. Or, you might be handed a pen (or some other object) and told, "Sell me this pen." The interviewer will be looking for an ability to sell benefits and to ask for the order. This question used to be asked exclusively of salespeople, but is asked more frequently than in the past because every employee who has customer contact is viewed as a salesperson. See question 47 on page 178 for more on how to sell an object handed to you in an interview.

Prepare for simulation interviews by anticipating the kinds of things an employer might want to test you on through the use of simulation. Pick one or two and think through how you would handle it.

Being prepared psychologically is critical. The biggest problem people face is high anxiety when simulation is introduced into an interview. In simulations the key thing to remember is that there is rarely only one way to do something. You will generally be judged on your thought process. For example, if the interviewer takes on the role of an angry or difficult customer he is observing your ability to stay calm, to calm down the customer, to listen effectively, and to come up with good solutions.

SITUATION INTERVIEWS

With situation interviews, a situation is described and you must explain what you would do in those circumstances. It can be as simple as, "A customer calls and starts yelling because it is now five p.m. and an important package was to have arrived from the warehouse at one What do you do?"

more sticky when you're given a situation where it appears g to lose no matter what you do. Consider this: You're the sales manager and the production department is fabricating parts for a new and potentially huge customer. The parts are supposed to ship today. A long-time and major customer calls with a complaint that 10% of his last shipment of parts is bad and he absolutely must have good parts tomorrow morning. One of the two is going to get their products late yet both say they absolutely must have them on time.

These are difficult questions because you can't anticipate them or specifically prepare for them. These questions are a test of your judgment. People face new situations frequently and they have to rely on their wisdom, their ability to think clearly under pressure, and their ability to get at the heart of an issue.

If you have been in a similar situation you could state that and ask if you could describe your actual experience. This will probably be permitted. If this question has a formal method for scoring (as they often do) the interviewer will insist that you answer the question as it was presented. You would then describe what you would do and why.

In situation interviews it is important to realize that how you arrive at your decision is often as important as the decision or action you propose to take.

This question should virtually never be answered with a simple "I would do such and such." In addition to stating what you would do, you should also indicate the options you considered and why you selected the ones you did. Demonstrate that you are willing to make tough decisions and that you are prepared to defend your decisions and live with the consequences. As you finish describing which actions you would take you could then briefly mention a similar situation and how you actually handled it.

ON-SITE INTERVIEWS AT HEADQUARTERS

You've succeeded. You did well in telephone interviews and local interviews; now you've been invited to corporate headquarters for more interviews. Knowing what to expect and how to prepare can increase the odds you'll get an offer. Throughout the process demonstrate enthusiasm for the job and the company.

From the beginning, make sure you understand the process. The invitation will come from a human resources professional. Ask any questions you have at that time, but don't worry if you forget something since you can always call later to clarify any points. Your plane tickets will be sent directly to you. The company will make a direct payment to your hotel.

Make your trip as worry-free as possible. If you're not sure how to get from the airport to the hotel, ask your contact person. If you're not sure if you are to take a taxi to the corporate headquarters or will be picked up at the hotel, ask. It is your responsibility to get the information you need. Also ask how you should handle your incidental expenses such as taxis and meals. You will typically be reimbursed after submitting your receipts.

Know the schedule. Some companies will send you a schedule in advance, but others will give you the schedule only when you arrive. To be psychologically prepared, it is best to know in advance who you will meet and their titles. Ask your contact person who the people are and what they are likely to want to know. For example, sometimes one of the interviewers is a technical specialist, and that person's primary task will be to test your technical knowledge.

You will normally arrive the night before your interviews. Being well rested for six to eight hours of meetings and interviews will be critical.

Your first appointment will probably be with a human resources specialist who will provide information about the company and will ask a few questions. Your next appointment will likely be with the person who would be your direct supervisor. After that you may meet future colleagues and perhaps your boss' boss.

Lunch may consist of a quick bite at the company cafeteria or a long lunch at an expensive restaurant. Lunchtime is often used to chat in an informal way. In such a setting, relax and enjoy lunch, but remember that you are still being interviewed. Use the time to demonstrate that you are an interesting, knowledgeable person capable of speaking on numerous topics.

Be nice to everyone you meet. Some managers make a point of asking their secretaries what they thought of a certain candidate. Word that the person was rude is usually the kiss of death.

In the afternoon you may get a tour, particularly if you are interviewing at a manufacturing facility. The tour could be guided by your prospective boss, but it is more likely to be someone from human resources or a department staff person. Show enthusiasm by looking attentive and by asking questions. Tell them when something you are being shown genuinely impresses you. Ask questions about what they _____ to improve quality, or ask about any new products coming _____ ually talking, you can ask what the person likes or _____ t the organization. When asked tactfully, and after _____ gotten to know each other, this is a very acceptable

_____ ointment of the day will likely be with the human _____ you met at the beginning of the day. The person will _____ remaining questions. If you are still unsure of growth potential, this is the time to ask. This person will also want to discern whether you are likely to accept an offer if extended. If you know you would, do not hide your enthusiasm.

Before the interview, research the region you'll move to. Learn about the cost of living, climate, and culture. Try to determine in advance if there is anything about the region to cause you to not want to move there. While on your visit, ask people what they like and dislike about the area.

The Ethics of On-Site Interviewing

Recruiters and placement directors are in agreement on the ethics of on-site interviews. If you have no interest in a company that invites you to an on-site interview, or if you know you would be unwilling to relocate there, do not accept an offer for an on-site interview just to get practice at interviewing or to explore a new city.

Go to each on-site visit with the intention of exuding enthusiasm and confidence, and of selling yourself at all times.

CAMPUS INTERVIEWS

For college students about to graduate, the campus interview can make a tremendous difference in how well their careers begin. The organizations that visit campuses tend to be large companies which may be local, but more likely are from out of state.

The main factor of success in campus interviews is preparation. Read the recruiting literature that the company will have sent prior to sending the recruiter. Follow the instructions of your placement office because failure to follow the rules will jeopardize your effectiveness. Seek out opportunities to do practice interviewing with counselors at the placement center so you will be relaxed and confident. Get advice on how to dress.

Be sure to do your homework on the organization. This "tragic" story shows you why. In the very first question of the interview, the recruiter asked the candidate what he knew about the organization. He stared at the floor, saying nothing. After waiting for about 30 seconds the recruiter asked, "Did you read our literature?" At that point the young man looked up and said, "No sir." The recruiter then stood up and said, "This interview is over!" He may have been a great candidate for the job, but one lapse in judgment cost him dearly. Recruiters are looking at the seemingly smallest things to try to assess you. In this case the candidate revealed a lack of initiative and preparation.

The campus interview is a screening interview and will last 20–30 minutes. Recruiters are especially looking for enthusiasm, potential, maturity, and a sense of whether you will fit into the organization's culture. Recruiters from private corporations are looking for evidence that you value free enterprise and have some understanding of what business is really all about. This is especially important if you are a liberal arts major.

Remember, your competitors for these jobs will be people just like you: recent grads who have probably had the same type of low-level summer and part-time jobs that you've had. For that reason you are selling qualities and skills. Try to squeeze two or three quick stories into the interview which reveal your personality skills and transferable skills. Don't be embarrassed by your summer jobs. Instead, speak about them with pride and describe how you strengthened your work ethic through those jobs and learned how to cooperate with others. Of course if you have gained any work experience which is directly related to the type of position you are interviewing for, make the most of it. If you had an internship in a related field, work hard to identify all of the skills you gained or refined, and look for ways to discuss your experiences during the interview.

Thank the recruiter for the interview, indicate that you would very much like a second interview at corporate headquarters, and be sure to send a thank-you note.

STRESS INTERVIEWS

Stress interviews, which are seldom used these days, consist of questions and situations designed to put the interviewee under heavy stress. Supposedly the interviewee will reveal how he or she will actually react to stress on the job. It supposedly also reveals the "real you" and the level of poise one possesses. The stress is so artificial, however, that little is learned. Classic examples from the past included making the interviewee sit in a chair that had one leg significantly shorter than the others, or positioning the interviewee so a bright light shined directly in his or her eyes. Such interviews included making such accusatory statements as "You're hiding things from us, aren't you?" Put-down questions would include, "What's wrong with you, why aren't you making more money at your age?" While these bizarre techniques were seldom used, even during the peak use of stress interviews during the 1950s and 1960s, they reveal the lengths that employers were willing to go in order to select the right person.

Rapid-Fire Questions

Another form of stress questioning involves asking rapid-fire questions so that the candidate barely has time to think. A client once had an interview in which two interviewers sat at opposite ends of a rectangular table. While answering one person's questions, his back was turned to the other. These two interviewers would each ask yet another question before the interviewee had finished the previous one, so he was constantly turning one way and then the next. Had he realized that he was being put through a stress interview, he could have simply turned to the one asking the fresh question and stated, "That's an important question and I would like to answer it, but before I do I feel I need to fully answer Mr. X's question." Using this approach once or twice would have stopped their childish game.

Silence

A common form of stress is to use silence. You may have just completed an answer, yet the interviewer maintains silence and simply looks at you. If you break the silence, you lose. If you were truly finished with your answer you should remain silent. Maintain a soft look at the interviewer and begin to silently count the seconds. It is almost guaranteed that the interviewer cannot hold out for more than 15 seconds. If you find it difficult to maintain eye contact during the silence, look down, but do not show any nervousness or discomfort with the situation.

Interviewers May Confront You

An interviewer may begin challenging or disputing some of your statements. Immediately realize that you are being tested—probably to see if you can handle confrontations. One solution is to take the attention off yourself by eliciting your interviewer's feelings. It could be as simple as, "What do you feel the best approach is?" or "How are you trying to deal with that at XYZ?" Another response is to tactfully ask, "Why do you feel that way?" While you should avoid arguments with a prospective boss, you need to show that you don't cave in as soon as a more senior person challenges your beliefs or assertions. You can defend your positions without becoming defensive.

The Antidote

Although the pure stress interview is seldom used today, some employers still like to put people under stress at different times during an interview. The primary antidote to the stress interview is to simply recognize it. As soon as you realize the interviewer is intentionally putting you under stress, say to yourself, "Aha, I know what you're doing, and you're not going to get me to panic or get angry or become defensive." Then become assertive, as the person receiving the rapid-fire questions should have.

JOB FAIR INTERVIEWS

With today's tight job market, employers are looking at all the possible ways to find high-quality job candidates. Job fairs are one cost-effective way to accomplish that. Here are the reasons why you should attend job fairs:

> There are real jobs there.
> You get a chance to practice your "Two Minute Sell."
> You get a feel for what employers are seeking in the
> current market.
> You'll gain solid interview practice by having several
> low-stress interviews.
> You can scout out organizations that you may be
> interested in.
> You'll come away with a nice collection of pens,
> yoyos, and other trinkets.

Before attending a job fair, determine who you most want to meet. A couple of days before the job fair, a full-page ad in the major local paper will list which organizations will attend, and will provide a floor layout indicating where each organization will be located. For many job fairs there will also be a web site where you can learn more about the job fair. Often there will be links to the web sites of the organizations attending. At a company web site you should be able to read about the organization and learn what their current openings are.

After reviewing a company's web site, you should know what they are looking for. If not, many organizations will post at the booth a list of the types of positions they are filling. Most organizations will spend a few minutes with anyone willing to wait in line, so if you are really interested in the organization but don't have a background they are currently seeking, stand in line anyway. While they will quickly realize your background does not match current openings, if they see potential in you, they will still give you some quality time.

You'll meet all kinds of people at a job fair. One organization may send a recruiter who has been on the job for six weeks and knows little about the organization or the openings available. Others will send hiring managers who are there to conduct serious screening interviews with top candidates. Most will rely on their HR people who will be knowledgeable and helpful.

With some recruiters you'll sense that they are genuinely trying to get to know you and your capabilities to assess how well you might fit into their organization. With others it will appear that they are just collecting resumes. Some will not only tell you about the organization and the available positions, but will screen you by asking two or three interview questions. The more closely you appear to meet their needs, the more time they'll spend with you.

You'll get about five minutes with a recruiter, so make the most of it. You'll usually begin by presenting your two-minute sell—your well-rehearsed-but-not-canned-sounding sales presentation. (For tips on the two-minute sell, see page 76.) Pack as much valuable content as possible into two minutes. Each recruiter will speak to 8–10 people per hour during a ten-hour job fair, so you have to determine what will have the most impact. Your goal is to cause the recruiter to attach a note to your resume recommending that you have an in-person interview or at least a telephone screening interview. The recruiter will typically not know all the details about the jobs available or those that will be available soon, so it is especially important to sell the fact that you work hard, you're a team player, you have an excellent background, and you'd fit well in the organization.

If you give your two-minute sell and answer a couple of questions, you'll probably have time for only one or two questions about the organization. Determine in advance what you want to learn about it. Having visited the web site will help.

Be sure to get the business card of the recruiter you speak with. If you are truly interested in the organization, state that you look forward to an on-site interview. Add that you'll call the recruiter in a couple weeks if you haven't heard from anyone. Then follow up as you stated unless they give you other options.

If they don't have any appropriate openings for you, ask for the name, title, phone number, and e-mail address of the manager who would hire someone with your specialty. Or, ask for the same information about a recruiter who specializes in people with your background.

Chapter 11

PLAYING THE INTERVIEW GAME

There are rules to playing the interview game. Job seekers who know and understand the rules recognize that there are ways to make themselves stand out from the rest. Knowing how to handle ambiguous questions, when to pause, and how much eye contact to maintain, will make a major difference in your interviewing success.

The Pregnant Pause

Interviewees often feel they must give instant responses to every question. While you certainly would not want long pauses after every question, a significant pause is often the best response to a difficult question. If you answer an obviously difficult question too quickly, you can leave the impression of being a person who "shoots from the hip." A pause can demonstrate that you are a thoughtful person who wants to provide the most appropriate response. Pausing also gives you time to select the best example and therefore provide the best answer possible. When a question is asked, and you realize it is going to be difficult, look away from the interviewer and begin to consider a response. Looking away is the natural way all people ponder a question.

To try to maintain eye contact while thinking is unnatural. With difficult questions, a pause of 10–15 seconds is reasonable. If you need to buy some time you might say, "That's a good question," "That's a difficult question," or "That's a tough one." This will give you another few seconds to think.

In *Sweaty Palms,* Anthony Medley tells a classic story about Jackie Robinson. Branch Rickey, general manager of the Brooklyn Dodgers, asked Robinson if he was willing to become the first black player in Major League Baseball. Robinson knew that if he accepted, he would face harassment from fans throughout the league. Robinson also knew that if he did not respond well to that pressure, it might prevent other black players from coming into the league for another decade or two. After pausing for several minutes, Robinson said he felt he was mature enough to handle the taunting and ridicule he would face in the coming years. Had Robinson responded immediately with, "Sure, I can handle it," Rickey would have had serious doubts and might have sought another player.

Getting and maintaining eye contact can be overdone.

Darren had read about the importance of
maintaining strong eye contact.

Eye Contact

Interviewees are frequently told to maintain constant eye contact during an interview and that anything less will be interpreted as weakness. Actually, that type of eye contact is completely unnatural. Studies reveal that in normal conversation, the speaker typically looks away 30–70% of the time. As a person begins to speak, he turns away while speaking, then periodically returns his eyes for several seconds to the person being spoken to, and then looks away again. It is the extremes that should be avoided. Appearing to stare at the person being spoken to makes that person feel uncomfortable and shows the speaker lacks social graces. On the other hand, I've also seen people who speak for several minutes at a time and look at the person being spoken to only as they finish speaking. That also is unnatural and needs to be corrected.

Eye contact *must* be maintained, however, by the listener. Whenever the speaker returns his or her eyes to you, your eyes must be on that person. The interviewer should not catch you looking around the room, looking out the window, or staring at the floor. Active listening requires you to keep a soft look on the interviewer to demonstrate interest and attentiveness.

Truthfulness

A reputation for integrity and honesty is priceless. Never say anything in an interview that would cause an interviewer to question your integrity or honesty. Lying in a resume, application form, or during an interview is simply too risky, and any short-term gain you might achieve would not be worth it. Besides, being able to sleep well at night is a great asset. As John Wooden, the great basketball coach, put it, "There is no pillow as soft as a clear conscience." Those who have lied about having college degrees often admit that they always worried about being found out. Most application forms have a stipulation at the end stating: "I understand that any false answer or statement on this application or any other required documents may result in denial of employment or discharge." Another application states: "I certify that answers given herein are true and complete to the best of my knowledge. In the event of employment, I understand that false or misleading information given in my application or interview(s) may result in discharge." These comments are pretty serious stuff, and they are not idle threats.

It's not uncommon to hear of a person who's been fired because some disgruntled employee decides to check up on a boss or colleague, only to discover that the person never actually graduated from college. It's so easy to verify college graduation that no one should ever falsify that information. Granted, most companies do not check up on such things, but enough do that it just isn't worth it to lie.

Mark Twain put it best when he said "If you tell the truth you don't need such a good memory." During the stress of an interview it is hard for the person who is stretching the truth to remember what has been said to whom. Interviewers can spot inconsistencies. If they catch you, they may not bring it to your attention—they simply won't invite you back for another interview.

There may be other situations in which interpretation, not truth, is the issue. Opinions and interpretations of events cannot be proved or disproved. For example, during an interview you may be asked what you liked most and least about your last boss. Even though the person may have been a total jerk, don't say that in the interview. Instead, find a major quality about him that you liked, and a fairly minor quality that you disliked. Bite your tongue if you feel the urge to say more. Are you being dishonest? I don't think so. You're being discreet.

Another common question asks about your reason for leaving each position. Whether you left of your own accord or were asked to leave, there were probably several reasons, not just one. My recommendation is to mention only one or two reasons. Those reasons should be described in such a way that the interviewer believes he would have left under those circumstances also.

Really touchy areas need a lot of thought. A client of mine was "semi-terminated." That is, he was given an option of going to another department, but there was no promise of it being permanent. The position was not desirable, so he chose to resign. In one sense he was terminated, but in another sense he quit. When he was asked why he left this job, he mentioned the impact the recession had on his company and stated that his position, as well as several similar positions at other branches, had been eliminated. He also described the position within his company that was offered to him, and explained why he had declined it. All of these statements were true, and the interviewers were satisfied with the explanation.

Along with being truthful, it is important to remain consistent. Once you decide how you are going to deal with a certain issue, maintain consistency in the way you describe and talk about it.

Employers want people they can trust implicitly. Therefore, during the interview demonstrate openness and genuineness. Make positive statements about yourself but avoid exaggeration. Such demonstrations of openness and genuineness will foster the sense that you are trustworthy. Being consistent will allow the employer's trust in you to build throughout the interview.

Skeletons And Other Touchy Subjects

Many people have a skeleton or two in the closet. It's important, therefore, to know how you're going to respond if they are brought up. If the very thought of having to explain a particular fact or issue gets your heart racing or causes you to break out in a cold sweat, you'll need a lot of thought and practice, and perhaps some professional assistance, to learn how to handle the situation. Your challenge is to put the situation in the best possible light to minimize its negative effect. Depending on the situation, there may be no way to look good. Your goal may simply be to minimize and control the damage.

These skeletons include situations such as being fired from a job, having spent time in prison, having failed at a business venture, going through bankruptcy, and having been out of work for over a year. If there were five reasons for the situation, pick the two or three reasons that are easiest to discuss. It is important to provide enough information so the interviewer does not feel compelled to probe further. Practice discussing the situation until you sound confident and can explain everything without getting tense or defensive.

Safe Answers

As you read my suggestions, you may have noticed that I often recommend safe answers—answers that are not controversial. There is, in fact, a strong case to be made for safe answers, but always within the context of truthfulness. It is important to give the interviewer a sense of your openness and credibility. But this also requires discretion.

Your challenge is to get the employer to make a job offer. You want the opportunity to accept it or reject it and you do not want to give the interviewer any excuses for rejecting you. So discretion is the key. If you are asked why you want to leave your present job, you may have six reasons. Discretion tells you to mention only three of them. The interviewer may ask about your greatest weakness or the biggest job-related mistake you ever made. By all means share a genuine weakness and reveal a real mistake, but it need not be your greatest weakness or your biggest mistake. Revealing either might hurt your chances for a job offer.

This is a tricky topic to cover because I believe in the importance of honesty. With all of this in mind, however, there are times when you must choose not to reveal something. Whatever you say should be true, but there are times when you may withhold additional information. Use this as a principle to determine how you will respond to some of the really tough questions.

The honesty issue and the safe answer issue are not identical, so let's return to safe answers. Controversy will never benefit you and should be avoided. During an interview, an issue might come up that you would just love to go after with all of your views and opinions. Don't do it. In fact, the interviewer may even be baiting you just to see how you will react.

Base your answers on what you have already learned about the job and your prospective boss. Say you have twenty strengths that you are prepared to discuss during an interview, but you quickly realize that four of them would simply not sell you in this particular job with this particular supervisor. Naturally you would choose not to mention those four, but would sell the other sixteen at every opportunity. That is safe and prudent.

You may be a person who relishes independence on the job. Yet when asked what your job-related needs are, you might choose not to mention this because you have sensed that this supervisor likes to maintain close oversight of employees.

Some might suggest that it's better to clear the air right away. I call this the let-it-all-hang-out syndrome. It is justified by the belief that "if they don't like me the way I am, then I don't want to work there anyway." While this may be a rather noble approach, it does not yield the desired result—a job offer. Get the offer, *then* decide if you want to work there.

Harry decided this was the time to determine if they would accept him just the way he was.

Answering Ambiguous Questions

Employers often ask questions that can be interpreted in more than one way. Examples could be, "What is the biggest mistake you ever made?" or "What was the biggest crisis you ever experienced?" In both, it is unclear whether the employer wants job-related experiences or personal experiences. Generally it is better not to ask for clarification. Take a direction that is easier for you, safer, or will show you in a better light. Take, for example, the question about your biggest mistake. It may be easiest and wisest to simply mention a personal experience. The employer can always come back and say he wants a job-related example. But at least you gave an honest answer. Usually, if you give a good answer, the person will be satisfied and will go on to the next question.

One reason to not ask for clarification on these types of questions is that it breaks the continuity of the interview and can seem awkward. You may seem too cautious and afraid to take risks.

I am not saying never ask for clarification. At times you must. If the question is important, and the ambiguity is so great that you dare not take a wrong direction, by all means ask for clarification.

When seeking clarification you could simply ask, "I'm not quite sure I understand your question. Could you rephrase it?" Or, "I want to be sure to give the answer you're looking for. Do you mean A or do you mean B?" In this request for clarification the person is showing that he is trying to interpret the questions and just needs a little help. By seeking clarification in this way the interviewer will invariably provide more clarity and will often give you clues about what is expected.

I Don't Know

Sometimes we just don't know or don't remember the answer to a question. The best response is usually candor.

I don't remember the formula for calculating that problem, but I know where to find the formula and how to use it.

I don't remember what our raw product wastage rate was, but I know it went down substantially as soon as we installed our new software which made more efficient use of our textiles.

I'm not sure how to solve that programming problem. I haven't done any C programming in three years. During the last three years I've primarily been programming in Java Script and Visual Basic, so I don't remember the coding for that kind of problem. I know I could come up to speed quickly, though. I always do.

I don't remember how many inventory turns we had that year, but I do have the records on that. I could call you with the figures tomorrow.

Don't be embarrassed when you don't know an answer. We all forget things. Your candor and lack of defensiveness will usually more than make up for your inability to answer the question.

Chapter 12

THINGS TO DO AND REMEMBER

Bring Work Samples/Portfolio

It can often be very effective in an interview to show work samples. These could include spreadsheets you've developed, reports created by using databases or spreadsheets, a computer program or newsletter you developed, a drawing or advertisement you created, an engineering design you produced using a CAD program, a research paper you wrote, or a mechanical part you machined. There are literally hundreds of things that job seekers have appropriately taken to interviews.

Artists, photographers, and designers have long been putting portfolios together. In school they are often taught how to create a portfolio, but rarely taught how to present it. The principle with work samples is, if you think that under some circumstance you would want to show your work, bring it with you.

Begin by considering all of the things you've worked on that you're proud of. What visual item could you use to enhance a story or demonstrate a skill? Determine if there are items that you could give to the interviewer. Giving something for the person to keep can be powerful. Mark, an architect who wanted to concentrate on architectural renderings, spent hours and a couple hundred dollars developing a brochure with great drawings of five unique Pacific

Northwest homes. That brochure left a lasting impression. Leaving something with the interviewer causes the person to think about you each time the item is looked at.

Once you've selected your items, practice using them. If the person will be flipping pages in your portfolio while you speak, practice talking while you're looking at it upside down. Know what points you want to make about each page or item. Explain what problem you were working on or what problems were solved. An artist or photographer might mention what techniques were used to create an interesting effect. An engineer or product designer might bring the actual product produced or, more likely, would bring drawings and photographs. Be selective. In any given interview you might just show a few items. Keep it interesting. Watch the interviewer's face and body language to determine how interested he or she is in your material.

Know what's in your portfolio and where it is. Nothing is more frustrating for an interviewer than to watch a candidate flip page after page and then looking elsewhere in their briefcase saying, "I know it's here somewhere, I saw it just yesterday." Don't overwhelm an interviewer with all of your material.

Do Something Unique Or Different

Throughout your job search, keep asking yourself if you can do something unique, something creative, or something unexpected that will make you stand out. Consider what happened to Jason when he used such a strategy. A major software company was interviewing three candidates for a purchasing manager position. Jason's last interview was held on Thursday, and he was told he would be given the decision by Monday. Thursday night after his interview, he wrote a plan for purchasing that would help handle the firm's rapid growth. On Friday morning he had a messenger deliver the proposal. On Monday he was notified he had the job because "We knew you wanted it." Clearly, the extra effort and creativity Jason applied in this circumstance gave him the outcome he was hoping for.

Send A Thank-you Note

Sending a thank-you note, even one as short as three sentences, can be one of the most important things you do. When employers receive thank-you notes, they immediately remember you. Sending a note also makes you stand out positively because so few people send them. Most of all, you should send a thank-you note because it is the courteous thing to do. Thank-you notes can be handwritten or typed. Handwritten is more personal, but typed is more professional. Stationery that is monarch-sized (7" x 10"), or the standard 8½" x 11", are generally preferred to sending a card, especially one that says "thank you" on it.

Let the interviewer sense your enthusiasm for the job. Even specify those parts of the job which you are looking forward to or which would make excellent use of your skills. Do not hesitate to mention that you see the job as a challenge that you are more than ready to take on. Tell the interviewer that you want the job. Sell your confidence.

If you did not handle an objection well, the thank-you note provides a wonderful opportunity to cover it in a positive way. Sometimes, however, it is better to let those missed opportunities alone and stick to more positive points. Bring up the objection only if you think that without covering it in your thank-you note you have virtually no chance of being invited back for another interview.

A typical thank-you note might read like this:

> Thank you for the opportunity to meet you on Thursday. The position sounds quite interesting and challenging. I believe I can make a significant contribution. If you would like any additional information, please contact me at (207) 454-6952.
>
> I would welcome the opportunity to work for (name of company).
>
> Sincerely,
> Sandra Pendergast

A somewhat expanded thank-you note might read:

> I really appreciated the opportunity to meet with you today. The position sounds very challenging and I am convinced it would make excellent use of my talents and experience. I know that I can make a significant contribution.
>
> I am especially interested in the project management aspect of the position. For the past three years project management has been a major function of my job. Because of my ability to get tough projects completed on schedule, I've developed a reputation as the person to give the really difficult projects to. The system conversion project and the office renovation projects that I mentioned in our interview are just two of the many projects that I'm proud of.
>
> I would very much like the _____ position and I am especially looking forward to working with you.
>
> Sincerely,
> Roger Hinen

It's hard to go wrong with any note as long as you say thanks.

Check With Your References Before Using Them

Make sure your references are truly willing to speak on your behalf. When asking for their help, give them an out by saying, "If you're really busy, I'll understand." If they don't want to be references, don't use them; they won't do a good job for you. If you've had a major interview, call them and let them know to expect a call. Give them the background of the job and tell them why you'd be effective in the position.

Know How To Deal With Probing Questions

Whenever an interviewer feels obligated to ask probing questions, it is bound to hurt you. The key to handling probing questions is to eliminate the necessity of being asked such questions. Probes occur because the interviewer is not satisfied with the information obtained. The interviewer may follow up with another question simply because the initial answer was incomplete, or because the interviewer believes you may be withholding something. Your challenge is to provide enough information to satisfy the interviewer, but not so much information that it hurts you. Probing questions might arise around such issues as your weaknesses, why you were terminated, or why you've had four jobs in the last five years. Clearly, you can't score points with questions like these, so the tendency is to provide an extremely brief answer. If interviewers suspect you're avoiding something, however, they often go for the jugular. An interviewer could ask three or four additional probing questions and use up 10–15 precious minutes doing it.

Several approaches can help you preempt probing questions:

1) Know in advance what questions could potentially hurt you. If you were recently fired, you know what the difficult question will be. When you've decided which questions might hurt you, practice your responses.

2) Avoid sounding anxious or defensive in your answers.

3) Provide enough, but not too much information. Interviewees lean toward one of two extremes. Some are too brief in their responses and appear evasive. Others provide long-winded explanations in an attempt to cover every possible detail. Such long responses usually just provide more material for probing questions.

Effectively Answering Technical Questions

All interviews include questions that assess how closely your knowledge and experience match the job requirements. Your responsibility is to predict what the technical questions will be and then prepare for them. Technical questions are those questions that clarify whether you have the specialized knowledge and experience needed to fulfill specific job responsibilities. You may be asked how much experience you have with spreadsheets, developing marketing plans for software companies, or designing heart monitoring equipment. The list of technical skills is endless, but for your specific field you should be able predict what the technical questions will be.

If you interview with several people at an organization, one of them will often be the most knowledgeable technically. That person will ask you the toughest technical questions.

You can rarely fool the technical person, so don't even try. Microsoft is famous for using at least one highly technical person to really test you. If you say you are a power user of Excel, the Microsoft Excel specialist might ask you how you would go about creating a macro that would automate a particular function. If you claim expertise in the C++ programming language, you will be asked to go to a white board and solve a problem. You won't leave until the specialist has thoroughly assessed your knowledge level.

You'll want to claim as much expertise in your resume as possible without overstating it. Understating can result in no interview, but you will be unceremoniously dumped out of the interview process if you overstate it. Try to accurately project your real knowledge and experience level.

To predict technical questions, you need to know as much about the job as possible. Do everything you can to get a thorough job description. Ask questions of the recruiter or HR person before the interview. While the information may not always be available, no one can fault you for trying to obtain it. You can even be so bold as to ask the HR person or even the hiring manager, "What technical skills and experience are most important in this position?" Even if you don't get all the information you'd like, you'll be way ahead of your competitors, who will rarely ask for such information.

Many interviewees do not bother to evaluate their technical skills (also called work content skills; see page 258). They say to themselves, "There's no way to prepare for it—I've either done it or I haven't, and I either know it or I don't." While there is a certain logic in this thinking, it is really just an excuse to be lazy. Remember the balance scale concept covered on page 3? The balance scale reminds us that the person who gets the job is the one who has the most weight on his or her side of the scale at the end of the interviewing process. It means that you must get as much weight added on your side of the scale with each question, because it is the combined weight of all questions, not just one or two, that makes the difference.

If you prefer to think in terms of points scored, the goal is to score as many points as possible on each question. If you're asked what experience you have in planning for trade shows and you've never even attended a trade show, let alone coordinated one, you're in danger of getting no points on that question. If caught unprepared, you should quickly recall things you've done that are similar (see page 14) and try to get a few points.

If you knew that one of the duties of the position is to plan and coordinate three trade shows annually, you would first read up on trade shows, and, if time permitted, talk to people who coordinate trade shows. You would try to learn the jargon so you could appropriately use all the right terms. Just for speaking the language, you'll get some points. You would also describe the things that need to be done and demonstrate that you are more than capable of handling each task.

Having predicted that you'll be asked about trade show experience, you'll work hard to recall one or more experiences that are related or similar to trade shows. If you've attended trade shows but never coordinated one, you would point out that you know what goes on at trade shows and that you observed some of the planning or setting up at trade shows. If you worked closely with the person who coordinated trade shows for your company, you would describe what you learned from that person.

Here's the problem when you haven't done a particular thing that is called for in a job description: managers tend to forget that there was a time when they also had not done that thing. They also tend to forget that someone gave them the opportunity to learn it on the job. Often they learned it very quickly. You can do the same if given a chance. Don't forget to sell the fact that you learn new things quickly. You could even say something like:

> While I haven't specifically coordinated trade shows, I certainly have all of the skills needed to do it. I have a good understanding of what needs to be done. I'm very good at coordinating events, which I've done on several occasions. I view a trade show as an event that has some unique features to it. I also plan well and I have an extensive history of completing major projects on schedule and at high quality. I'm sure in your career you've been assigned tasks that you had never done before, but with a little assistance from others and some experience, you became quite adept at. I've also been given new tasks and I always rise to the challenge. I would really enjoy coordinating your trade shows.

It is nearly impossible to have all the knowledge and experience an employer might like. Despite having some shortages, you may in fact be the virtually perfect candidate. The employer will see that if you 1) effectively describe your relevant experience and knowledge, 2) sell all the benefits you bring, 3) vividly describe appropriate past successes, 4) convince the person that you have related experience in areas where you're weak, and 5) prove that you learn new tasks quickly. In addition you must show that you are a flexible, easy-to-work-with person who will fit right in with the other staff. To get the offer you must make all of these things happen. That's why effective interviewing requires lots of preparation.

Getting Feedback From An Employer

Usually the interviewer's facial expression will indicate whether a point you just made has been thoroughly understood, but not always. If you've just described something technical, and you're not sure the interviewer understood, get feedback. It can be as simple as looking directly at the person and tactfully asking, "Was that clear?" If you are not sure you truly answered what the interviewer was asking you could ask, "Is that what you were looking for?" or "Am I giving you the information you need?"

Sometimes during an interview you can't tell if the interviewer is truly interested or just polite. If you would like to say more about an experience or topic, but you've already spoken for over a minute and you're not sure the person wants to hear more, simply ask, "Would you like to hear more about my experience with . . . ?" That enables the interviewer to respond, "That's probably sufficient," or, "Sure, it sounds like that was an important experience."

Disagree Tactfully

Generally you should resist the temptation to overtly disagree with the interviewer. The interviewer may say something negative about a politician you admire or about a social policy you support. The interviewer may disparage a management concept that you believe strongly in. With few exceptions there is simply no need to inform the interviewer that you disagree. It just doesn't matter. Any two people are bound to disagree on some issues, yet they are capable of working well together. Most disagreements are simply unimportant to your goal—getting the job offer. So, bite your tongue if you must, but stick to things that will help you score points. Disagreeing will rarely do that.

There are times when you must disagree. When you must, do it tactfully. The time to tactfully disagree comes when the interviewer makes a statement about you which you know is either untrue or is not as serious as the interviewer seems to think. The statements might include, It seems that you:

are a little too sensitive

don't like to deal with details

have trouble getting along with people

tend to rule with an iron fist

find it difficult to stay with one company for long

One way to deal with the situation is to show some amount of agreement, but then state where you don't agree. "I would agree that I _____, but I wouldn't say that I'm _____." In response to "It doesn't seem that you like to work with details," it might work out this way: "I would agree that a detail orientation is not my greatest strength. I really am more of an ideas and big-picture person. But when I'm overseeing a project I keep very close track of the details while keeping my eyes on our goals. When I can, I'll delegate some of the details to others but I make sure those things are getting accomplished. I hold my people accountable."

To make this work, anticipate criticisms or objections that might arise and determine how you would deal with them. See pages 11-13 for more on objections.

Create Positive First Impressions

Interviewers tend to arrive at quick conclusions about interviewees and are heavily influenced by negative impressions. A study published by the *Canadian Journal of Psychology* indicated that 85% of interviewers' decisions were based on information obtained in the first four minutes of the interview. Just one unfavorable rating on one aspect led to a reject decision 90% of the time. This research merely confirms what we've known all along—first impressions are important. Make sure yours are positive.

Many first impressions occur within a minute and are primarily nonverbal. A warm smile as you greet your interviewer gets things off to a good start. Firm handshakes create positive impressions while limp or bone-crushing handshakes get the interview started in a downward trend. From the beginning demonstrate your enthusiasm and energy. Be friendly and open. When you arrive for the interview take a quick visit to the bathroom to check yourself out in a mirror. Check your hair, blouse, or tie to make sure everything is looking right. Make sure that buttons are buttoned and zippers are zipped.

Chapter 13

INTERVIEWING TIPS

Know The Time And Place

Leave nothing to chance. Know the exact time and location of your interview. Purchase a pocket calendar and put all of your appointments in it with the name and correct spelling of the person you'll be meeting, as well as the person's title, and the name and address of the organization. If you're unsure about the location, get explicit directions or drive by the day before so you'll know exactly how to get there. Leave early for the appointment to allow for traffic tie-ups or other problems.

Dress Appropriately

Stories abound about men who have gone to interviews in jeans, with dirty fingernails, or unkempt hair, and women who have attended interviews wearing curlers or low-cut cocktail dresses. Those folks did not get job offers. Some use their clothing to make a statement, justifying such dress with the self-defeating logic, "If they don't like what I wear, I don't want to work there anyway." Such an attitude, however, only hurts the applicant.

The emphasis is on appropriate dress; there is no rule which fits all people. For male and female professionals, a conservative and properly-fitting business suit is recommended. Pant suits for women may be acceptable on the job but should rarely be worn for interviews. If in doubt, dress up. You may know in advance that office dress is casual, but don't use that as a cue to dress down. It's fine to be dressed in a suit while being interviewed by someone dressed casually. Everyone knows that when appropriate, people can dress down, but they have much less confidence that people are willing to dress up. Scents used by men or women should be subtle, with just a *touch* used. Jewelry should be conservative and limited. Unless you know it is highly accepted, a man's earring should be removed for the interview. Beards and mustaches are generally accepted when nicely groomed.

Bring Pen And Pad

When the interviewer gives you some key information that must be written down, such as the name of a person or organization, you'll want to have a pen and pocket-sized note pad handy. Otherwise save your note-taking for later. Upon leaving the interview, jot down notes from the interview in the lobby of the building or in your car. Jot down your impressions about the job and the organization. List any questions that you feel were not adequately answered. Begin with the company name and the division, the name of your interviewer and the person's title, date and time of the interview, and the length of the interview. List the people you interviewed with and met (do your best to get people's business cards) Then jot down a detailed description of the job, including what you like about it and don't like about it. Indicate the key points you made and the specific experiences (accomplish ments) you described. List the interviewer's major concerns and how you responded. Consider for a moment what your next steps should be, and list those points. Then list points you wish you had made and things you said that you wish you hadn't. Close with the actions you intend to take.

While I prefer the approach of taking notes immediately after the interview, some people would rather take notes during the interview. If you take notes during the interview jot down only key points, do it as unobtrusively as possible, and maintain eye contact as you take your notes. Your notes may be a little hard to read as a result, but you can always rewrite them later. The important thing is to give total concentration to what is being said by the interviewer.

Remember The Interviewer's Name

Nothing is so important to people as their name. Anthony Medley, in his book *Sweaty Palms,* recalls an applicant who kept referring to him as Mr. Melody. She didn't get the job. My pet peeve is people who insist on putting an r in Washington, making it Warshington. If you're unsure of the pronunciation of the interviewer's name, ask the receptionist. Do not call the person by his or her first name unless invited to do so.

Shake Hands Firmly

Offer your hand as soon as the interviewer makes the first move. If you are a woman, offer your hand first if you feel comfortable doing so since men are sometimes cautious about offering a hand to a woman. Most people like a firm handshake but detest both the limp and bone-crushing types.

Wait Before You Sit

Allow the interviewer to invite you to be seated and to indicate where to sit. If no indication is made, you can ask or simply sit down in the chair which is most obvious.

Look For Clues About Interests

Photographs or mementos on a desk or wall can often provide clues regarding a person's interests. Discussing a shared interest can help build rapport at the beginning of an interview. For example, if a person's office has a nautical theme, it may mean that the person loves to sail or study the subject, or it may simply mean that this person likes the visual effect of such a theme. Rather than assume too much, broach the subject with an exploratory question such as, "Do you sail?" The person may respond with, "I love to sail, how about you?" If you share a love of sailing, the two of you will probably have an interesting conversation and the interviewer will begin with the belief that the two of you share numerous values and interests. That will help you. If you don't sail, you might respond with, "No, I don't sail but I've always wanted to," or "No, but I love to watch sailboats. It must be an interesting sport." The interviewer might then share a few past experiences before getting fully into the interview. Listen attentively. Avoid overstating your interest or experience in a hobby, however; it could come back to haunt you.

No Smoking Or Gum Chewing

If you're a smoker and your interviewer lights up a cigarette and offers you one, tactfully decline. You cannot fully sell yourself with a cigarette in your hand. Chewing gum during an interview is considered rude.

No Profanity

Even if your interviewer uses salty language, keep yours totally free of profanity. Even among those who swear themselves, hearing it out of the mouth of an interviewee is a turnoff. Some interviewers will even use profanity as a test to see if you will join in. Don't.

Keep It Interesting

Throughout the interview you must keep your responses interesting. One of the worst sins of interviewing is to bore the interviewer. Long-winded, rambling responses will cause the interviewer to lose interest. Responses that are concise and packed with key information, however, will maintain the interviewer's interest. When you're through, the interviewer may be so interested in the experience you've just described that he or she will ask a follow-up question. Anytime you sense you've lost the interviewer, finish your response as quickly as possible.

Well, to begin with I'm trustworthy, loyal, helpful, friendly, courteous, kind, obedient, cheerful, brave, clean, and reverent.

Go In With An Agenda

The employer has an agenda and so should you. In your pocket-sized notebook, using your own shorthand, list the points you want to get across and the examples you want to give. List a few questions that you can ask if the employer invites you to ask questions. Toward the end of the interview, you can glance at your agenda to see if you've missed anything.

Practice Your Intuition

Throughout the interview try to detect the biases of the interviewer. Everyone has biases, and sensing the biases of your interviewer can be a real advantage to you. For example, if your interviewer appears to be quite conservative, you as a liberal would be careful during any discussion of social issues. Other biases might include a belief that teamwork increases productivity, or that when quality is emphasized, profit will follow. When you detect a bias or belief that you personally hold as well, look for opportunities to demonstrate that you share those beliefs. It is human nature that most managers prefer hiring people who share their values and beliefs.

Ask About Needs

If you are interviewing with someone other than the hiring manager, ask about the needs or challenges being faced in the department. Such people are often less reticent to share these types of things than hiring managers.

Don't Ask Throwaway Questions

In the first and second interview you will usually have the opportunity to ask only a few questions, so they should be questions which are truly important to you. Never ask a question just because you think it will show how smart or knowledgeable you are. Often people will pick up an interesting tidbit during their research and then will try to squeeze in a question about it in order to look good. The problem with this, however, is that most employers can detect the true intent behind such a question. Instead of scoring points, such questions can actually cause you to lose points.

Share Credit

Throughout your interview demonstrate that you value and appreciate team members. Show that when you work with a team there is synergy. Acknowledge the help you received from a mentor, a boss, or teacher, and specify how that person helped you. By doing these things it demonstrates that you are a self-confident person who trusts others and seeks out their help.

Don't Assume

Many an interviewee has gotten into trouble by assuming too much. Don't assume the interviewer knows exactly what he wants or needs in an employee. And don't assume the interviewer knows all the right questions to ask. Help the interviewer decide that you are the right person by revealing as many strengths as possible during the interview.

Don't assume that you did well or poorly in the interview. People have left interviews feeling they performed masterfully only to learn that the interview was a disaster. Others, who felt certain they'd blown it, have been surprised to get an offer. After each interview, spend a few minutes evaluating how you did and determine how you'll do better next time. Do not waste time considering how poorly you did. Energy spent beating yourself up over what you assume has been a poor interview is self defeating.

Leave The Interview On A Positive Note

As you exit the interview, express your interest in the position. Do not ask how you did, as doing so can be embarrassing to both you and the interviewer. It is fine, however, to ask what the next step will be and how soon you might expect an answer. Your goal is to get invited back for the second round. Everything you say and do should be geared to that purpose.

Follow-Up Phone Calls May Be Appropriate

Do not even consider a follow-up phone call unless you've already sent a thank-you note. A follow-up call can be made to express interest and thanks, or to clarify a point. You can come right out and say, "I just wanted you to know how interested I am in the position." Because you may be interrupting the person, keep it short. You can also ask about the status of the position, but don't do this unless it is past the date when you were told a decision would be made.

If your first interviewer has subsequently passed you on to the hiring authority, or someone higher up, call and thank that person. Feel free to ask for some advice on how to prepare for that interview or even ask what that person will want to know about you. Your statement could be, "Mr. Weirman, I really appreciated the opportunity to meet with you, and I wanted to thank you for referring me to Janet Carlson. I'm looking forward to meeting her. What do you think are the main things she's going to be looking for?"

Look For Buy Signals

As soon as you hear phrases such as, "I think you could do a good job for us," "I like [a particular quality such as determination] in a person," or "If we offer you the job how soon could you start?" you know the employer is seriously interested in you. It does not mean, however, that the job is sewn up. Maintain a high level of enthusiasm and be sure to ask for another appointment. By all means state that you want the job.

Closed-Ended And Open-Ended Questions

All questions are either closed-ended or open-ended. A closed-ended question is one which can be answered with a yes or no: "Are you a college graduate?" "Do you believe the U.S. should sell high-tech equipment to China?" and "Are you a team player?" The first question requires only the simplest of answers—"Yes, I am." Although the latter two could be answered with a yes or no, each of them invites a broader explanation. When a question is thoroughly and completely answered with a yes or no, stop—there is no need to go further. Most questions, however, really do invite elaboration. Inexperienced interviewers are the ones most apt to ask closed-ended questions. If you're going to sell yourself in such an interview, most questions will require a 15–45 second response. Technically, "Do you work well under stress?" is a closed-ended question. No interviewer, however, is merely seeking a yes or no response. Clearly these types of questions require explanation even though they are asked in a closed-ended fashion. Remember the first rule of interviewing: every time you open your mouth, it is to sell yourself.

When You Blow An Interview

Occasionally you'll come out of an interview knowing you blew it. You may have been overly nervous, or lacked enthusiasm, or there were questions that stumped you and you know it hurt you. In such cases it may be appropriate to call the interviewer and simply state that you feel that you blew the interview and that the person did not see you at your best. You might go on to explain that since you believe you are ideal for the job, you would like another opportunity to sell yourself. After your explanation you could simply ask, "Could I meet with you to give you a half-hour of my best?" Obviously this tactic should be used sparingly, only for those jobs you really want, and only when you absolutely know you blew it.

Chapter 14

THINGS TO AVOID

To be effective in interviewing you not only need to know what to do, but also what not to do. The following tips will make you more effective.

I've-never-done-it-but

Avoid saying, as if it is all one word, *I'veneverdoneitbut*. Rarely will you need to confess, "I've never done it, but . . . ." Instead, concentrate on what you've done that is similar. For instance, if the company uses dBase for a database manager, and you've only used Access, you would not say "I've never used it, but I'm sure I could learn." Instead you would say, "I do have excellent experience with relational data bases (which dBase is), primarily using Access. I became highly proficient with Access in about four weeks. Having four years of heavy experience with databases, I'm sure I could master dBase in two or three weeks."

Both dBase and Access are known as relational databases. That means that while the commands they use may be different, the way they operate is quite similar. Knowing one will make it easier to learn the other. In fact, you could even say that they are similar in more ways than they are different. In this case, the person should go on to describe some of the uses that were made of Access so the interviewer can see how closely the skills really match those he is looking for.

If the interviewer wants someone who has done grant writing, a job candidate might sell the fact that she publishes a newsletter for her professional association and has raised money for the Boy Scouts. By combining her writing and fund-raising experience, she may still have a shot at the job.

Always start with the assumption that you have done something similar to what the employer is looking for. If you assume it, you will usually find it. Don't apologize for the fact that it is not a perfect fit. Just go with what you do have and sell your experience the best you can. Even if the interviewer concludes that the skills or experience don't match what she needs, she will at least respect you for your effort and will have enjoyed a good story.

Do Not Let The Interviewer Feel Threatened By You

Occasionally you'll get a sense that an employer feels threatened by you. This most often occurs if the person is not competent, has less knowledge than you have in your specialty, or has not been in the job long enough to have gained the full confidence of upper management. Books on management typically discuss the importance of hiring the best person possible, even if that person knows more than you. The idea is that you can't be promoted until your replacement has been trained. People who are secure seek the best because those employees will make them look good and help them get promoted. In spite of this management premise, some managers will consciously or unconsciously not want to hire someone who is more knowledgeable or capable than they are.

On your part, don't do or say anything that might cause the person to feel threatened. Giving the impression that you intend to come in and shake things up immediately (assuming that would not be your mandate) will ingratiate you to very few. No matter how talented you are, it is expected that you will survey the situation adequately before you start changing things. A statement like, "I certainly think we should be able to get this department shaped up very quickly," will come across as threatening and egotistical to nearly anyone, especially a manager who has given a great deal of thought to the existing problems but has not yet solved them. A nonthreatening, yet positive statement might be, "I believe I can certainly play a key role in tackling some of these issues. At Datacom we faced some similar issues and I think we came up with some good solutions. Some of them may be appropriate here as well."

If you sense that your interviewer feels threatened by you, tone down your experience and results a bit. This is the only circumstance in which you might intentionally undersell yourself. If you determine that you are more knowledgeable than the interviewer, do nothing to give an impression that you feel superior. Avoid discussing things the interviewer may know little about. Do not correct him if you detect an error in something he has said. Of course, you should *always* be careful about correcting anyone during an interview.

As always, do your best to sell yourself into the position. Once you get the offer, determine whether you want to work for this person. Try to talk to people who have worked for him before. Incompetent people rarely make good managers and often seek to sabotage those around them. If you find, upon further investigation, that this person is incompetent, you must take this into account as you decide whether to accept a position in the organization. If such a person is entrenched in the organization, he may make it difficult for you to get promoted because he will rarely get promotions himself.

Avoid Foot-In-Mouth Syndrome

To prevent saying something you might regret, practice telling your stories and giving answers to the common interviewing questions. This will give you a clear sense of how your stories will be received. I once interviewed for a claims adjuster position with an insurance company. In the middle of the interview, I was asked why I wanted to leave my present claims position. Taken by surprise, I stated, "Mainly because they give us too many assignments." As soon as I said it, I knew it didn't sound right; the look on the faces of both interviewers confirmed this suspicion. I'd stuck my foot in my mouth, and I spent the next five minutes extricating it. (I must have done a pretty good job since I did get an offer.) I quickly explained that my company gave us so many claims that we were unable to thoroughly investigate each one. I told them how many claims I handled each week and they determined it was about three times more than their adjusters handled. I came out of it all right, but I certainly learned a valuable lesson. Preparation is the best way to avoid foot-in-mouth syndrome.

Don't Reveal Company Secrets

Don't offer proprietary information even if asked. Employers have been known to interview people for the sole purpose of gaining proprietary information or trade secrets. If an interviewer keeps pestering you for inside information from your current or most recent employer you'll need to clear things up by saying you simply cannot divulge that type of information. "I can't reveal that type of information, just as I wouldn't reveal inside information about this company if I were working for you."

If the interviewer inadvertently touched on a sensitive area he or she will actually gain greater respect for you because you have just demonstrated a high degree of integrity. This indicates that the organization will benefit from your integrity in various ways. It is always better to demonstrate a quality than to simply state that you have it. Demonstrating integrity will score many points for you.

Don't Assume The Interviewer Sees Your Qualifications As Clearly As You Do

When you describe accomplishments, most interviewers can discern additional skills even if you don't label each one. They may not discern all of your skills, however, so don't be too subtle. One method which can ensure that your interviewers get a clear picture of your skills is to state which skills you demonstrated in a particular accomplishment. For example, you might say: "I think my greatest strength is my ability to get people excited and motivated about projects. For example . . ." Then, tell a two-minute story which illustrates your point. Go on to say, "So I really do think I can get people excited about projects and really motivate them. At the same time, I can keep people focused and bring out the best in them." Notice that two additional skills were identified and demonstrated in the accomplishment, even though the person started to describe only one skill, the ability to motivate people.

Interviewees often assume and act as though interviewers should be able to magically see what wonderful qualities they possess. While some interviewers are very perceptive, many are not. Unperceptive interviewers will only pick up on your most obvious strengths. Thus, it's your responsibility at every opportunity to reveal your strengths and demonstrate why you are the right person for the job.

Avoid Self-Centeredness

One of the biggest turnoffs for employers is the candidate who seems self-centered and cares only about what the company can do for him or her. Employment is certainly a two-way street and there must be give and take, but during the interview the emphasis *must* be on how you can benefit the organization.

To paraphrase John Kennedy's famous challenge, "Ask not what your company can do for you, but ask what you can do for your company." After the offer is made, there is plenty of time to talk money and benefits. Until then, emphasize what you can do for the organization.

Chapter 15

ATTITUDES AND INTERVIEWING STYLES TO AVOID

How you approach an interview, and the attitudes you adopt, will have a tremendous impact on your success at interviewing. There are eight attitudes and interviewing styles that can destroy your interviewing effectiveness: being apologetic or defensive, providing inappropriate information, expressing anti-business feelings, demonstrating negativity, showing an unwillingness to reveal your true self, being overly modest, bragging, and trying to take charge of an interview.

Apologetic/Defensive

Many job applicants come across as apologetic or defensive. This usually occurs because they feel insecure and believe their background is weak in certain areas. Consider the following responses to the comment, "Ted, we're looking for someone with six years of computer programming and systems analysis."

An apologetic response: "I'm sorry, I only have four years of experience. I wish I had gone to school earlier in my career, then I'd have the six years. I really blew it."

A defensive response: "Well, I don't have six years of experience, I have four years. Every place I go they want more experience than I have. What's wrong with my background?"

Whether apologetic or defensive, Ted's lack of confidence comes through loud and clear. If the applicant lacks self-confidence, how can the interviewer be expected to have confidence in his or her ability?

Now consider Ted's response after he's had some interview coaching: "Mr. Jenkins, I've had four years of programming experience. Because of the variety of my experience, however, it's equal to what most people gain in seven or eight years. During these last four years I've taken on every challenge I could so I'd be ready for this type of responsibility."

Ted has learned the art of overcoming objections. The interviewer was probably impressed with Ted already when the question was asked. The job description specified six years of experience, but the interviewer realized it was not just a matter of years, but of the quality of experience. He was testing Ted, and Ted passed.

Inappropriate Information

Giving inappropriate information in an interview can be disastrous. Let's assume an interview has just started and the two people are still involved in small talk:

Interviewer:	Did you see the latest Gallup Poll? It indicated the number-one goal of college students today is to get a good job and make a lot of money. Things sure have changed since the '60s, haven't they?
Sandy:	I think they've sold out. Everything now is "what's in it for me?" When I was in school people cared and they took action. Look at what we did with the marches on Washington and the 1968 Democratic Convention.

Job interviews are not the place to discuss religion or politics. Both are emotional issues. You can win in such discussions only if your views coincide with the interviewer's. It's seldom worth taking the chance. In principle, any statements that do not help to sell you should be left out.

Unless your opinion on a specific matter is requested, it is generally inappropriate to express opinions. Have you known people who are so opinionated that they constantly insist on telling you what they think, whether you want their opinion or not? For instance, it would be very inappropriate to say something like, "Mr. Bertram, it's probably none of my business, but have you noticed how old fashioned your logo looks?" Do you think this person scored any points?

The exceptions to the no-opinions rule: 1. Your opinion on an issue has been requested. Be honest in your response but also use discretion. 2. You are expressing an opinion in an area that you believe will help sell you. For example, "Mr. Johnson, I've studied virtually all of the Japanese and American theorists on management, and have tested many of those methods. What I've learned is that some of them are just fads and have no lasting impact. I'm still quick to embrace ideas that have been proven to work in U.S. companies, but I really look hard at them to see if they will work with my particular department." Here the person has intentionally expressed an opinion. The comment demonstrates that this manager is very knowledgeable and that she has learned to be selective about introducing new management techniques.

Anti-Business

Especially during the 1960s and 1970s, many college graduates went into interviews expressing a strong distaste for big business and capitalism. Today, liberal arts graduates are the ones most likely to consciously or unconsciously express an anti-business bias. Throughout the interview, demonstrate that although you majored in history or speech, you have an appreciation for private enterprise. Business people do not feel the need to defend the profit motive, neither do they want to enter a debate regarding their record on pollution control. Raising these and other anti-business issues merely raises questions about you.

If you have strong views on various issues, however, there is a solution. Research the company prior to the interview to determine how well it matches your values. If you like the organization and you're called in for a second interview, research the organization more thoroughly. Even if your research doesn't give you a definitive answer about the organization, go to the interview and thoroughly sell yourself. If the matter you're concerned about is an emotional issue for you, it is probably best not to ask questions concerning the issue until the job is actually offered to you. When you do ask your questions, ask in a calm, objective fashion. If the company passes your test, you have an employer who shares your values.

Negativity

A common problem I observe among job seekers is that they often create their own problems. They commonly do this by showing a streak of negativity. During interviews they often identify certain aspects of a job which they would not like. Unlike those who merely become less enthusiastic about the job, these people actually raise barriers. They will point out to the interviewer the perceived negative aspects of the job during the first interview. Remember, employers are often looking for reasons to exclude people from further consideration. If it appears a person has a negative attitude or really doesn't want the job, the employer needs no further reasons for rejecting the person. The first or even second interview is not the time or place to raise issues such as the long hours, the long commute, or the inadequate medical plan. Keep silent on these issues and go right on selling yourself. After the job has been offered to you, then these issues should be raised and discussed. That is the proper time.

Unwillingness To Reveal Yourself

The person who carefully measures every response, and who seems fearful of revealing anything which could possibly be construed as negative, quickly creates a negative impression. The interviewer becomes frustrated by this total lack of self-disclosure. After the interview the employer knows about past job titles and duties, but has no sense of the person—he or she remains an unknown entity. While it's important to be careful in what you say, you must also come across as genuine and real. Striking the right balance between openness and discretion is a matter of preparation. If you know the points you want to sell about yourself, if you are prepared to answer all of the typical questions, and if you are prepared to handle any difficult questions with tact and discretion, you will be able to relax more and be your true self.

Meek And Mild Doesn't Make It

Some people are so concerned about the appearance of bragging that they are unwilling to say anything positive about themselves. Their attitude seems to be, "I probably won't get the job, but at least I didn't toot my own horn like a lot of people." This is a self-defeating attitude. If you don't say positive things about yourself, who will? Interviewing is all about selling yourself. To sell yourself you need to believe that you're a pretty good product and that any company which hires you will be fortunate. If you tend to undersell yourself, it's especially important that you take a good look at your accomplishments and identify the skills you demonstrated in those accomplishments.

To avoid the appearance of bragging, simply talk about your experiences. In this way, you can let the experience speak for itself. If the interviewer wants to be impressed, he can be; if not, he won't. If the interviewer is not impressed, you haven't hurt yourself because you did not create huge expectations. It's better to respond in this way:

Employer:	Are you effective at completing projects on schedule?
You:	I'd have to say I'm very effective. Last year I . . .
	or
	I would say so. In June I. . . .
	or
	That's one of my top strengths. I've worked on numerous projects that had very tight deadlines. One of them was already three months behind when I took it over, and I had only six months to complete it. . . .

In the beginning of each of these statements, the person sounded fairly modest but also confident. I don't believe that anyone would think the person was bragging. So, go ahead and feel confident. As your story unfolds, it will speak for itself.

Avoid Bragging

Interviewees are more apt to be too modest than to brag. Nevertheless, some do come across as bragging, and it always hurts the interviewee. Often the job seeker has no intention of bragging; it just comes out that way. The antidote to the appearance of bragging is sharing specific examples and letting the example speak on your behalf. The sense of bragging usually comes through because the interviewee merely makes claims yet never backs them up. Employers want to sense your confidence, but confidence should not spill over into conceit. Avoid saying you are outstanding in a certain area. Even if you provide a good, solid example, the interviewer may be disappointed because expectations were set so high. It is better to sound somewhat modest, and then share an impressive example, than to claim greatness and give an example demonstrating you are "only" excellent at that skill.

Taking Charge Does Not Work

Some interviewees feel compelled to take control of the interview. They dominate the conversation and take it in directions the interviewer never intended. Generally, this approach makes an interviewee seem arrogant. A client recounted how he began interviewing an applicant, and was still in a rapport-building stage, when out of nowhere the applicant said, "Well, let's roll up our sleeves and really get to it." This created an instant feeling of dislike. The applicant did not get the job. Another applicant entered the room, took off his coat, and announced, "Let's get comfortable." The results were the same.

Chapter 16

OFFENSIVE AND ILLEGAL QUESTIONS

Personal And Offensive Questions

Personal, offensive, and illegal questions pose real problems to interviewees. If you object to the improper questions, you may offend the interviewer, yet by saying nothing it seems that the interviewer is being encouraged to continue his or her discriminatory ways. Knowing what is legal and what is illegal, and knowing effective techniques for combating improper questions, will enable you to respond appropriately when confronted by offensive and illegal questions.

Occasionally you will be asked personal questions which, while not illegal, are certainly inappropriate. If you are asked such a question, you must quickly decide whether you will answer it or tactfully decline. Because the interviewer will generally realize he's touching a sensitive area, a gentle rebuff will usually cause the person to back off. It could be, "Mr. Hanson, I try not to get into personal issues during interviews." Examples of such personal questions might include, "Do you have a boyfriend?" "Are you planning to get married?" or "Are you living together?" These questions are inappropriate and should not concern the interviewer. Just knowing that you don't have to answer such questions often helps. Tactfully declining is the key. Don't try to make the person feel ashamed, since that certainly would not help you. And don't make too many negative assumptions about the person or the company because of the questions. The explanation for why the question is being asked often has more to do with curiosity than discrimination.

Some personality tests have been found illegal by the courts because they ask highly personal questions about religion, sexual practices, and one's inner thoughts ("Have you ever considered suicide?" "Have you ever been so angry you wanted to kill someone?"). Even though the employer rarely actually sees how the questions were answered, and they are either scored by a computer or a psychologist, several tests have been found unsuitable for employment screening. People are frequently very offended by the questions and have refused to answer them even for jobs that they really wanted. There is no place in employment interviewing for that invasion of privacy.

Illegal Questions

Because most interviewers are untrained either in the art or legality of interviewing, it is fairly common for interviewees to be asked illegal questions. You should know your rights and know in advance how you plan to handle illegal or inappropriately prying questions. Virtually all states have laws or regulations prohibiting discrimination on the basis of race, color, religion, national origin, ancestry, medical condition, physical handicap, marital status, and age, particularly as it pertains to application forms and interviewing.

Generally, questions about your or your spouse's national origin, including questions about your native language, are illegal. Employers cannot ask about your marital status or the number or ages of children or dependents. Nor can they ask questions regarding pregnancy or birth control use, or plans for having children. Employers are allowed to ask questions about disabilities in the following form: "Do you have any physical condition or handicap which may limit your ability to perform the job applied for? If yes, what can be done to accommodate your limitations?" They cannot, however, ask questions regarding an applicant's general medical condition or illnesses, or regarding an applicant's having received Worker's Compensation. Nor can they ask questions such as, "Do you have any physical disabilities or handicaps?"

Employers are not allowed to ask questions regarding religion. A question such as, "Are there any holidays or days of the week you can't work?" would probably be held illegal, even if religion was not specified. However, it would probably be acceptable to ask, "We often work holidays and weekends. Is there anything that would prevent you from doing so?"

You'll notice that there is often a fine line between acceptable and illegal. Those who really want to find out a particular piece of information can probably find a legal way to do so.

Employers can ask if you have ever been convicted of a felony, but cannot ask if you have ever been arrested. In some states even the question about a felony would have to be worded very carefully. In those states the felony conviction in question must be job related. The question posed to a controller might need to be, "Have you ever been convicted of embezzlement?" rather than "Have you ever been convicted of a felony?"

Dealing With Illegal Questions

There are several ways to deal with illegal or prying questions. Each of them can be effective, but it is important to have decided in advance which you will use and then practice it. Without practice it is unlikely you will handle this tricky process effectively. There are several alternatives when addressing illegal questions:

1. Simply answer the question without revealing that you are the least bit offended. For most illegal and prying questions, that is my recommendation. To respond in that way, simply assume that the person means no harm, is simply curious, and is unaware that some people might be offended by such questions.

2. Address the real and more basic concern of the interviewer rather than the surface concern. For example, if the interviewer asks, "Do you have any children [an illegal question]?" the employer is not specifically concerned about children, but whether you will likely miss any work because of caring for a sick child. Your response could be, "I have three children in school and they have excellent full-time child care."

3. Tactfully remind the interviewer that the question is illegal. You might say: "That's not a legal question. I'd rather cover other points." If you do respond in this way, it is important to continue the interview by demonstrating the same professional manner you had prior to the question. The interviewer may already feel somewhat foolish for having asked such a question, or may feel perturbed at you for being so sensitive. So it's important to proceed with the interview as if nothing happened. In a sense it has become your responsibility to put the interviewer at ease so both of you can concentrate on the key issues of the interview. Because you've demonstrated both your assertiveness and your knowledge of the law, it is unlikely you'll be asked another illegal question.

4. A very simple response is to merely have a quizzical look on your face and tactfully ask, "Why do you ask that?" The interviewer will likely go on to another question, but if the person persists, you'll need a different tactic.

5. Ask how the question is relevant to the position. "That question really does not seem relevant to the position. Could we concentrate on areas that relate directly to the job?" Once again, a statement like this must be said with a great deal of tact.

Generally it is good to answer questions the best you can, without confronting the interviewer about legality. At the same time, you should be looking for a pattern of discrimination. One illegal question can be written off as a simple mistake, but several such questions will indicate something quite different. If you think you want the position, continue answering the questions or tactfully decline if you have taken that approach, but make a mental note of each illegal question. Write them down immediately after you leave the interview. If you don't get the job and you decide to claim discrimination, your notes will be critical. If you feel you have been discriminated against, you may get good results by speaking to the company's director of human resources and describing what happened. If you do not receive satisfaction, you must hire an attorney or work through your state's human rights department.

*Sandra let him have it when he asked
if she had children.*

Predict which illegal questions you are most likely to face and decide in advance which approach you will take. You can also choose to reveal information about yourself even though it would be illegal for an employer to ask about it. Parents, for example, will sometimes voluntarily tell an interviewer that they have children, but then go on to explain that because of their ages, there will be no problem with overtime or travel. It might be stated like this after being asked to talk about yourself: "I've been working in this field now for ten years and I continue to enjoy it. I have two teenagers who are both very independent. I'm able to travel, and I have never hesitated to work overtime when that was necessary. I'm known as a can-do person who gets a lot accomplished." A person in a wheelchair might indicate that she drives a car, is an athlete, or has no work limitations. As with any issue, your challenge is to remove any objections an employer may have, whether the objections are fair or not.

If you feel you may face discrimination, be clear on the laws and regulations of your state. Most states have a Human Rights Commission or an equivalent agency. Each organization will have published examples of questions it considers legal and illegal. You could also speak to a representative to receive specific advice about your own unique situation.

State Guidelines On Legal And Illegal Questions

The following guidelines will help you to better understand which questions are legal and illegal. Each state provides guidelines specific to that state. The guidelines shown here have been borrowed from California, New York, and Washington. Your own state may vary, but most states share a great deal of agreement on what is legal and illegal.

Name
> **Acceptable:** "Have you ever used another name?" or "Is any additional information relevant to a change of name, use of an assumed name, or nickname, necessary to enable a check on your work and education record? If yes, please explain."
> **Unacceptable:** Maiden name.

Residence
> **Acceptable:** Place of residence.
> **Unacceptable:** Do you rent or own your home?

Age

Acceptable: Statement that hiring is subject to verification that applicant meets legal age requirements. "If hired can you show proof of age?" "Are you over eighteen years of age?" "If under eighteen, can you, after employment, submit a work permit?"

Unacceptable: Age, birthdate, dates of attendance or completion of elementary school or high school, questions which tend to identify applicants over age 40.

Birthplace/citizenship

Acceptable: "Can you, after employment, submit verification of your legal right to work in the United States?" Also acceptable would be to make a statement that such proof may be required after employment.

Unacceptable: Birthplace of applicant, applicant's parents, spouse, or other relatives. "Are you a U.S. citizen?" (some states permit this question) or citizenship of applicant, applicant's parents, spouse, or other relatives. Requirements that applicant produce naturalization or alien card prior to being offered a position.

National origin

Acceptable: Languages applicant reads, speaks, or writes.

Unacceptable: Questions as to nationality, ancestry, national origin. "What is your mother tongue?" or language commonly used by applicant. How applicant acquired ability to read, write, or speak a foreign language.

Gender, marital status, family

Acceptable: Name and address of parent or guardian if applicant is a minor. Statement of company policy regarding work assignment of employees who are related.

Unacceptable: Questions which indicate applicant's gender or marital status. "Do you wish to be addressed as Miss? Mrs.? or Ms.?" "Are you married? Single? Divorced? Separated?" Number and/or ages of children or dependents. Questions regarding pregnancy or child bearing. Name or address of relative, spouse, or children of adult applicant. "With whom do you reside?" or "Do you live with your parents?"

Birth control

Acceptable: None.

Unacceptable: Questions regarding birth control, inquiry into capacity to reproduce.

Race, color

　　Acceptable: None.

　　Unacceptable: Questions as to applicant's race or color. Questions regarding applicant's complexion, or color of skin, eyes, or hair.

Physical description, photograph

　　Acceptable: Statement that a photograph may be required after employment.

　　Unacceptable: Questions as to applicant's height and weight. Require applicant to affix a photograph to application. Request applicant, at his or her option, to submit a photograph. Require a photograph after interview but before employment.

Physical condition, handicap

　　Acceptable: Statement by employer that offer may be contingent on applicant passing a job-related physical examination. "Do you have any physical condition or handicap which may limit your ability to perform the job applied for? If yes, what can be done to accommodate your limitations?"

　　Unacceptable: Questions regarding applicant's general medical condition, state of health, or illnesses. Questions regarding receipt of Worker's Compensation. "Do you have any physical disabilities or handicaps?" "Have you ever been treated for any of the following diseases . . . ?" "Do you have now or have you ever had a drug or alcohol problem?"

Religion

　　Acceptable: Statement by employer of regular days, hours, or shifts to be worked.

　　Unacceptable: Questions regarding applicant's religion or religious days observed. "Does your religion prevent you from working weekends or holidays?"

Arrest, criminal record

　　Acceptable: "Have you ever been convicted of a felony, or within [specified time period, such as five years] a misdemeanor which resulted in imprisonment? Give details." In California and perhaps other states, such a statement must be accompanied by a statement that a conviction will not necessarily disqualify applicant from the job applied for. In some states questions about convictions must be limited to a specific time period (seven years in Washington). Some states require that questions about convictions only be asked if relevant to the position, such as questions about theft or embezzlement of a person who would handle money. Statement that bonding is a condition of hire.

Unacceptable: Arrest record or "Have you ever been arrested?"

Bonding

Acceptable: Statement that bonding is a condition of employment.

Unacceptable: Questions regarding refusal or cancellation of bonding in the past.

Military service

Acceptable: Questions regarding relevant skills acquired during applicant's U.S. military service.

Unacceptable: General questions regarding military service such as dates and type of discharge. Questions regarding service in a foreign military.

Economic status

Acceptable: None.

Unacceptable: Questions regarding applicant's current or past assets, liabilities, or credit rating, including bankruptcy or garnishment.

References

Acceptable: "By whom were you referred for a position here?" Names of people willing to provide professional or character references for applicant.

Unacceptable: Questions asked of applicant's former employers or acquaintances which elicit information specifying the applicant's race, color, religion, national origin, ancestry, physical handicap, medical condition, marital status, age, or gender.

Notice in case of emergency

Acceptable: Name and address of person to be notified in case of emergency.

Unacceptable: Name and address of relatives to be notified in case of accident or emergency.

Suggested Answers To Illegal Questions

Unfortunately, illegal questions still occur. You should predict which of the illegal questions you are most likely to be asked. If you're over 50 or if you're a woman, you know what they are likely to be. Don't wait until faced with the questions. Decide now how you will handle them. Remember that your goal is to get a job offer. Once you get the offer you can decide whether you want to work for the person or the organization. The following responses are geared for those who decide not to confront their interviewer when asked one or more of these illegal questions.

Are you married?

The interviewer is really trying to determine how dedicated you'll be to the organization and to what extent family obligations will interfere. Of course, this question is usually addressed to women. If you are married but without children your response might be, "Yes I am. My work is very important to me, though, so I make sure nothing interferes with my giving 100 percent to my job. I'm very career oriented. I can travel and work weekends when necessary." That's a fine statement for the person who is willing to work 50 or more hours per week, work weekends, and travel occasionally, but not every woman or man is so inclined. That's why you've got to phrase your response as positively as possible while still being true to yourself.

A person who really does not want to work a lot of overtime might phrase it: "Yes I am. My work is very important to me so I make sure nothing interferes with my giving 100 percent. I do whatever is necessary to get all my work done and do it at a very high-quality level." Notice the difference. The first person is claiming that nothing will interfere, and that overtime and travel are quite acceptable. Whether the person has children does not matter since the person either has excellent day care or the spouse is able to take over when there is a sick child. The second person is indicating that work is important but that it has some limitations. This person is closer to the norm. Most men and women, while being ambitious, really do want to work a 40–45 hour week and will go to great lengths to keep it to that. Because they know their limitations, they typically work very hard at being efficient and productive during those 40 hours. In fact some of them get more real work done than those who put in 55 hours. The point is, the second type of answer is very acceptable and is certainly appropriate for the person who takes that point of view.

When do you plan to start a family?

This is another question that is asked almost exclusively of women. If this is a well-crafted question on the part of the interviewer, he knows it will reveal whether you are married, whether you already have children, and what your future plans are. This is a blatantly discriminatory question, and there is no excuse for it in these days when even small companies should have enough sophistication to know something about the law. The small employer, of course, will have trouble covering for someone who takes six months maternity leave. You can put this person at ease with a couple of responses: "No, we're not going to have children. We're both very career oriented." Or, "I do intend to have children, but not for several years, and when I do my leave would be very short." Of course, there are some jobs where the employer is not necessarily needing a ten-year commitment; they simply don't want to train you and have you leave in 6–12 months.

What religion are you?

Some would ask this question in order to discriminate, while others are concerned that those who are actively religious will seek to convert people and will interfere with employee productivity. Your goal is to keep either from happening. Do not let the interviewer trap you into debating some specific doctrine. Even if you argue with supreme logic or emotion, you will lose.

If you practice a religion you might say, "I attend church [syn-agogue, mosque] but I don't mix religion with work. I've always been very dedicated to my work. I get along with everyone regardless of their religion." If you said synagogue or mosque, you have revealed your religion. If you merely say, "I attend services," that has not revealed your religion. Decide in advance how you will handle it if a person presses you to be more specific and name the denomination or religion you belong to. Of course if you feel perfectly comfortable saying "I'm

*As part of the over-55 crowd, John took the advice
to demonstrate high energy a little too far.*

Baptist" or "I'm Jewish," then feel free to say so. Just realize that some may discriminate against you merely because you are Baptist, Jewish, or Buddhist.

If you do not practice a religion, you might say, "I do have my own beliefs that are very important to me, but I'm not involved with any organized religion. And I certainly don't involve my beliefs with my work."

How old are you? or What is your age?

When answering this question, show that you are comfortable with your age, that you are proud of what you have accomplished, and that you are a person full of energy. "I'm 54 [or, I'm in my fifties], and I have 28 years in this field. I love this industry as much as I did 20 years ago, and I've never stopped learning." If appropriate go on to mention some of the benefits you offer because of your maturity or because of your vast experience. If you know that many of the people who interview you will be younger than you, plan your answer and wow them with your energy and enthusiasm. When interviewed by a person who would be your boss and is younger than you, look for opportunities to indicate you are adaptable, open minded, and work easily with people from other cultures and backgrounds. That will help remove the younger boss' concern that you'll be difficult to supervise.

Chapter 17

ASKING QUESTIONS

Employers like being asked questions. In fact, most are disappointed if you don't ask a few questions; they may even interpret a lack of questions as a lack of interest. Giving the interviewer a chance to answer your thoughtful questions makes the interview interesting and makes you seem more interesting as well. Asking questions also gives you the opportunity to gather useful information and clear up any confusing issues.

Ask your questions selectively since asking too many questions can leave a negative impression. Ask only those questions you really care about. Also, avoid a probing or belligerent tone which could make the interviewer feel under interrogation. Don't ask the questions too early in the interview. Instead, give the employer an opportunity to cover them first. Later in the interview, if some key points have not been covered, that is the time to ask your questions.

Questions Reveal You've Done Your Research

When asked properly, questions reveal that you've done your homework. For example, "What will the impact on exports be if the World Bank cuts loans to Taiwan?" Or, "What will the impact be if you have a long labor strike in June?" Or, "I saw that BAX is coming out with a complete new line of ultrasound equipment. What will you do to counter it?" These can be good questions.

When asking questions, be careful not to overwhelm the interviewer with your knowledge. Don't try dazzling the person with your knowledge of earnings per share if you're interviewing with the purchasing manager. Such questions may be perceived as obvious and deliberate attempts to impress.

Questions Can Prevent Misinterpretations

If you need to ask a few questions in order to remove confusion or clear up a possible misinterpretation, you might say, "Do you mean that earnings this quarter will determine whether you can expand next year?" Or, "Does that mean I could complete the training program in three months instead of six if I learn the process quickly?" Or, "I'm not sure I know what you mean by _____."

Some of your questions can be planned, but ask them only if they seem appropriate. Good general questions to ask might include: "Would you describe your management style?" "Would you describe your management training program?" "Where is the company (department) strong and where does it need to be strengthened?" "If I'm as effective as I think I will be, where could I be in five years?" "Is there anything else I should know that would help me understand the position?"

When you have a clarifying question, ask it as soon as it comes up by tactfully interrupting the interviewer. Often all you need to ask is, "Would you elaborate on that?" If even a tactfully worded interruption concerns you, wait for the first break in the employer's speaking to ask your question.

Ask your questions in such a way that they invite full and complete answers. Closed questions, which can be answered with a yes or no, or with a very brief, incomplete response, won't work for this purpose. A closed question might be, "Are you going to implement a computer network?" An open question would be, "If you're going to implement a computer network, how would you go about doing it?"

Ask Questions The Interviewer Can Answer

Ask questions your interviewer can answer. Do not ask questions the interviewer could not reasonably be expected to know. That can be embarrassing and seem threatening. For instance, asking the sales manager a technical question about inventory control would be inappropriate. Also, do not ask questions that would result in giving away trade secrets. The employer won't tell you anyway, and it will appear that you lack discretion.

If you do ask a question the interviewer is obviously sensitive about, back off and perhaps even apologize. This is true for all questions *except* those tough questions you must ask after the job has been offered to you. At that time, you will need a lot of data to help you decide whether to accept the position.

Avoid Dumb Questions

Do not ask dumb questions! An IBM recruiter shared a story with me that illustrates this perfectly. Right after the interview began, the interviewee asked, "What does IBM stand for?" Although the interview continued for a few minutes, it was over at that moment. Had this person really wanted to know what the initials IBM stand for, she should have found out on her own. Not only was this a dumb question, it also revealed that the interviewee was unwilling to do even a minimum amount of employer research. So, before asking a question, determine whether it's something you need to know or should know, and whether it is something an interviewer would normally have told you by that stage of the interview. If the answer is something you could come up with fairly easily on your own, don't ask the question.

Avoid Loaded Questions

Beware of asking loaded questions that reveal strong beliefs. Such questions can convey a sense of superiority or even contempt. A typical loaded question might be, "Do you really believe you should be operating plants in the People's Republic of China where they use slave labor?"

Ask Your Probing Questions Only After The Job Is Offered

Your probing questions should be withheld until the job has been offered to you. Then it is your *duty* to ask whatever questions are necessary to help you determine whether the job is right for you. While you never want to offend an employer, you may need to ask probing questions to get the information you need. Just as you may sometimes seek to withhold information, an employer may be motivated to do the same. If you need to know how stable the company is financially, the employer may resist giving you these details. Therefore you may need to ask follow-up questions in order to obtain it. You need to ask tactfully, but if you really do need the information, you must also ask assertively. The answer to your question must be important enough that if the true answer is what you suspect, you would turn down the offer. Continue asking until you get a satisfactory response.

Many candidates have paid the supreme price for not asking enough questions once the job offer was made. The supreme price is getting fired because of misunderstandings, or feeling obligated to quit because promises were not kept. Terminations have occurred because expectations were never clarified. Typically in such circumstances, the new employee feels he or she is doing fine, while the manager does not. Be sure you know what the expectations are, and be sure you can meet them. Clarification before accepting a job is critical.

Be prepared so that when the time is appropriate, or when you are invited to ask questions, you'll be ready to do so. Before the interview, jot down some things you hope to learn about the job and company. If those issues don't arise during the interview, you should be prepared to ask about them.

SAFE QUESTIONS TO ASK IN A FIRST INTERVIEW

Some questions are safe to ask during a first or second interview while others are simply best left unasked until a job has actually been offered to you. Each of the following questions could be appropriate during a first, second, or third interview.

By asking the right questions you'll be able to determine more accurately if the job is right for you. Go through this list of questions before each interview to determine which ones are most important to you. They are listed to help you select questions that are safe to ask at any stage of the interview process. Many of these questions could also be asked after the job has been offered to you in order to clarify points that were never fully covered in earlier interviews.

Questions About The Organization
How would you compare this company to others you've worked for?
What types of people seem to do well in this department/company?
What are the opportunities you see for this department/company in
    the next year?
What do you like about working for this company?
What are the challenges facing this company?
What would you change about this company if you could?

Do you see growth opportunities for yourself?

How would you rate top management? Do they have a vision for the future?

Is the company prepared to deal with technological changes in the next five years?

Will the company continue to be competitive? How?

Is the company quick or slow to adopt new technology?

What type of growth for the organization do you foresee in the next few years? Why?

What would you say drives the company—sales, marketing, engineering, or finance?

Where in the company do you hope to be in five years? (This is a good way to sense potential growth.)

What are the current plans for expansion or cutbacks?

What kind of turnover rate does the company have?

What is it like working here in terms of the people, work loads, and rewards?

How would you describe the politics of the organization?

How strongly does the organization try to promote from within?

How financially sound is the organization?

Questions About The Job

What do you look for in people you promote?

Why is this position available?

How many people have held this position in the last three years? (If the turnover rate seems high, ask for an explanation.)

Who would I report to?

Can you show me how this position fits in with the total department?

What are the challenges that have to be faced?

What kind of things have worked before when facing these challenges? Will they work in the future?

What would be my first assignment?

Where is the person who had this position before? (If the person was promoted, ask where the person is now; if fired, ask why.)

How well did the previous person do in this job?

What was the person like who previously held this position?

Questions About The Work Environment

How does the company promote personal and professional growth?

What is needed to get ahead in this organization?

How would you describe your management style?

How would you describe the corporate culture (environment)?

Notice that all of these questions are basically neutral. They do not reveal a preference on your part, you simply want to know. This is unlike questions such as "Is there a lot of overtime?" "Is there a lot of travel?" "Am I likely to be relocated?" These questions raise red flags about you. Even if you are unlikely to be relocated, merely asking the question raises a question about your flexibility and ambition.

Chapter 18

QUESTIONS TO BE PREPARED FOR

Many people perform only passably in interviews. The cause is almost always lack of preparation. Since nearly every conceivable question can be anticipated, you'll gain a real edge over others through preparation.

Thoroughly preparing for the following 101 questions can easily take 15–25 hours. That may seem like a lot of time, but your success in interviewing will make the time spent a great investment. Few of your competitors will spend anywhere near that time in preparation, enabling you to stand out. If you apply only for those jobs that you are eminently qualified for (meaning you are not trying to stretch), then perhaps you could get by with 10–12 hours and still do well. Perhaps. The danger you face is that someone out there without the level of experience you have will become an outstanding interviewee, and will cause you to finish a close second. For the average job perhaps that's okay, but what if you were a close second for that dream job?

Following are 101 questions which are frequently asked or cause great difficulty for interviewees. Write each question on a sheet of paper, and then briefly list the points you would like to make in response to them. Do not write out your responses word for word or try to memorize the answers. In an interview you may forget parts and stumble. Besides, your answers would sound canned. Instead, briefly list the main points you'd like to cover, then practice speaking the answers. This will enable you to give thoughtful but spontaneous-sounding answers.

An outline might look like this:

What is your greatest strength?
Developing solutions to difficult problems
      Able to recognize root causes of problems
      Effectively present the problem to management and gain support
      Able to pull together the necessary resources
      Develop excellent plans of action
      Get others to buy into solving the problem and gain their support
      Won't quit until the problem is solved
      Examples: 1) Found cause for defects in valve covers and resolved
        it, 2) decreased absenteeism 32%

In the next eight chapters the principles for answering the following questions will be covered in detail.

See our web site at www.cmr-mvp.com in order to print out a complete list of the questions with space already provided so you can write in your points as you prepare.

Chapter 19
Selling Personal Strengths

1. Tell me about yourself.
2. What is your greatest strength?
3. What can you offer us that someone else can't?
4. What are your three most important career accomplishments?
5. How would you describe yourself?
6. Why should I hire you?
7. Describe the biggest crisis in your life [career].
8. What is unique about you?
9. How would your supervisor describe you?
10. Rate yourself on a scale of 1–10.
11. Tell me a story.
12. How have you benefited from disappointments?

Chapter 20
Overcoming Negatives And Objections

13. What is your greatest weakness? (similar to, What do you most need to work on?)
14. Have you ever been fired or asked to resign?

15. Why have you changed jobs so frequently?
16. Why have you been out of work so long? What have you been doing?
17. What is the biggest mistake you ever made?

Chapter 21
Responding To Questions About Your Personal Factors

18. What are your career goals?
19. What do you really want to do in life?
20. How long have you been out of work?
21. What personal, non-job-related goals have you set for yourself?
22. Are you willing to relocate?
23. Are you willing to travel overnight?
24. How do you feel about overtime?
25. What have you learned from your past mistakes? What were some of them?
26. What do you think determines a person's progress with a good company?
27. Who has exercised the greatest influence on you? How?
28. What public figure do you admire most, and why?
29. What are your primary activities outside of work?
30. Would you have any concern if we did a full background check on you? What would we find?
31. What qualities do you most admire in people?
32. What have you done to increase your personal development?
33. What types of books and magazines do you read?
34. What was the last book you read [movie you saw] and how did it affect you?
35. How do you feel about your career progress?
36. What was the most useful criticism you ever received?
37. What is the biggest change you've made in your life in the past ten years?
38. If you won the $5 million lottery today, what would you be doing a year from now?

Chapter 22
Selling Personal Qualities

39. Can you work well under stress?
40. Do you prefer to work individually or as part of a team?
41. Are you a team player?
42. Tell me about the last incident that made you angry. How did you handle it?
43. What are the things that motivate you?
44. How do you handle people that you really don't get along with?
45. What have you done that shows initiative?
46. What personal qualities are important for success in this field?
47. Sell me this pen.
48. Are you willing to take calculated risks?
49. Can you establish effective methods and procedures?
50. We have some very difficult and demanding customers. Can you handle that?
51. We need someone who is resourceful.
52. What has been your greatest challenge?
53. Describe a team project where you are proud of the team's result, as well as of your personal contribution.
54. Describe a difficult decision you've made, and the process you went through to reach that decision.
55. Give me three qualities that are really helping you get ahead and three qualities you must work on if you are going to achieve your career goals.
56. What is the most important lesson you've learned in the last ten years?

Chapter 23
Job Factors

57. Describe your perfect job.
58. What is most important to you in a job?
59. Why do you want to change careers?
60. Why do you want to get into this field?
61. Why did you leave your last job?
62. How long will it take before you make a positive contribution to our organization?

63. What do you like least about this position? Most?
64. Tell me about your duties at your present job.
65. What is the most important aspect of your job?
66. Describe a time when you were criticized on your job.
67. What is the most difficult situation you ever faced?
68. What frustrates you about your job?
69. What jobs have you enjoyed most? Least? Why?
70. What duties have you enjoyed most? Least? Why?
71. What is the worst thing you've heard about this organization?
72. Describe a typical work day.

Chapter 24
Questions Regarding Organizations And Supervisors

73. What position do you expect to hold in five years? (similar to, Where do you expect to be in five years?)
74. Why would you like to work for us?
75. What is your opinion of your present [or past] employer?
76. How long would you stay if we offered you this position?
77. What do you know about our company?
78. Why do you want to leave your present employer?
79. Starting with your first job out of college, tell me why you left each organization.
80. What kind of recommendations will you get from previous employers?
81. Describe your relationship with your last three supervisors.
82. What are your supervisor's strengths and weaknesses?
83. What kind of supervisors do you like the most? Least? Why?
84. How has your supervisor helped you grow?
85. What did your supervisor rate you highest on during your last review? Lowest?
86. What kind of supervisor gets the best results out of you?
87. What is your boss like?

Chapter 25
Are You A Good Manager?

88. What actions would you take if you came on board?
89. Can you supervise people?
90. Describe your management philosophy and management style.
91. How many people have you hired? How do you go about it? How successful have the people been?
92. How many people have you fired? How do you handle terminations?
93. How would your subordinates describe you as a supervisor?
94. Some managers watch their employees closely while others use a loose rein. How do you manage?
95. How have you improved as a supervisor over the years?

Chapter 26
College: How Did You Do?

96. Why did you pick your major?
97. What kind of grades did you have?
98. What courses did you like most? Least? Why?
99. How has your schooling prepared you for this job?
100. Do you feel you did the best work at school that you were capable of doing?
101. How did your summer jobs benefit you?

In the following material, I've given you principles you can use to answer each of these questions. In some instances I have given examples of what could be said. When examples have been provided, it is not with the belief that these short responses are adequate to answer the entire question. Your responses will almost assuredly be longer. Use this material as a guide, then develop your own responses.

Chapter 19

SELLING PERSONAL STRENGTHS

---

1. *Tell me about yourself.* Most people hate this question. By preparing for it, however, and knowing what a wonderful opportunity it is to sell yourself, you should look forward to it. It is the most frequently asked question in interviewing. It usually serves as a bridge to go from small talk to the real interview.

Briefly describing your education or your work history are appropriate responses to this question. Even though the employer has your resume at hand, describing interesting aspects of each job can add a nice touch. Expand briefly on some of your results. This will likely cause the interviewer to select an accomplishment and ask you to tell more about it. That is exactly what you want; you score points every time you discuss results. After bringing the employer up to the present, you could describe one of your top strengths. You might summarize your strength by saying:

> Basically I'm an analytical person. For example, at Dependable Services, no one really knew how much our services were costing the company. I had taken courses in cost accounting in college, so I figured out the actual costs, taking depreciation of our equipment into consideration. I discovered that one of our services actually cost us 7% more than we charged for it. We raised our fees immediately. That alone earned an additional $17,000.

*Any other accomplishments besides
training Tippy to roll over?*

You could wrap up by asking, "Could I provide more detail on some of this?" A well-thought-out answer will usually require two to four minutes.

2. *What is your greatest strength?* The question asks for your number-one strength, skill, or asset and requires you to analyze yourself. Going into the interview you should have several strengths in mind. Share the strength you feel will score the most points. Begin with a brief statement and provide a clear example. A person interviewing for a management position might respond:

> I would say it's my ability to train and motivate people. At XYZ there was a severe turnover problem among our first-line supervisors. Even without the benefit of a pay increase, which they deserved, I reduced the turnover from 20% to 7% in just six months and to 5% by the end of the year. My analysis indicated that our leads were receiving inadequate training when they were promoted to supervisors. Most were unsure of their authority and how to use it. Many quit out of frustration. I developed a training program which really gave them confidence. Once we got the supervisors trained, productivity in the plant rose substantially.

3. *What can you offer us that someone else can't?* Since you can't possibly know what backgrounds the other candidates have, you must respond by describing your known strengths. If you feel certain that you have some valuable or unique experience, you would certainly want to use that as an example.

4. *What are your three most important career accomplishments?* Choose accomplishments that are related to the job you are interviewing for, and ones which your interviewer can relate to. Avoid unnecessary detail. A question like this gives you a fantastic opportunity to sell yourself. Take full advantage of it. Allow 45–60 seconds for each accomplishment.

5. *How would you describe yourself?* Discuss only positive attributes and then describe them or give examples to show how you typically demonstrate those attributes. Emphasize your personality skills. See pages 69-71 for more on personality skills.

6. *Why should I hire you?* This question is often asked at the end of an interview and allows you to summarize your strengths. Since this is a summary, you can discuss points that you've already covered and mention new points as well. Sell yourself. This may be one of your best opportunities. Be prepared to take up to four minutes. Try to focus on everything you have learned about the job, your future boss, and the needs of the company. With such limited time, you must cover only those points which will have the greatest impact. You can create that impact by describing a combination of personality skills, transferable skills, and technical skills.

7. *Describe the biggest crisis in your life [career].* Describe a genuine crisis or difficult situation, not necessarily the biggest crisis you've faced. While the wording of the question will help you determine whether to mention a personal crisis or a work-related crisis, be prepared to describe either. Select an example that will demonstrate positive qualities and one in which you ultimately came out on top. Tell it concisely yet vividly to reveal as many qualities as possible. This is an opportunity to sell qualities such as maturity, perseverance, emotional stability, effectiveness under stress, and sound judgment. If you don't feel you've ever faced a true crisis you might say, "I don't think I've ever faced a true crisis, but I've certainly dealt with difficult situations. One that comes to mind would be..."

8. *What is unique about you?* In essence the interviewer is asking what is special about you. The interviewer is not asking what is absolutely unique about you. You are being given an opportunity to discuss some of your best qualities. So, reach into your mental check

list and pull out some of your strengths. You might say, "Well, there are very few people who have the combination of experience that I have. I have experience in _____, _____, _____, and _____ which some others may have, but I've also done _____, _____, and _____. I'm sure that very few will have experience in all those areas. With that breadth of experience I can help you improve productivity and quality."

9. *How would your supervisor describe you?* This is an opportunity to mention positive statements that you know or assume would be made about you. Discuss the qualities that you received high ratings on during reviews. Also give quick examples that demonstrate why your boss would see such qualities in you. Quote from your reviews or things bosses have said about you in the past.

10. *Rate yourself on a scale of 1–10.* To succeed with this question you must demonstrate that you like yourself, but not too much. The employer is testing your self-esteem. With this in mind you should rate yourself an eight or nine. A seven would be too low and a ten would indicate you are egotistical. High-caliber people never think they are tens because they are so aware of how they can get better. Explain why you feel you are a nine (or eight), stressing your strengths. Then indicate what you expect to do to move up a notch or two. That will demonstrate a strong desire for personal growth.

11. *Tell me a story.* With a question like this you have an option— you can simply share an interesting experience or you can ask for clarification. You would seek clarification by asking, "Are you looking for something in particular, perhaps from my personal life or my work life?" The interviewer may answer one of two ways. One response is, "Just tell me any story you like." In this instance the interviewer is testing your ability to handle ambiguity. Or the response could indicate that the story should have a certain theme. Interviewers who ask such an ambiguous question usually do it with a purpose and are testing you. My recommendation is to treat this question the same as you would, "Describe an experience which reveals a key strength of yours."

12. *How have you benefited from disappointments?* The key word is disappointments. Notice it does not ask how you have benefited from failures, which would be different. In life some disappointments are bitter experiences and remain bitter for years, while others quickly have a happy ending. It may be that the disappointment led directly to a major accomplishment or a peak experience. If you have such an experience, use it. If not, think of an experience in which you truly learned a great lesson. Perhaps the disappointment prepared you later to take full advantage of an opportunity which presented itself.

Chapter 20

OVERCOMING NEGATIVES AND OBJECTIONS

---

13. *What is your greatest weakness?* This is one of the most frequently asked questions, yet interviewees typically do poorly with it. Avoid trying to score points with this question. The interviewer who asks this question will ask it of virtually every interviewee, so everyone will have to reveal a quality that is somewhat negative. Some "interviewing experts" advise people to select something which is really a strength and disguise it as a weakness. They suggest statements such as, "I guess I'm a workaholic," or "I'm too much of a perfectionist," or "Sometimes I'm too aggressive." The intent is to get the employer thinking, "That's not a bad weakness to have." Most interviewers readily see through such ploys and the interviewee immediately loses credibility. Show yourself to be genuine and willing to reveal things about yourself.

Be prepared to discuss personal weaknesses as well as technical weaknesses. A personal weakness could be a tendency to procrastinate, while a technical weakness could be a lack of experience with Microsoft Excel.

When asked this difficult question, it is best to state a genuine weakness, but choose one which will not automatically disqualify you. It cannot be a trivial weakness, however, such as a manager saying he or she is all thumbs when it comes to keyboarding.

Any other weaknesses beside the fact that you crack your knuckles?

Fred was ready for the "What's your biggest weakness?" question.

Usually you would indicate that you have known about this weakness for some time and have taken definite steps to overcome it. You don't need to demonstrate that you have totally conquered it, but show that you've made major progress with it. Examples of weaknesses that people have used successfully include: "I'm not good at working with repetitive details," "It's hard for me to get to know people at first," and "Sometimes I'm not assertive enough." There are many possibilities, but it may take time to come up with one which is safe to use. In interviewing you can score anywhere from minus ten to plus ten on any question. On this question you are trying to remain in the minus two to plus one range. Something in the minus six range can seriously damage you, while trying to score plus five or better will jeopardize your credibility and sincerity. The goal is to provide a short answer which satisfies the interviewer, and allows you to move to other questions that you *can* score points on.

After you decide which weakness to use, begin developing a response. Your response must show how it is a genuine weakness. In other words, you need to show how it has hurt you. Numerous clients have used their perfectionism as their greatest weakness. That can work, but you must show how perfectionism has caused problems for you. When I asked one client during a practice interview how perfectionism had hurt her, she replied, "Well, I guess it hasn't, but I just know that I shouldn't be so much of a perfectionist." I responded, "Then give me a real weakness." She had not convinced me that perfectionism was a genuine weakness, so when I asked for a real weakness she got flustered and did poorly throughout the remainder of the interview. So, you can see how important it is to answer this question properly.

Perfectionism can work, but let me show you how it might be used to better effect than the situation described above:

> I think probably my greatest weakness is my perfectionism. It seems that I want everything done just right, and it's hard to let go until it's almost perfect. Sometimes that means I'll spend too much time on a project when I really should go on to other things, since it's probably just fine the way it is. But then I'll look at it again and realize that it could be better with just a little fixing up. Sometimes I'm through in an hour, but other times I might dig into it again and spend another day or two on it. Last year that happened on a project, and because of it, another project had to be rushed and it was definitely not the quality it should have been. So now as I'm finishing up a project I'll just tell myself, 'It's fine as it is, just put it to bed.' Or I'll have a coworker look at it and if she thinks it's fine, it's usually easier to wrap it up. I know that I'll always be a perfectionist, but I think I've got it pretty well under control.

Where do you think she scored? I would put her around zero, or neutral, which is right where she should be. She came across as sincere and genuine. She was willing to open up and show that her perfectionism gets her in trouble at times, but she also demonstrated that it is almost under control. Undoubtedly an employer would have been satisfied with her response and would have gone on to other questions.

In addition to showing how the trait has hurt you, you can also show how it sometimes benefits you. In the case of our perfectionist, she might add:

> Of course, as a perfectionist I'm also very thorough. Last year we were having a quality problem with one of our cold cream products. Customers were calling and complaining that when they got the product home, the oil had separated and risen to the top. Our chemists and manufacturing engineers were unable to find out what the problem was and we were getting ready to shut down production. As the marketing manager for that product, solving a production problem is not my area, but I did not want to lose the market share that we had gained in the last two years. I starting researching the problem. One day I was chatting with a purchasing agent and asked

him if any of the ingredients had been changed in any way. He said no, but then something clicked. I asked if we had changed any suppliers in the last four months. It turned out that we had started buying an emulsifier from a new vendor who claimed the product was identical to what we were using, but cost about 20% less. We checked the emulsifier, and sure enough it was substandard. We immediately returned to the previous vendor and the problem was solved. So I guess sometimes my perfectionism and thoroughness can pay off.

This example demonstrates that there are always two sides of a coin: The very quality that causes problems in one situation can be very useful in another. When sharing a genuine weakness, it is fair to show the other side of the coin as well.

Another way to share a weakness is to describe one which has almost been overcome:

I absolutely hate firing people. In the past I held on to a couple of people longer than I should have just because I hoped they'd turn around. I was just plain avoiding the inevitable. To prevent that from happening in the future, I've been holding extensive interviews with the top candidates and performing thorough background checks. That way, I hire only those with the greatest potential. If I don't find what I want, I won't hire second best. I'll keep looking until I find the right person. The last five people I've hired have been really good choices.

You should be prepared to share three weaknesses. If one seems inappropriate for a particular job, you still have two others to choose from. You could also run into an interviewer who loves to ask about several weaknesses.

14. *Have you ever been fired or asked to resign?* For those who have been fired in the past, this is perhaps the most difficult question of all. Fortunately, many of your interviewers will have at some time in their career been fired. Studies indicate that about 80% of firings are over personality issues rather than competence: good chemistry becomes bad chemistry, the company changes but the employee is unable to adapt, or new managers come in with different values and expectations. Being fired is not the kiss of death to a career.

Your goal is to develop a response that demonstrates maturity. If you can handle this question with dignity and maturity, you will gain the respect of the interviewer. Cause the interviewer to realize that regardless of the reasons for the termination, you are a person with a great deal of potential. Speak in such a way that the interviewer neither questions your competency nor integrity. For this reason you must never attack your former boss or company. Everything you say must be said without the hint of defensiveness or rancor.

Another goal is to go into interviews calmly and with confidence, with no fear of this question being asked. I have worked with clients whose dread of this question was clearly communicated by their nervousness. To overcome this problem, I usually have clients work on the response and the delivery until it becomes merely another question.

If you were recently fired, one approach is to tackle the question head on. Admit that you were fired, and then without any defensiveness, explain the reasons. While explaining the reasons, be sure to describe your strengths and contributions as well. If you believe it was unfair, or simply not a good decision, say so, but avoid calling your former boss names, raising your voice, or losing your temper. People have said, "I know they had to reduce overhead, I just don't feel eliminating my position was the best way to do that." While not blaming yourself for the outcome, you could mention things that, looking back now, you wish you had done differently. Concentrate on describing the situation and explaining that under those conditions a termination occurred. The key to this approach is explaining things in a totally nondefensive manner. Because of the understandable concern of the employer, your task is to convince the person that this was a one-time occurrence which will not affect your future performance.

It is perfectly acceptable to indicate that you were a top-quality employee who received excellent reviews. You might indicate that you got caught in a political squeeze. In such a case, state that you understand that this is simply part of business. Sometimes you can say you supported the wrong person during a power struggle. Frequently if the boss is fired, the subordinate's termination soon follows.

You may want to admit that had you been more astute, you would have quit months earlier. You might mention that sometime prior to the termination, the organization began experiencing serious problems. Looking back you should have started looking for another job, but out of loyalty to the company and a desire to make things work, you stayed too long. In your answer you can admit that you and your boss differed in management style and philosophy of management. You could say, "She's a very good manager—we just had different ways of getting the job done."

If your position has not been filled since you left, that could give you an out. You could explain that the company was having financial difficulties and that you were laid off.

By the way, it is always more positive if you can say you were laid off rather than terminated or fired. It may be beneficial to work out such an arrangement with your former boss or the human resources director.

Generally a past employer has no desire to hurt a terminated employee's career. If that's true in your case, discuss your situation with your former boss and reach an agreement on what both of you will say when asked. Agreement is essential. Your former boss needs to know what you will be saying so he or she can back you up. In these days when people are suing their former employers for defamation of character, your company has every reason to want to help you.

If you were fired from a job several years ago, you should contact your former boss. You might explain that getting fired was the best thing that ever happened because it shook you up and you got your act together. You would go on to explain that you have been successful since that time. You might then suggest some things the former boss could say if contacted by a prospective employer. The former boss will probably be glad to hear from you and will be more than happy to assist you. Surprisingly, the negative things which caused the termination are often forgotten, with only positive qualities now being remembered.

Even if you still hate your former boss, the two of you need to talk. I have had clients who strongly resisted this and absolutely never wanted to see or talk to that person again. Once accomplished, however, I have never seen anyone regret having done it, even when the outcome was a less than total success.

If you've been fired, you **must** know what your former boss is saying about you! The issue is often taken care of in your discussion with your former boss, and can be confirmed by having the person write a letter of recommendation for you. When someone has *written* nice things about you, it is much harder to *say* bad things about you. If the recommendation seems half-hearted, have the person write it again. You are not powerless. One client had her boss revise the letter three times before she was satisfied. Her request was tactful but firm; she virtually forced him to write a better letter.

Having the discussion with your former boss and getting a letter of recommendation may be enough, but often it isn't. Sometimes you just won't trust your former boss. If you have any doubts regarding what is being said about you, obtain the help of someone who can find out. An executive recruiter or employment agency counselor would be good, but a friend or anyone who does hiring could do it just as well. The person making the call may indicate you are being considered for a position and should then ask what type of an employee you were. You should provide the person helping you with a job title and brief description of the type of position you would be seeking to help make this process more effective.

The person should not only write down what is said, but also indicate the tone of voice. The tone of voice can totally change the meaning of what was said. Often, it is the *way* a former boss gives a reference, rather than what is said, that makes the reference a bad one. Imagine someone saying, "Yes, he was a good employee." Consider enthusiasm coming through in the voice. Then imagine the same words with a couple of pauses and a complete lack of enthusiasm. The identical words can create two distinct impressions.

Documented Reference Check (DRC) is one company that will, for a relatively small fee, check your references for you. They have people from legitimate businesses who will call on your behalf and act as someone who is considering hiring you. In this way they will act as any employer would who is seeking to gather reference information. Since the person is from a real business, if the employer asks for a phone number and calls back later, it will reveal that the caller is from a real business. The benefit is that the employer will have no idea that you are the one who has instigated the reference check. The person calling will engage the human resources director or your former boss in a conversation and record what is said. A report will be sent to you. The only drawback is that DRC will not comment on the tone of voice or the "feel" of what the employer was saying. They have chosen not to provide this information based on legal advice. Much of their work leads to defamation of character lawsuits and for that reason they concentrate solely on the exact words and not on tone.

My recommendation is to find someone from a real business who could conceivably want to hire you and have that person call on your behalf. That person should report to you not only the words but also the impression given by the former employer. If that is not possible, see if DRC can help you. Call the toll-free number (1-800-742-3316) to speak to a representative and have your questions answered. Or check out their web site at www.badreferences.com.

I've had many clients who were fired from positions. One person had been fired from an executive position. Due to his past successes he was highly marketable and began getting interviews throughout the country. He was flown to interviews in several major cities. Although the interviews seemed to be successful, he was not offered any of the positions. After three months and interviews for seven high-level positions, he discovered that his former boss was giving him negative "recommendations." He confronted the person and it was agreed that a more favorable person would provide future recommendations. The client then quickly found another job. Numerous opportunities, however, had been lost because he waited so long to find out what was being said about him.

If you know your boss is going to be a bad reference, seek out someone else in the company to provide a reference for you. If the boss who fired you was not always your boss, list a previous boss, even if that person is no longer with the company. Sometimes your boss's boss will do an excellent job, since he or she is not hindered by the emotional issue which may be affecting your ex-boss. Of course, whoever you use, he or she must know what you are doing and must agree to assist you.

Because of their concern regarding defamation of character lawsuits, many companies will not allow managers to give references. In those cases, people trying to check references will be referred to the personnel department where only job titles and the dates of employment will be confirmed. If your company has a strict policy of giving out only dates of employment, your task is made easier and you won't have to be concerned about what your boss might say.

If you were fired from a job years ago and there is no way for a company to discover that, you must decide whether you will reveal the firing or not.

I've given you some principles that should help you answer this difficult question. If your situation is particularly sticky, however, and you just can't come up with a good response, I would recommend obtaining the advice of a career specialist or executive recruiter. If you seek the help of a career counselor, make sure the person has extensive experience with interview coaching.

15. *Why have you changed jobs so frequently?* An interviewer asks this question when something in your background has given the appearance that you're a job hopper. If, at the end of your response, the interviewer still views you as unstable and unlikely to stay long enough to really contribute, you probably will not get the offer. If you have worked for three different companies in the last six years, you have not been the epitome of stability.

To overcome the objection, you might begin by stating that there have been good reasons for leaving each position (there's usually no need to detail the reasons unless specifically asked) and that long-term employment is certainly your goal. If you have simple explanations such as a plant closure, a major layoff, or the company went out of business, then you should mention these things. Sometimes a person has spent fifteen years with one company and then has a string of three one-year jobs. Emphasize the long-term position and indicate that your stability in that job reflects the true you. If there are only three or four changes to account for, do so briefly.

If you have not been stable, you might point out that you are now married, own a home, or any other point that might convince a person that stability has entered your life.

16. *Why have you been out of work so long? What have you been doing?* This question is usually only asked of those who have been out of work for over six months. The concern is that while you seem capable, other employers have apparently discovered something negative

enough not to hire you. Prepare for this question by listing on paper what you were doing at each period. Did you take a long vacation or drop out for a while?

One approach is to show that you really have not been looking for long. Numerous things can account for your situation: you were waiting on a job which was promised you but never came through, you took care of a sick relative, you were managing the estate of a relative, or you took a long vacation. You may have worked briefly for a friend who needed help, decided to work on a temporary basis for awhile, or you took a break from work to recover from your last job. You may have spent considerable time deciding what you really wanted to do and just recently made that decision. You might mention only one item that kept you from your job search, or you may mention several. Plausibility is the key to a successful answer here. Explaining the reason for a long period of unemployment, by using an example like those mentioned here, is a form of damage control. In other words, such explanations won't help sell you, but they will reduce the concerns an employer may have about you.

You may have been looking steadily for a job for the past six or nine months. Sell the fact that you have been working hard at the job search just as you work hard at everything you do. You might indicate you have been quite selective and that this is one of the few jobs that has been attractive. If you have had offers but turned them down, mention them.

If you have been looking for over a year without success, you should seek out the help of a professional career counselor who can help evaluate any weaknesses in your search and can get you back on track.

Even if you are having trouble paying the rent, do not allow any sense of desperation to show through during your interviews. Emphasize that you are a confident person merely waiting for the right opportunity.

In these situations women actually have an advantage. When women have long gaps in employment, it is assumed that child rearing was involved, even though this may not be the case. If you have chosen to stay home and raise children, however, merely explain it without sounding the least defensive about it. There is no need to defend this choice, even if a fast-climbing career was temporarily put on hold as a result.

17. *What is the biggest mistake you ever made?* If asked in this way, you can decide whether to mention a personal mistake or a job-related mistake. Personal mistakes are a little safer to discuss than job-related mistakes, but be prepared to discuss either. A personal mistake

could be that you wish you had selected a different college major or had not dropped out of college. As a rule, pick something that happened two or more years ago. This will enable you to discuss what you learned from the experience with more insight and objectivity.

If there is an obvious and glaring mistake in your background that the employer will be aware of, this might be the chance to deal with it. For instance, if you have three years of college but never finished your degree, this question gives you an opportunity to discuss that situation. Since you are providing information about an issue that the interviewer is already curious about, you are also defusing a possible objection before the interviewer brings it up.

Reveal a mistake, but don't feel obligated to reveal the absolute biggest mistake you ever made in your life. Revealing a major mistake may cause an employer not to hire you, more for the lack of discretion than for the mistake itself.

Chapter 21

PERSONAL FACTORS

---

18. *What are your career goals?* This question tests whether you've established career goals, and whether your goals match what the organization has to offer. Sound clear and definite about your goals, but express yourself based on what you know about the organization. Mention only those goals that you feel the organization can help you attain. Express them in terms of the experience you hope to receive and the expertise you hope to develop. You could use the opportunity to describe your present level of expertise and then how you want to further develop yourself. You want to leave the impression that you are a growth-oriented person with realistic expectations regarding promotion opportunities.

19. *What do you really want to do in life?* Sometimes this type of question is inserted so the interviewer can think of the next question. Still, you want to be prepared so that your every response will demonstrate enthusiasm and potential. This could be a time to share one of your dreams. Perhaps you want to enjoy a cruise around the world someday. Or you could select a job-related dream. Perhaps you want to help produce affordable housing in your city, in a volunteer capacity. Almost anything will be positive as long as you are genuinely enthusiastic about it.

20. *How long have you been out of work?* The employer who asks this question may simply be curious, in which case you would merely mention the month by saying, "I left in June." The employer could also

be implying that he knows you've been out of work several months and wants to know why you haven't found a job yet. If you had to take care of certain personal or business-related responsibilities before you could get fully into your job search, you might want to mention those responsibilities. If you've had some job offers, mention that and state that they just weren't what you were looking for. Demonstrate that you intend to be selective. Then state that you are excited about the position you're interviewing for because you are being selective.

Do not be defensive when answering a question like this. Emphasize that you've been carrying out a systematic job search and that you've met many interesting people. Also see question 16, *Why have you been out of work so long?*

21. *What personal, non-job-related goals have you set for yourself?* If you take time to consider your goals in life, both job- and non-work-related, the answer will be easy. The interviewer will be determining if you are a thoughtful person. Goals related to your family are always acceptable and often preferred because they demonstrate stability. Anything related to personal growth is very acceptable, such as taking night classes, learning a foreign language, building your own home, or jogging.

22. *Are you willing to relocate?* The only response is, "Yes, I'm prepared to make a move." If you answer "no," the interview is over. At this stage no harm is done by saying "yes;" you merely keep the interview alive. Actually what you're saying secretly to yourself is, "Yes, I'd relocate for a great opportunity." Of course by the time the job is offered, you should know whether you would actually be willing to relocate. It helps to know where you would likely be relocated, how soon it would likely occur, whether moves always include a promotion, and how much the company helps you when you move. Some companies, for example, will buy your home at market value if you have been unable to sell it. Others will pay a wage differential if you are moved to an area with a much higher cost of living. Some, unfortunately, will squabble over the cost of hiring a moving company.

23. *Are you willing to travel overnight?* The question may be worded as generally as this, or it may be more specific: "This job involves at least four nights on the road each month. Is that acceptable to you?" Prior to the interview you should have an idea of whether the job you are seeking typically involves overnight travel. Even if the amount of travel mentioned in the interview is more than you had anticipated, respond with, "That's no problem." This response will simply keep the interview alive. Later you must determine whether you are willing to do it. If the amount of travel is more than you want, but

you believe there are ways to reduce it, keep selling yourself. Get the offer, then negotiate the travel issue.

24. *How do you feel about overtime?* If you've had jobs that required overtime, simply describe how you handled it. If you have not had a job which required much overtime, you might respond, "I'm the type of person who will do whatever it takes to get the job done right." Before accepting the job, however, you will need to know whether you will be expected to work overtime regularly or only occasionally.

25. *What have you learned from your past mistakes? What were some of them?* We all have made mistakes. Often, there were lessons to be learned from these mistakes. So, when you answer this question, share some mistakes, but not major ones. Determine in advance whether you will discuss personal mistakes or business-related mistakes. The best mistakes to share are those that you were able to recover from. For instance, you might describe a mistake that created a temporary setback for you, or one you recovered from by putting in extra time. If a mistake cost you or your employer money, show how the lesson ultimately benefited you or your employer. With some mistakes, enough time has elapsed that you are able to laugh about them. Thus, they may offer an opportunity to inject some humor into the interview. In any event, use your mistakes to show how you have matured and grown from these experiences.

26. *What do you think determines a person's progress with a good company?* A survey by Korn-Ferry, the international executive search firm, indicates that senior executives believe that hard work, high integrity, intelligence, and excellent human relations skills got them where they are today. Your answer should reflect those main points plus factors such as the ability to get results and sell ideas.

27. *Who has exercised the greatest influence on you? How?* This question is designed to discover what type of person you are and to reveal a side of you that the interviewer might not otherwise see. People will often mention parents, relatives, former bosses, coaches, and teachers as having influenced them. Being asked this question is an opportunity to describe what they taught you. Emphasize that these qualities are deeply ingrained in you.

28. *What public figure do you admire most, and why?* Identify two or three people you admire. Generally they should be people who are widely admired but not overly controversial. Political figures are more risky, but can be used effectively. In the late 1970s I had a client who indicated he admired both Menachem Begin and Anwar Sadat for the courage they showed during the Middle East peace negotiations.

Another person, preparing for an interview in 1989, did a good job with Richard Nixon. He said he did not like everything Nixon ever did, but he admired him for the way he opened up contact with the People's Republic of China. A local figure who is well known would also be an acceptable choice. Usually the question will be worded in such a way that the interviewer clearly wants a living person, so don't use historical figures such as Abraham Lincoln. Generally, your reasons for admiring the person are more important than the specific person.

29. *What are your primary activities outside of work?* All of your activities reveal things about you so choose your answers carefully. You may want to mention one activity and then balance it with another. For example, mentioning family activities shows certain positive qualities, but might be balanced with mentioning that you enjoy reading trade journals in your field.

30. *Would you have any concern if we did a full background check on you? What would we find?* The immediate response should be a simple, "Not at all." If damaging information would be discovered, however, this might be the time to share it so you can put it in the best light. But be discreet. This is not the time to bare your soul and confess everything you ever did.

31. *What qualities do you most admire in people?* Pick four or five and explain why you value them so highly. This tells the employer more about you and your character.

32. *What have you done to increase your personal development?* The employer is trying to determine whether you are a growth-oriented person. You might mention courses, seminars, or self-study you have undertaken. Whether you were engaged in these activities on your own time or company time does not matter. The things you mention need not all be work-related unless the question was worded that way. You may have started studying a foreign language, taken up karate, or joined Toastmasters. Be prepared to discuss why you started these things and how they have helped you.

33. *What types of books and magazines do you read?* This question may be asked to determine whether you are growth-oriented and whether you keep up on the technical side of your profession. If you subscribe to any periodicals that keep you up to date in your field mention those, along with any recent books you've read which do the same. You can also mention novels, biographies, or other genres, as well as any specific books or authors you've liked. It's fine to mention news magazines, business magazines, or periodicals that deal with a

hobby of yours. If you've recently read a book which is highly recognized in your field, you could mention it and describe what you found useful in it. Avoid mentioning trashy novels or other types of reading that would not help sell you.

34. *What was the last book you read [movie you saw] and how did it affect you?* Your response need not necessarily be the absolute most recent book or movie, but you would certainly want it to be recent and one that you can discuss easily if the interviewer asks follow-up questions. Mention a book or movie that makes a positive statement about you and shows you to be a discerning individual. What you say about the book or movie is more important than which one it was. The interviewer is assessing how thoughtful you are. If you've recently read a book that deals directly or indirectly with the work you do, mention it and describe what you gained from it. With movies you would generally not want to mention the most recent action thriller you've seen. Instead you would select a movie which dealt with major themes and emotions, perhaps one in which people show uncommon courage. Or it could be a more "artsy" movie which plumbs the psyches of its characters.

35. *How do you feel about your career progress?* If you are not feeling good about your career progress, you could mention that as one of the reasons you're looking for a new position, particularly if career progress in your current company is blocked. Indicate that you have done the right things and have received excellent reviews, but that lack of company growth, or some other factor, is preventing you from moving ahead. Indicate that you know patience is important, but state that your strong ambition to take on more responsibility is also important to you.

If you've made rapid progress in your career, you should acknowledge this and supply the reasons for your progress in terms of your results and accomplishments. Be sensitive to your interviewer's situation, however. If you know that the interviewer has not been promoted for some time, you might want to tone down your own success, so as not to appear to be a threat. In such a situation, you would also have to determine whether your prospective boss's lack of progress could block yours.

36. *What was the most useful criticism you ever received?* This is a difficult question since criticism is usually given in ways that are not very helpful. You could begin by stating that on several occasions you have received constructive criticism and that you always listen to criticism, constructive or not, in hopes of learning from it and getting better at your profession. Think back to some of your best bosses and

coworkers and try to recall advice or criticism that they gave you. Jot down several such occurrences and write down any action that you took as a result. Then select an instance in which the criticism was difficult to accept, and perhaps you initially rejected it or planned to ignore it. Within a day or so, however, you began to recognize that the comment had validity and that you needed to take some action. Then describe how you used the advice or changed a behavior. Then describe how it has made you a better employee and better at your profession.

37. *What is the biggest change you've made in your life in the last ten years?* Select a change that has made you a better person or a better employee. It could include giving up a bad habit or starting a good one. Perhaps you stopped smoking, started exercising more, began attending professional seminars on a consistent basis, or became a better listener. Describe how this change has benefited you and past employers.

38. *If you won the $5 million lottery today, what would you be doing a year from now?* The most important thing is to be genuine. I'm going to exaggerate to make a point, but you would not say, "Well, I just love to work so even if I won a $100 million Powerball lottery I would still keep working, and I would keep working here to help us achieve our mission." Give me a break. Don't just say, "I would probably retire and travel for a year." Or, "I would want to keep working because I think I need to work." Give a thoughtful answer. Admit that you would be tempted to quit your job and do something you really wanted to do. Even though some people who win big lotteries continue to work in their current job, don't be so sure that you would. Describe the process that you would go through. You might indicate that you would want to stay in the job and not make any major changes in your life until you adapted to your new financial status. You might add that if you were enjoying your job, you would probably stay because you like to work. You might add that you have had a dream of starting a foundation that would help dying children or help people get off welfare. After a year or two you might quit to do that work. This is sincere and employers will appreciate it and learn a lot about the kind of person you are.

Chapter 22

SELLING PERSONAL QUALITIES

---

39. *Can you work well under stress?* You don't have to say that you like stress, but you should provide an example or two demonstrating that you work effectively under stress. Most stress comes from deadlines and long hours. Perhaps the question is asked since in the past people have quit because they could not tolerate the stress. You should know in advance whether this organization, field, or industry typically requires long hours or faces lots of deadlines.

40. *Do you prefer to work individually or as part of a team?* The best response depends on what you know about the job. If the organization is looking for a decisive person, you would emphasize your individualism and independence. If most work is done by committees and task forces, emphasize your ability to work as part of a team. If you are not sure of the best response, describe how you enjoy both aspects.

41. *Are you a team player?* With the question worded in this way you are virtually assured that they are looking for a team-oriented person. Describe how you are philosophically committed to working as a team. Indicate that you do not hesitate to state your beliefs, but when the group makes a decision, you willingly go along with it. Show that you are flexible and cooperative. Provide evidence that people

enjoy having you on their team. Use an example where effective teamwork was essential to the success of the project.

42. *Tell me about the last incident that made you angry. How did you handle it?* Pick an example that would have made anyone angry. Describing *how* you reacted is particularly important. Make sure your reaction was mature, rather than childish. If it was a somewhat childish reaction, describe it in a humorous way so both of you can laugh about it. Being cut off in traffic or seeing someone blow through a red light makes most of us angry. Use such common occurrences rather than an argument with a spouse, child, boss, or coworker.

43. *What are the things that motivate you?* Challenge, creativity, success, opportunity, and personal growth are the motivators most frequently mentioned. You can also mention specific skills that you are motivated to use. These might include troubleshooting, problem solving, planning, speaking, writing, or counseling people.

44. *How do you handle people that you really don't get along with?* If you are one of those fortunate types who get along with almost anyone, tell the interviewer so. However you answer the question, indicate that you work hard to get along with others. Think through how you really do respond to difficult people. The interviewer is using this question as an opportunity to learn about your human relations skills. As a follow-up question, the interviewer could ask you to describe an actual instance in which you dealt with a difficult person.

45. *What have you done that shows initiative?* Pick an example where you decided to do something on your own initiative because you knew it would benefit you, your boss, or your department. It should be something that was immediately embraced by your boss and coworkers, or became widely accepted after its benefits were readily seen. If it was something which primarily benefited you, explain how it saved you time and enhanced the quality of your work. Developing a new process or procedure can be very useful. A person who uses spreadsheets, for example, might describe creating a macro which enabled a complex procedure to be calculated in much less time than before. Or it could be some type of report that benefited you or your boss by creating useful information in a very concise form. Indicate that this experience is just one of several examples that you could use. An interviewer who asks such a question is obviously looking for someone who has a history of taking initiative. It would also indicate that this person does not want someone who will need a great deal of supervision, so use the opportunity to sell the fact that you are self-motivated and very disciplined. Be sure that when you took initiative

it was not something which went against company procedures or policies. Supervisors frequently want people who take initiative, but they won't want you breaking company policies or department policies they established.

46. *What personal qualities are important for success in this field?* To answer this effectively, list four or five key qualities. After listing them you might add, "I think that there are other important qualities as well, but those are the key ones." Then go on to give 20–30 seconds describing how you demonstrate each of those qualities. To keep the answer fairly short, you might remind the interviewer of a story you have already told, and show how that experience demonstrates each of the characteristics you've just mentioned.

47. *Sell me this pen.* While this question has historically been asked of salespeople, today everyone must understand the concept of features and benefits because virtually everyone in a company must sell. Of course the item to be sold may not be a pen, but it often is. Like so many interview questions, it is artificial, since no one is ever asked to sell a product without having received training in how to market it. Nevertheless it is an increasingly used question for nonsales positions. The primary principle is to know the difference between features and benefits. A feature of a pen may be that it is plastic; a benefit is that plastic makes it lighter and less expensive. In other words, you would mention the feature that it is plastic, only if you were going to join it with the benefit that the plastic makes it lighter and cheaper. Sell benefits, not features. Years ago I developed a strategy for my sales clients which worked wonders, and it can do so for you as well. Decide that you are going to have fun with this question. Study the object for one or two minutes and make up some benefits that, if true, would help you sell this product. After all, how can you know for sure what the benefits are if you don't have a price guide and sales literature? So you have to make it up. With a pen, for example, you might answer like this:

> I think you'll be very interested in our product. Hold this pen for a moment as you would while writing (a sales technique is to get a customer involved and to actually hold and closely examine the product). Notice how comfortable this pen is. Our engineers spent over 1,000 engineering hours developing the absolutely perfect ergonomic design. You can write with this pen for hours without experiencing writer's cramp. Our research shows that people love their pens so much that they become extremely upset if they lose them or if they run out of ink. So we ingeniously added two very interesting benefits. This pen has three times more ink than a normal pen. In addition, we added a very inexpensive chip which

memorizes your unique grip. If someone accidentally or intentionally walks off with your pen, it will emit a very slight beep which will cause the person to immediately return it to you and ask how they can obtain one of their own. That's why nearly half the pens we sell are used for marketing purposes—companies give them away with their name and logo on the pen. They come in five standard colors as well as four neon colors. We can give you delivery in three weeks for the pens with your company name on them and one week without. How many gross do you think you'll want?

In a real sales situation you would spend time asking questions and you wouldn't try to close so quickly. Since this is an interview, you must quickly demonstrate that you know how to sell benefits and ask for the order. Study the brief sales presentation and notice what the person did. First he created a benefit by saying the pen is so well designed that people can write for hours without getting writer's cramp. Next he added another benefit—the ink lasts three times longer than the competition's. Mentioning the chip which memorizes a person's grip brought a little lightness and humor to the interview. Then the person gave some useful information about colors and delivery times. Ultimately the person asked for the order. When you are asked this question, the interviewer will always be looking to see if you ask for the order.

48. *Are you willing to take calculated risks?* Be careful. Before you answer you should have a sense of what the interviewer is looking for. If you are interviewing with a rapidly growing, highly entrepreneurial firm, they may be looking for people with good judgment and a track record for taking risks that have worked. On the other hand, if you're interviewing with a slow growing organization in a very mature market, they may be hoping to find that you are not a risk taker. It's fair to discern what the interviewer is really looking for so you can adjust your response. After all, you are probably a risk taker in some areas of your personal and business life, and a very conservative, risk-averse person in other areas of your life. You merely need to decide which side of your life you will describe. Obviously whatever risks you discuss will be those in which you succeeded.

In any case you must begin by stating that while you are willing to take calculated risks, you do everything possible to reduce the risk or reduce the cost in case you are wrong. Describe the work you typically do or the research you do to gain assurance that the decision you are about to make is the right and prudent one. What complicates your answer is that everyone realizes that if you are too risk-averse you will miss opportunities. Frequently the window of opportunity is very short and decisions must be made quickly, often with less information than you would want to have. If you are unsure of how to respond, discuss how in one case you were cautious and events of the future demonstrated that you were wise to hold back. Then share a brief example of how you took a small gamble and got a high reward.

49. *Can you establish effective methods and procedures?* This question is usually directed to people in supervisory and management positions where change is continual and where both methods and procedures for doing things must constantly be updated. Sometimes this question is posed to lower-level staff because today nearly all employees are in a position to improve methods and procedures. Those working daily in a job are often the first and best people to recommend and implement improvements. In essence you want to show that you are a person who is constantly looking for better ways to do things. Begin with an overview describing your history of improving processes. You're the type who is never satisfied with "good enough." You don't subscribe to the concept that "if it ain't broke, don't fix it." Even when a process or technique is not "broken," there may be a better way to do it.

Show that you involve bosses when appropriate, such as when a change you make will affect others. Your future boss who is interviewing you does not want to hire a loose cannon who makes major changes without consulting others. When you make a change that only affects you it is okay to show that you did it totally on your own. This can also be a good opportunity to show that you are a team player by describing how you and one or two others came up with the idea and implemented it. You should always provide an example to demonstrate that you truly are a person who seeks improved methods. Describing things you did on your own shows initiative.

50. *We have some very difficult and demanding customers. Can you handle that?* This question begs an example. Begin by emphasizing that a customer has the right to expect a lot from its vendors. Then point out that some customers are not very tactful about the way they make demands and can be downright rude. You would indicate that you don't prefer that kind of behavior, but that you have learned how to deal with it: you are always polite, you always listen to the customer and his complaints, and then assure the customer that you will take care of it. Indicate that you always follow up with the customer to indicate what is being done to fix the problem. Then give an example of how you tactfully handled a complaint from your most obnoxious customer.

51. *We need someone who is resourceful.* Resourcefulness is the ability to make do when you don't have all the tools or support that is usually required for a task or project. Somehow, resourceful people always find a way to get it done. They are can-do people. These people

find ways to obtain the necessary resources through other than normal channels. To answer this question state that it is always nice when you have all the tools and resources available to you, but that they are often not available. Your attitude is that the task still must be completed. Show that individually or with your team, you brainstorm and come up with creative ways to get it done. Wrap it up with your most creative and resourceful solution to a problem.

52. *What has been your greatest challenge?* This is different from "Describe your biggest crisis." Keep in mind that while many challenges involve problems, a challenge can also be viewed as an opportunity. A problem occurs when something is going wrong and must be fixed. A challenge occurs, for example, when you can see that a competitor is developing a technology that you must match or exceed quickly or else lose market share. You still have a fine product, but you realize you must stay ahead of the competition. Another type of challenge occurs when you are working on a project and you can see numerous road blocks that must be overcome. List a few challenges and then practice sharing two or three of them.

53. *Describe a team project where you were proud of the team's result, as well as of your personal contribution.* List some of your best team projects, some where you were a lead person and others where you contributed but had no leadership responsibility. Recall some where there were real conflicts among team members or where there were arguments about how to proceed or how to solve certain problems. If you played a role in getting that group to resolve its differences, that would be an excellent experience to share in the interview. If there was a particularly difficult person on the team, but you helped everyone else get along better with that person or helped that person feel part of the team, that would be an excellent example. If you were part of a team where everyone clicked and the team came up with really creative solutions, that would also work well.

54. *Describe a difficult decision you've made, and the process you went through to reach that decision.* Recall and then list several difficult decisions you've had to make. Pick one that was truly difficult but had a good outcome. It may have been difficult because you didn't have all of the information you might have wanted. It may have been difficult because key people opposed the decision or told you that it would have negative consequences. Then list the steps you went through to arrive at it. It might be good to have one example where you did a great job of analyzing tons of information and distilling what you needed to decide. Then recall a decision where you primarily used your intuition, even in the face of contradictory data. As you think about difficult decisions

you've made, determine if there are methods that you almost always use. If you use different methods under different circumstances you could show that you are quite flexible and that you use strategies that fit the situation.

55. *Give me three qualities that are really helping you get ahead and three qualities you must work on if you are going to achieve your career goals.* You are well on your way to answering this question if you have worked on, "What is your greatest strength?" "Why should I hire you?" and "What is your greatest weakness?" You should identify 8–10 strengths and be prepared to describe any of them. If the question asks you to describe three areas you must work on, they do not have to be weaknesses. You could have a fairly good ability in some area yet realize that to achieve your goals you'll need to improve upon this skill some more. Be prepared to describe what you are doing to become stronger in those areas.

56. *What is the most important lesson you've learned in the last ten years?* Clearly the interviewer wants to know that you learn from experiences, challenges, opportunities, and even mistakes. Basically the question requires a lesson learned and it should include information about the specific experience. Use a positive experience with a positive outcome. List several experiences where there were lessons learned so you can pick just the right one for each particular interview.

Chapter 23

JOB FACTORS

57. *Describe your perfect job.* This is not the place to describe your dream job. Select those *parts* of your dream job, however, that you think could be found in the job you are interviewing for. If you dream of a job that would take you to Europe twice a year but this job offers no chance of that, don't mention your desire to travel. The greatest danger here is in becoming too specific. If you mention things that cannot be fulfilled in the job, the employer may assume you would soon become dissatisfied.

58. *What is most important to you in a job?* What do you value in a job—challenge, good working conditions, friendly coworkers, a boss you respect? Mention one or two items and explain why they are important.

59. *Why do you want to change careers?* I define career change as a change of fields, such that the skills and knowledge required to adequately perform the new occupation appear *on the surface* to be significantly different from what was required in the former occupation. The key phrase is *on the surface*. Most would agree that moving from teacher to sales representative is a career change. But when you get below the surface, you will see the similarities in these careers. Both motivate—one to buy, the other to learn. Both must be able to simplify and explain difficult concepts. Granted, the teacher will have to develop product knowledge and learn specific closing techniques. But, because

of the underlying similarities in these careers, teachers frequently make excellent salespeople.

Here's my point: In most cases, refuse to accept the label of career change. You might say:

> I don't feel I'm changing careers. Basically I'll be using the same skills I've developed during the last eight years of my career. My knowledge base will be somewhat different, but I took several college courses in this area, and during the last three years I've been subscribing to three trade journals and devouring every article in this specialty.

This is not just a question of semantics. The employer has stated that he or she believes you are making a career change. In essence, the employer has raised an objection about you. The employer is actually saying, "You don't have a track record, so how can I judge your ability to perform this job?" Unless you can overcome the objection, no job offer will be made. Respond by saying, "I don't feel I'm changing careers." Avoid defensiveness and sell those skills which are similar to ones required in the new field.

60. *Why do you want to get into this field?* This is different than "Why do you want to change careers?" This interviewer is looking for evidence that you really know what you're getting into. People getting into personnel work often respond, "I enjoy helping people." That is the worst possible response and indicates a total misunderstanding of personnel work. In answering this question, it's important to let the interviewer know that you are aware of positive *and* negative aspects of the field.

61. *Why did you leave your last job?* Here you must overcome the interviewer's natural desire to hire someone who currently has a job. Even when a person has been laid off during a recession, the question in the interviewer's mind is, "Most people in her company are still there. Why was she laid off?" The concern is that perhaps you sound impressive, but are not able to produce under pressure.

If you left voluntarily, make that clear and then explain the reason. A resignation due to a personality conflict must be handled carefully. Your explanation should make your leaving seem like a mature and responsible thing to do.

If you were fired, terminated, or laid off, you must handle this question very carefully. Do not become defensive and do not start criticizing your former boss. A good answer will require a carefully considered response. It is wise to know what your former employer will say about it. See question 14 for additional help if you were fired.

62. *How long will it take before you make a positive contribution to our organization?* This question tests your self-confidence. A good response might be, "After a brief orientation to your methods, I think I can contribute almost immediately. The duties you've outlined are very similar to the ones I've been performing at Jersey Central." The interviewer will be looking for a realistic, self-confident response. You do not have to come across as a miracle worker.

63. *What do you like least about this position? Most?* By asking these questions, the interviewer is trying to get below the surface and force you to make some definite statements. This is a hard one to prepare for because you won't usually know enough about the job prior to the interview to prepare adequately. An effective way to deal with these questions is to describe a minor duty as one you like least and a major duty as one you like most.

64. *Tell me about your duties at your present job.* This question provides an opportunity to really sell yourself, yet many miss this opportunity. Mention only those duties that will help sell you. Sometimes this even means overlooking a major duty simply because that duty would not be related to the job you're interviewing for. As you describe your major duties, describe an associated accomplishment as well.

A good overview will require two or three minutes. Be concise, however. Because people know their duties so well, many go on and on, adding unnecessary details that bore the interviewer. Based on what you know of the job you will be interviewing for, select those duties that you would like to discuss, then practice sharing them concisely and with enthusiasm.

65. *What is the most important aspect of your job?* This is another question which tests your judgment. Although you have numerous responsibilities, the interviewer wants to have your view of what you do that contributes the most to your organization. You could begin by mentioning the four most important things that you do, but then finish by saying, "But I think the aspect that has the greatest impact on the success of my department [division, or company] is . . ." Then explain why it is so important and show that you have been very effective in that area.

66. *Describe a time when you were criticized on your job.* Describe a situation where you were criticized by coworkers, but make it one in which your idea or program was ultimately adopted and shown to be effective. Or you could describe a program you were responsible for which was not immediately achieving the desired results. You began to

receive criticism, but you continued according to the plan and it worked out just fine. Or select an idea which was criticized, and demonstrate that you were mature enough to recognize its merit. Then show that by changing your plan you were successful. Try to avoid describing a situation where the criticism originated with your boss unless the interviewer absolutely insists on it. Be sure to have such an example handy. It should be one in which your boss was right, you then made the appropriate changes, and everyone lived happily ever after.

67. *What is the most difficult situation you have ever faced?* Typically your answer would be work related, but not necessarily. Your most difficult experience may have been going through a divorce and a child-custody dispute, but do not mention those types of experiences. Whatever example you choose it should be one in which you demonstrated maturity and good judgment, and perhaps even courage. This is similar to question 7, "Describe the biggest crisis in your career."

68. *What frustrates you about your job?* Give concrete examples when answering this question. If you feel strongly about a particular frustration, and would refuse future job offers if you would continue to face that frustration, describe that frustration in bold terms. For example:

> When I started in quality control, Acme was producing very high-quality drill bits. We applied stringent tests before they passed inspection. Because our new plant superintendent gets his annual bonus based on the quantity rather than the quality of production, I've seen quality really slip this past year. That's why I'm especially interested in Best Tools. All of our tests on competitors show that you consistently produce high-quality drill bits.

If you don't feel so strongly about any of your frustrations, or you wouldn't let them stand in the way of accepting a job, you'll want to choose more minor frustrations. Another quality inspector might say, "There really aren't any major frustrations. I was frustrated a few times when I wasn't allowed to buy new testing equipment when I felt we could use it, but we got by." Your response should sound justifiable, such that your interviewer will think, "I'd be frustrated too, if I were in that situation."

69. *What jobs have you enjoyed most? Least? Why?* To prepare for this question, think through and recall each of your positions. Relive them. What brought you satisfaction? What was frustrating? If you've been out of college several years, do not bring up summer or part-time jobs—most people assume that such jobs are unrewarding and frustrating. You need not admit that you hated any of the positions. The question only requires that you discuss which jobs you enjoyed least.

70. *What duties have you enjoyed most? Least? Why?* Select your favorite and least favorite duties based on what you have learned about the job for which you're interviewing. In general, pick major duties to like and minor duties to dislike. A disliked duty might be one you have done in the past but would not be doing in the job being interviewed for.

71. *What is the worst thing you've heard about this organization?* If you've done your research, you've heard both positives and negatives. You could mention a negative you've heard, but then explain why you don't believe it is true. A response might be, "Some people say you're ruthless in the marketplace, but my observation is that you're just aggressive and fight hard to get your market share."

72. *Describe a typical work day.* Don't just cover all of the little details of your job. Use this question as an opportunity to mention some of your key functions and how well you do them. To prepare for this question list all of the types of things that occur on your job. This is for your benefit to gain a greater appreciation for all of the things that you do. While you may rarely perform all of these things on any given day, you could still mention all of your key activities. This question is similar to "Tell me what you did yesterday."

Chapter 24

QUESTIONS REGARDING ORGANIZATIONS AND SUPERVISORS

73. *What position do you expect to hold in five years?* This question tests how realistic you are. It's not realistic to say you want to be president in five years when you are five levels below that and there are four hundred people ahead of you. It's okay to have such a goal, but don't express it. Employers seek promotable people, but tend to be suspicious of the person who expects to turn the company upside down. If your interviewer will be your boss or your boss's boss, you might say, "I would like to move up the ladder with you. I realize you have other very capable people in this department, but through my contributions I'll seek to be the person who moves into your position when you're promoted. In five years I'd like to move up two or three notches."

74. *Why would you like to work for us?* If this question is asked at or near the beginning of the first interview, you have an opportunity to describe what you know about the organization by way of your research. If the question is asked after the interviewer has described the job and the company in detail, you could mention positive points that you had

discovered on your own, as well as some mentioned by the interviewer. This might include the reputation of the company or department, its rapid growth, or your personal attraction to the interviewer as a boss. You might also mention that the job itself is a factor in your wanting to work for the company.

75. *What is your opinion of your present [or past] employer?* The interviewer does not expect you to speak in glowing terms about your employer, but you should emphasize the positive qualities. If you really like your present organization, your response will be easy. If you hate it, be careful. Start by saying something positive, followed by one or two minor negatives, and finish with a strong positive. This is not the time to blast your employer. If you mention only negatives, the interviewer may assume you are a negative person who is difficult to satisfy.

76. *How long would you stay if we offered you this position?* This is an impossible question to answer since no one really knows how long he or she will stay. The best way to handle it is to lay out the conditions for your staying:

> I hope to stay for many years. Everything I know about the company tells me this is an ideal fit. The philosophy of top management matches mine and I like everything I've seen so far. Advancement and pay are certainly important to me. As long as my responsibilities and income grow with my proven worth, I expect to stay a long time.

Notice how stating the conditions made it seem like a much more realistic and honest response. You are unlikely to be believed if you say that you expect to stay with the company for 20 years and then retire. Furthermore, such a statement may make it seem as though everything you say is designed simply to match what the interviewer wants to hear.

If you have an unstable work history, you must develop a convincing statement which clearly shows that those days have ended. Actually, you should begin dealing with this issue as soon as you can in the interview; don't wait for the interviewer to bring it up. At the first opportunity mention what makes this job appealing. You could also sprinkle in subtle hints that there is more stability in your life at this time and that you would value a stable job as well. These comments will help you emphasize that you are a very reliable, responsible person.

77. *What do you know about our company?* The employer asks this question to determine your interest, enthusiasm, and initiative. There's no faking this answer—either you've done your homework or you haven't. Typically you would describe what you know about their products or services, the reputation of the organization, the size of the organization in relation to its competitors, and any financial infor-

mation you've picked up. If you've thoroughly analyzed the company's annual report, don't overwhelm the interviewer with financial data. Share any interesting knowledge about the company you've gathered, such as a new product or acquisition.

78. *Why do you want to leave your present employer?* The four most acceptable reasons for leaving an employer include the desire for more money, more responsibility, more challenge, or more job satisfaction. Less acceptable reasons might be a personality conflict with your boss, not wishing to relocate, or having to work too much overtime. These last three reasons may be real, but they cast suspicion on you as a worker. Be prepared to offer two or three reasons since employers realize that changes are seldom made for one reason alone. Every employer understands someone wanting more money. A good response might be:

> With my level of expertise, I should be earning more. Of course I realize my company is not going to pay me more than my boss earns, so I've decided to look elsewhere. I've gained some outstanding experience there. I'm interested in Prodata because of the quality of your products.

Top-quality people seek greater challenges and more responsibility; some companies allow faster growth than others. Companies that promote primarily by seniority and those with slow growth make promotions more difficult. You could explain your reason for leaving by saying:

> Western Gear is an excellent company and I've learned a lot, but right now it's in a slow growth pattern. My boss has told me I'll have his spot when he moves up, but both of us realize that could take four or five years. I just want to use my abilities to the fullest.

79. *Starting with your first job out of college, tell me why you left each organization.* Generally, people will have several reasons for leaving a company. Select the most appropriate and acceptable reason for each move. Do not use such negative statements as "I had a personality conflict with my boss," or "It was a lousy company to work for." Learn how to soften your statements. Your answers may require some elaboration since the reasons for leaving are often complex. If you had four or five reasons for leaving, select one or two that will cause the employer to understand and accept your reasons.

80. *What kind of recommendations will you get from previous employers?* You should know the answer to this question. Although many companies are hesitant to make negative statements about former employees because of possible defamation of character law-

suits, some will say negative things. If you've been fired from one of your last three jobs, you would be wise to contact your former boss or the personnel department and ask what they will say. If the termination was justified, but you have since changed your ways, explain that to your former boss. Explain, too, how the firing was actually a blessing in disguise because you really learned from the experience.

If you know you will receive good recommendations you might simply say, "I'm certain each of my former bosses will have only positive things to say about me. We worked well together and I learned a lot from each one." You could also expand and describe some specific points the supervisors might make. In other words, let your supervisors sell you even though they are not present.

You may have had excellent relations with all but one former supervisor. How you would respond to the question, in that case, depends on what you find out when you recontact past supervisors. If you are confident that nothing negative will be said, simply respond by stating they will all say positive things. If you are fairly certain that a particular supervisor would say negative things about you, describe some of your results and indicate some areas where you and your boss differed. Your intent would be to soften or counteract what you believe your former boss may say. Psychologically it has less negative impact when an employer has already heard from *you* the negative statements that a former boss might make. Of course you need to be discreet about what you mention.

If your relations with that boss were poor, but you know the company has a strict policy about not giving out information beyond dates of employment, do not indicate that your former boss would say anything negative about you. Be sure to read the material covering question 14 regarding having been fired or terminated. Even if you have never been fired or terminated, there are several key points in that section which will help you respond to this question.

81. *Describe your relationship with your last three supervisors.* This question is easy to answer if you've had great relationships with your supervisors. If the relationships were less than sterling, you don't have to pretend they were wonderful, just accentuate the positive. If you had a hot and cold relationship with a supervisor, stress the things which you know your boss valued about you. It is acceptable to say, "We didn't agree on everything, but we both respected each other a great deal. We learned how to work around those differences. Once decisions were made, I would back her completely, and she valued that." A statement like this shows maturity on the interviewee's part. After all, even your interviewer has probably had four or more bosses. I can guarantee you that not all of them were wonderful. If you try to paint a picture that

your relationship with each supervisor was ideal, you will seem less credible to your interviewer.

82. *What are your supervisor's strengths and weaknesses?* Be prepared to answer this question for each of your supervisors. To answer it, concentrate on strengths. Play down weaknesses, even if they were many. Select a fairly minor weakness to discuss.

83. *What kind of supervisors do you like the most? Least? Why?* To prepare for this question, list all of the qualities you truly like and dislike in a supervisor. When the question is asked, select those that are most appropriate. For your preferred characteristics, select two or more that your future boss appears to have. For dislikes, select qualities that appear not to be true of this person. Be careful with a statement like, "I don't like a supervisor who won't give me enough independence." You may come across as a maverick. Don't just make a statement— explain what you mean. Instead of the above response, you might say, "It's frustrating working for someone who doesn't delegate effectively." See the difference? No one appreciates someone who does not delegate well. With this answer you would then go on to describe yourself as one who is highly reliable and self-directing, capable of taking on major challenges.

84. *How has your supervisor helped you grow?* Whether you have a great supervisor or a lousy one, every supervisor will add to your personal growth in some way. If, for example, your supervisor has no human relations skills, emphasize how the person has helped you grow in technical knowledge.

85. *What did your supervisor rate you highest on during your last review? Lowest?* Emphasize the positive and give a complete explanation as to why your supervisor valued that quality. Undoubtedly there are four or five things that you were rated highly on. Pick the one or two items that will score the most points with this particular interviewer. Of those things you were rated lower in, you might say, "Overall, I was rated quite high in everything. I suppose if there was anything that my boss wanted me to work on it would be to work on my presentation skills. That's why I'm now in Toastmasters." When possible, emphasize a technical skill that your boss simply wants you to work on, as opposed to a personality characteristic. It is always more acceptable to say you need to learn or perfect a technical skill rather than say, "My boss wants me to work on my tendency to be rude to customers."

86. *What kind of supervisor gets the best results out of you?* Base your answer on what you've learned about your prospective boss. If

you know this person keeps a tight rein on employees, you would not mention your strong need for independence. Think through and identify several qualities that really help motivate you and be prepared to share two or three. You might answer by saying you prefer a supervisor who is fair, open-minded, and has high integrity. You could also say you prefer a supervisor who leads by example and motivates people.

87. *What is your boss like?* This is similar to the question regarding your boss's strengths and weaknesses, but with this question you will only discuss your boss's strengths. No matter how bad a boss may be, every supervisor has strengths—concentrate on those.

Chapter 25

ARE YOU A GOOD MANAGER?

88. *What actions would you take if you came on board?* This question is usually asked to determine if you have preset ideas on what should be done. The person with all the answers after one or two interviews is usually not trusted. The people interviewing you consider themselves capable. If they've been studying a problem for months and don't have the answers, they don't expect you to have the answers either. Perhaps you really do have some solutions, but don't sound cocky. You'll be respected more if you admit it will take time to study the situation, than to say you will have a complete set of recommendations by next week.

This question also tests your thought process. The steps you would take to solve a problem can reveal more about your character and your expertise than the actual recommendations you might make.

89. *Can you supervise people?* A positive statement followed by an example works well. "Yes, I supervise people very well. At Somestates Insurance I supervised eight claims adjusters. Through my personal training I was able to teach more effective negotiating techniques. As a result, our average personal injury settlement was reduced 4% last year." Relate one or more good examples, always keeping them short and to

the point. When appropriate you might discuss your philosophy and techniques of supervision.

90. *Describe your management philosophy and management style.* To answer this question effectively you need to be clear on both your management philosophy and style. Management philosophy and style have to do with your beliefs regarding participative management, management by objectives, total quality management, methods for training and motivating employees, and dozens of concepts and techniques that are covered in books on management. Philosophy is the theory you follow, while style is the way you actually operate on the job. Spend a short time on philosophy, but what an employer really wants to know is how you actually manage on the job. Emphasize your strengths. If you're a good delegator or a good motivator, describe how those abilities help you to be an effective manager.

91. *How many people have you hired? How do you go about it? How successful have the people been?* By asking this question the interviewer is trying to learn about you and your processes. Describe your methods, but emphasize your results. If you have hired five or more people, it is highly unlikely that each of them has gone on to great success. You do not need to claim perfect insight or judgment. You do want to get across the idea that you are very careful in your hiring decisions, that you are a good judge of character, and that you provide adequate training so that employees achieve their full potential.

92. *How many people have you fired? How do you handle terminations?* Here the interviewer is trying to determine how decisive you are, and how "cleanly" you can fire people. Terminations are the ultimate test of decisiveness. Typically, managers agonize over firing decisions even when it is clear that the employee is hopelessly ineffective. As you describe your termination process, demonstrate that you were decisive as well as humane.

93. *How would your subordinates describe you as a supervisor?* Indicate that you work hard to gain their respect, but that being liked by everyone is not your main concern. You might add, "They would say that they enjoy working for me. I'm tough but I'm fair. I give them room for independence and I seek self-starters. They would say I'm an excellent trainer. I'm patient, but they know I can get pretty upset when I see the same mistakes recurring." Here is a chance to share some of your management philosophy. Use this question to demonstrate that you elicit maximum output from your employees.

94. *Some managers watch their employees closely, while others use a loose rein. How do you manage?* You should indicate that you manage your employees neither too closely nor too loosely. Employees should be monitored carefully when new to the job and until they demonstrate the ability to do the job with little assistance from you. Use this as an opportunity to emphasize results you have achieved through those working for you.

95. *How have you improved as a supervisor over the years?* The interviewer is assuming you have improved as a supervisor, which means you can admit to past mistakes. Management is learned through experience, not textbooks, so it is safe to admit that you were far from perfect in the past. You might admit that early in your management experience you had difficulty delegating, or that sometimes you were too demanding. Preparing for this question will give you an opportunity to reflect and see how you have improved over the years. Once you've done this, you'll be prepared to share some of those reflections with an interviewer.

Chapter 26

COLLEGE: HOW DID YOU DO?

Recent college grads will be asked all of the typical questions, but there are also a few questions that are rarely asked of anyone but recent graduates. Be prepared for the following questions, which could be asked of you up to five years after leaving college.

96. *Why did you pick your major?* Try to recall your reasons for choosing your major, then give only the most positive reasons. The question gives you the opportunity to demonstrate your forethought and planning ability. Indicate that the decision was made only after considerable thought. If you are not using your major—you were a psych major now looking to get into banking—indicate the strengths you were able to develop as a result of your major.

97. *What kind of grades did you have?* If your grades were medio-cre, you need to prepare for this question. If, while you were in school, you worked 20–30 hours per week you might say, "I was a good student and worked hard in my classes. I'm confident that if I hadn't had to work nearly full-time during school I could have maintained a 3.0 GPA." If you simply weren't a good student you might say, "I've never been a great student, but I do retain information well and I use a lot of com-mon sense. That's always been my strength."

98. *What courses did you like most? Least? Why?* For courses that you liked, mention those that are most related to the job you're interviewing for. Otherwise simply choose courses which excited you and explain why. It's safe to mention courses having little to do with the job as those you liked least. For instance, business majors can say they least enjoyed science courses and can even admit they disliked accounting.

99. *How has your schooling prepared you for this job?* If your education is directly related to the job you are interviewing for, emphasize that your education has given you a strong foundation upon which to build. If you are a liberal arts major, emphasize your broad education, your written and verbal communication skills, and your analytical ability. If you're a liberal arts major seeking a job in private enterprise, discuss any business-related courses you took, such as macroeconomics.

Also describe how your overall college experience has prepared you for work. You could mention that you matured while in school or that you gained excellent experiences by participating in extracurricular activities. Describing how you served on a committee and learned how to negotiate and compromise would be helpful. If you worked on any group projects you would describe how you learned teamwork and how you were one of the hardest working people on the team. If you became the team leader you would emphasize your experience in leadership. If you had an opportunity for study abroad you would mention how you have learned to adapt to other cultures. If you had an internship, even one in which you had little real responsibility, emphasize that you gained a good understanding of how business (or government) really operates.

100. *Do you feel you did the best work at school that you were capable of doing?* If you truly worked hard at your studies, you might say, "I worked very hard and really took my studies seriously. I graduated with a 3.2 GPA [or with honors]. Even the classes I didn't do so well in grade-wise really taught me something." Or you might say, "I worked hard and got good grades, but I also wanted to balance my education. I was active in [student government, debate, sports, dorm counseling, etc.]." If you received poor grades you could admit to a lack of focus at the time, adding that you are very focused now.

101. *How did your summer jobs benefit you?* If you had the typical summer jobs in which you had little responsibility, and they consisted mostly of grunt work, emphasize that you developed a strong work ethic and proved to yourself that you could handle physically demanding or highly repetitive jobs because you had a long-term goal in mind. One

client shared with me that his summer at a sawmill, where he was the only college-educated person, proved to him that he could get along with anyone. By the end of the summer he had gained the respect of the crew and was accepted as "one of the guys."

Other questions frequently asked of recent graduates include:
How did you choose your college?
How did you pay for college?
Which college professors did you enjoy most and why?
What are your career goals?
Were you active on campus? How?
Did you get involved in student government?
Do you like to cram for exams or study throughout the quarter?
Do you think grades are a good indicator of a person's success, or
    lack of it, on the job?

Chapter 27

BE READY FOR ANYTHING

By understanding the principles of these 101 questions, you'll be able to develop effective responses to any question thrown at you, including the ones provided below. You'll be better prepared to think quickly and assess what the employer is after. It is impossible to predict all of the questions that might be asked in an interview. By being prepared for the 101 most common questions, and by having experiences in mind for behaviorally-based questions, you'll be ready for just about anything.

Reviewing the questions below can also help you get ready. As with the 101 most commonly asked questions, write out each question and then list the points you would want to make, almost in an outline form.

Strange Questions

Sometimes you'll get questions which are really hard to prepare for, such as "If you were an animal, which animal would you like to be?" Don't panic with this type of question. Clearly, there is no right or wrong answer. The interviewer is observing you to see how you handle unusual things. Don't overanalyze it. In this case, you would simply think of an animal and explain why you would like to be that animal.

A client of mine was once asked to take the recruiter through a typical day at work. He was asked how he knew what to do, how he knew it was time to go home, how he felt when people doubted him, and what types of people intimidated him. Because these are unusual questions, it is impossible to prepare for them. You need to be so well-prepared and knowledgeable about yourself that you will always be able to come up with a good response, even to questions you didn't anticipate.

Examples of Other Questions

The following are additional questions that are worth preparing for:

1. Can you establish long-term relations with customers [vendors]?
2. Can you quickly establish rapport with people?
3. Can you handle working with people with big egos?
4. We need people who are detail-oriented.
5. What personal areas are you working on? (similar to, What is your greatest weakness?)
6. How do you resolve conflicts?
7. What project that you worked on has been most helpful in your personal growth?
8. Describe a time you had a leadership role. How did you gain it and why did you take it on?
9. Describe a stressful time when you performed well.
10. Describe the type of stress that hurts your efforts and the type that helps. Give me examples.
11. Walk me through a project when you demonstrated [human relations] skills.
12. In hindsight most of us can think of some things we wished we had done differently. What are some things you would have done differently, and what did you learn from them?
13. Describe a time when you were rejected or an idea was rejected. How did you handle it?
14. What is your feeling about job quotas [or any controversial subject such as abortion or gay rights]?
15. Are you tolerant of people with opinions and values different from yours?
16. As a manager, what have you done in the last couple of years to promote diversity in the workplace?

BEHAVIOR-BASED INTERVIEW QUESTIONS

Besides the types of questions mentioned above, you must also prepare to answer behavior-based interview questions. They are among the most unpredictable. There are literally hundreds of questions which can be asked. Although the actual wording will differ, in essence they will begin with, "Tell me about a time when . . ." While most of the questions will allow you to speak of positive experiences, you will also receive numerous questions that will require you to discuss negative or less positive experiences. You are not being singled out. This is simply part of the process. Virtually everyone will be asked the same questions, including the difficult ones.

The following questions are a sampling of behavior-based questions. Not all behavior-based questions begin with "Tell me about a time when . . . ," but I'm using that phrase as a convenient way to introduce to you the types of questions you can expect.

Tell me about a time when you:

achieved a great deal in a short amount of time.

were disappointed in your performance.

made a major sacrifice to achieve a work goal.

were unwilling or unable to make the necessary sacrifice to achieve a goal.

worked effectively under a great deal of pressure.

didn't handle a stressful situation very well.

really got angry over a situation at work.

felt under a great deal of pressure from an internal or external customer.

were really bothered by the actions of a coworker.

were especially creative in solving a problem.

were not as creative as usual.

organized or planned an event that was very successful.

planned and coordinated a project that was very successful.

were unable to complete a project on schedule despite your best efforts.

really had to remain flexible.

had to deal with a personality conflict with a boss or coworker.

were unable to sell your idea to a key person.

felt really good about a decision you made and the process you went through.

were very effective in your problem-solving ability.

used facts and reason to persuade someone to accept your recommendation.

utilized your leadership ability to gain support for what initially had strong opposition.

were able to build team spirit during a time of low morale.

were able to gain commitment from others to really work as a team.

used your political savvy to push through a program you believed in.

were particularly perceptive regarding a person's or group's feelings and needs.

were able to predict someone's behavior or response based on your assessment of him or her.

were particularly supportive and reassuring to a person who needed a friend.

built rapport quickly with someone under difficult conditions.

wrote a report which was well received by others.

were particularly effective at prioritizing tasks and completing a project on schedule.

identified potential problems and resolved the situation before the problems became serious.

were highly motivated and your example inspired others.

found it necessary to tactfully but forcefully say things others did not want to hear.

were particularly effective in a talk you gave or in a seminar you taught.

had to make an important decision quickly even though you did not have all the information you wanted.

had to make a decision you knew would be unpopular.

were in a situation when events and circumstances changed rapidly.

These are difficult questions. If asked such questions, take some time to come up with an example. To succeed:

1) Stay calm
2) Recall several potential examples
3) Choose one that feels right
4) Consider the ramifications of sharing it
5) Recall a few key points
6) Begin your story and share it with vividness and enthusiasm.

Your interviewer is likely to give you a minute or more before beginning to answer the question because he or she knows it is a difficult question that requires a thoughtful answer.

Preparation For Behavior-Based Questions

Because these questions can be so difficult, the best preparation is to simply recall dozens of different experiences that you have had, both positive and negative. These experiences need not be major events in your life. They may be experiences that started and ended in five minutes or five days. The best way to recall experiences is to begin with your current job. Just let experiences flow through your mind and as they do, quickly jot down a key word or two so you'll know which experience you're referring to. Pause just long enough to visualize it in your mind for a few seconds.

If this seems like a lot of effort, it is, but if you've ever been in a behavior-based interview and were not able to come up with an example, you'll understand why this process is important.

WHEN YOU DON'T SUCCEED

Regardless of how well one prepares and how effective one is in the interview, no one gets every job he or she interviews for. Clients often ask me, "Why didn't I get the job? I would have been perfect." Other than failure to fully sell your potential, there are four primary reasons why a person might not get hired.

More Experience/Right Experience. Job seekers are often told that someone else with more experience or just the perfect combination of experience was hired. Effectively selling potential will not always get you the job, and you cannot always have the ideal background. Sometimes the job responsibilities are so technical, or require such specialization, that even a social misfit—with the right background—would still get the offer. This might be the case, for instance, if the employer is in such a bind that there is no time for training.

Biases. Every interviewer has biases—some are conscious, others are unconscious. By being perceptive you can detect some of those biases, but you cannot detect all of them. Most of us are not proud of our biases and will go to great lengths to hide them. Interviewers are no different. Some biases are plain old-fashioned discrimination, others are more minor, but just as insidious. The 26-year-old manager who does not feel comfortable managing someone three or four years older may tend to hire people the same age or younger. A 50-year-old manager prefers secretaries who are "more mature" and will not hire anyone under 40. A conservative businessman still cannot tolerate someone with long hair. You can predict some biases and take actions to overcome them. For example, a man can trim the shaggy beard, shorten the hair, and dress up for the occasion.

Unfortunately some biases cannot be detected and some simply cannot be overcome. If a person has a bias against taller people, or those with college degrees, there's little you can do. Fortunately, most biases will not completely knock you out of the running.

Inside Track. Sometimes you won't be offered the position because the hiring decision was virtually made before the interviewing even began. There can be a number of reasons for this. The person offered the position may already work for the company and have a good reputation. The person offered the job may be a friend or former colleague of someone who's with the company. Or, the person who got the job may simply be a person who, four months ago, managed to get in for a 15-minute get-acquainted appointment.

Feeling Threatened. Sometimes because the interviewer feels threatened by a highly talented, knowledgeable applicant, he or she will not hire that person. A good manager welcomes talent and is never afraid of it. The insecure manager, however, is fearful and often hires lower-caliber people.

What Do You Do Now?

It is helpful to realize that one of these four reasons, or any one of a dozen other reasons, could explain why you did not get the job. The worst thing you can do is wallow in self-pity and complain of prejudice and discrimination. Instead, assume that someone with the perfect background came along and that no matter what you could have done or said, that person was going to get the job. If the job that got away was the one you really wanted, it's okay to feel down—for an hour, or even half a day. Then let go of it and move on. Cry, get angry, be sad, then let go. There is something better out there for you.

DISTINGUISH YOURSELF FROM THE COMPETITION

Ultimately there are eleven key things you can do to get more job offers. All of the tips and all of the techniques covered on interviewing are incorporated in these eleven points. Tell yourself that you will do everything necessary to fulfill each of these points at every interview.

1. Demonstrate enthusiasm and potential.
2. Tell vivid stories.
3. Exude confidence.
4. Be prepared.
5. Sell yourself.
6. Come across as a real and genuine person.
7. Listen intently.
8. Show you can solve problems.
9. Be interesting.
10. Know things about the organization.
11. Know yourself.

Chapter 28

NEGOTIATING THE BEST SALARY

Like most of the things you've been learning in this book, negotiating a salary is not difficult, but it does require preparation and practice. By studying and applying appropriate salary-negotiation principles, you can significantly increase your starting salary. You owe it to yourself to get the best salary and benefits possible. Salary, respect, and authority are interwoven.

All jobs have formal or informal salary ranges. Your goal is to receive an offer and negotiate for the high end of the range. To do so you must know the salary range for your geographical area. Your primary information will come from people who are knowledgeable about the field and industry. To get top dollar you must also clearly be the top choice.

As a rule, if you have a solid background and are making a job change rather than a career change, go for a 15–20% increase in salary. You can do this based on the fact that the employer has decided to look outside rather than promote from within and expects to pay a premium for your experience, fresh ideas, and potential.

KNOW YOUR WORTH

The first principle for getting a top salary is to fully sell your worth to the organization. You do so by demonstrating your ability to make or save money for the organization, solve problems, or reduce the stress and pressure that your future boss has been experiencing. Although companies have formal or informal salary ranges, those ranges are often ignored when someone with unexpected experience or potential becomes available.

At the early stages of your job search, you should determine your overall value in the field you are pursuing. Numerous resources exist to help you. The *Occupational Outlook Handbook* contains salary ranges covering about 300 major occupations. The *American Almanac of Jobs & Salaries*, by John Wright, is updated every two or three years and provides excellent information on an even larger range of occupations. Keep in mind, however, that both of these references provide national figures; salaries in your geographical area may be considerably higher or lower.

Beyond these tools, the most useful resources for determining salaries are people, including professional association officials, headhunters, and people who currently do the type of work you're interested in. Associations exist for every career field imaginable. They sometimes produce salary surveys for the benefit of their members. Even those which don't can often give you good information about current salary ranges. To find an appropriate association, use *The Encyclopedia of Associations* and *National Trade & Professional Associations of the U.S.* These references are available at most libraries. For local associations ask people in your chosen field what associations they belong to.

Once you locate an association, attend meetings and talk to members. With national associations find out if salary surveys are available and also ask to speak to the person most knowledgeable about salaries.

Headhunters are another good source of salary information and wage scales because they are privy to what people are being offered. Many will take two or three minutes with you to give you some advice. If you choose to call some headhunters, briefly sell yourself and ask if they are interested in receiving your resume as well. Recruiting firms and employment agencies often conduct wage surveys that they make available to the public as part of their marketing. You can call and ask these firms if they have such surveys available.

Talking to people who do the type of work you want to do can also provide excellent insight into salary scales. You can usually get this information over the phone. Explain the purpose of your call, and ask if they have a couple minutes. Then tactfully ask about salary ranges.

You might say something like, "I'm not asking what you make, but if you could give me a good sense of how much someone here in the Cleveland area might make with four years' experience in shipping and receiving, that would really be helpful." Taking them off the hook by specifically not asking how much *they* make invariably yields better results.

For a salary search using the Internet, go to Yahoo (www. yahoo. com) and click on Business & Economy, then click on Salary Information to find appropriate sites for your type of salary search. Most career web sites now provide salary information.

Complete your salary research at the beginning of your job hunt so you know what your career field is paying *today*. Then you won't end up turning down what will later look like a very good offer. Many people have turned down offers, only to accept something for even less several months later. This happens most frequently during a recession when many job seekers do not realize that salaries have fallen. By the same token, salaries tend to rise during a boom time, so don't short change yourself if you're job hunting at a time when the economy is strong.

KNOW WHAT YOU NEED

Knowing your worth as well as your financial and psychological needs is crucial. If you are currently paid well but are miserable in your job, you would probably be willing to take a pay cut if you could get greater job satisfaction. The question becomes how much of a cut you could accept.

To determine your financial needs, establish three budgets. If you kept track of last year's expenditures it will be easy. In the left column you would list all of the categories of expenditures that you have. The next three columns would consist of: 1) last year's expenditures; 2) a level of spending that is less but still comfortable; and 3) a bare-bones budget that enables you to keep your car and home, but slashes other nonessential items. By doing this you are not saying you want to live on a bare-bones budget. This process will simply give you an idea of how low you could go salary-wise and still maintain a modicum of normalcy.

Next, examine and define what you need in a job regarding your psychological needs. The right job is one that enables you to utilize your top skills and strengths. It also allows you to be and express what you already are, without trying to squeeze you into some pre-existing mold. The right job should closely match your temperament, values, and motivators. You should also define the type of organization you want to work for. The organization you work for is tremendously important and can often make the difference between a good job and a great job. Take time to define what would make for you a nearly ideal job, and then determine the lowest salary you would accept if this dream job was offered to you. Assume you are currently working. How much less than you are now earning would you accept?

Create a checklist to help determine how close a particular job is to what you want. On the next page is Debbie Wilson's checklist. It provided her with a useful guide as she evaluated jobs she interviewed for. You can use Debbie's checklist as a guide for creating your own checklist. Each item is listed according to its importance, with the most important things first. Debbie was looking for accounting management positions. Adapt the items to suit your career focus.

The following items are ones you might want on your list when defining the type of organization you want to work for:

Good salary
Benefits
Act on employee suggestions
Flexible
Innovative
Potential for advancement
High ethics and integrity
Pleasant physical environment
My own office
Minimal office politics
Pleasant place to work
Casual dress
Tuition reimbursement
Good opportunities for training
Excellent reputation in the industry
Relocation unlikely
Low turnover
Profitable company
Rarely have layoffs
Promotes from within
Facing challenges I'd like to be involved in
Short commute
Hours are reasonable, small amount of overtime
Well-managed organization
Top management is stable
Organization is doing interesting, valuable work
Team emphasis but also work independently
Organization has strong sense of direction
Management is open with staff
Management encourages new ideas

The list is intended to help you get started. Borrow items, but also come up with points that are important to you.

PRIORITIES LIST	definitely meets my needs	somewhat meets my needs	does not meet my needs	unsure at this time
Potential for advancement				
Company is financially secure				
Encourages growth in employees and pays for professional development classes				
Teamwork, professional, friendly atmosphere				
Allowed to work independently				
My boss expresses appreciation				
Company has strong sense of direction, purpose, growth-oriented, seeks new opportunities				
Strong integrity and ethics				
Company is doing interesting, valuable work				
Promotes use of new computer systems				
Management is open with staff				
Do hands-on work; not just directing				
Short commute				
Work mainly on projects, with some routine tasks				
Projects that last several weeks and are challenging				
Non-smoking environment				
Use of both mainframes and PCs				
Have my own office				
Analysis of financial data, work with management on financial result and setting up action plans				
Developing and enhancing Lotus spreadsheets				
Establishing financial controls				
Implementing computer systems				
Pay is good				
Complete benefits				
Hours are reasonable, small amount of overtime				
Stable and respected management				
Accounting department is respected and valued				
Management encourages new ideas and frankness				
Procedures to eliminate inefficiencies				
Nice building and physical environment				
Size of company 50–500				
Casual yet professional dress policy				

Debbie found this checklist very helpful as she evaluated jobs.
The job she currently has gives her almost everything she was seeking.

DO NOT DISCUSS SALARY UNTIL THE JOB IS OFFERED

Discussing your salary requirements before an offer is made hurts your ability to negotiate. For that reason you should avoid asking about salary, and you should deflect probes into your current earnings or salary expectations.

If the job seems challenging, assume it will pay adequately. Even if it turns out that the job will not pay enough, going through the interviewing process will at worst cost you some time. The following four things can happen only if you thoroughly sell yourself throughout the interviewing process and then go for the job offer:

1. The job is excellent and it pays what you want.
2. You succeed in convincing the employer that they need a highly capable person such as yourself, causing them to change the job description and to bump the salary up a couple notches.
3. You're overqualified for this position, but an excellent job in the company opens up a few months later and you are hired.
4. The employer hears of a suitable position with another company and refers you there.

None of these positive things can happen if you prematurely terminate the interview process.

If the job seems challenging, it is best to attend the first interview, learn as much as you can, sell yourself to your fullest ability, and do everything you can to get a second interview. If you are not interested in the position, and you believe it will not pay enough, you can always tactfully decline the offer for a second interview. I would recommend sticking with the process, however, with the intent of getting an offer. Then see where it can go. Any one of the four things listed above might happen.

The problem with asking about pay is that the interviewer will often turn the question around and ask you how much *you* make or how much *you* need to make. When that happens, you're in trouble. Of the three things that can happen, only one is positive. If you provide your income or your expectations, it will either be too high, too low, or about right. If the figure you give is too high, it will generally be assumed you will not be interested in the company's salary range, so the offer won't be extended. If you are making considerably less than they are prepared to pay, the assumption will be that you're a lightweight. This, too, results in no offer. Or, you might get the offer but they may lowball you, knowing that what they're offering you is 15% below the bottom of their range, but 20% above what you were making before. They know you will be hard pressed to turn down their offer.

Deflecting Questions

No matter how you look at it, talking about money before the time is right confuses things. Frequently of course, it's the employer who brings up the issue, so you need to know how to deal with it. Even in the first interview, the employer may ask you "What are you looking for?" "How much do you need?" "What's the minimum amount you'd accept?" or "What range did you have in mind?" Assuming no offer has been made and that the employer has not told you the salary range, your response might be "Perhaps we should concentrate on determining if I'm the right person for the job." Another response might be, "I always make it a point not to discuss money until a job has been offered." If you're fairly far along in the interview process you might add, "Can I assume you're offering me the position?" Although the employer was not actually offering a position, more than one job seeker has heard, "Well, yeah, I guess I am."

Usually these mild deflections work, but some interviewers persist. If the question comes again, tactfully, but assertively state, "If you don't mind, I'd really like to concentrate on making sure I'm the one who can help you reach your goals. When we accomplish that, I'm sure the compensation will be fair." A statement like that will usually work. In using any of these responses it is important to be as diplomatic as possible.

People are often concerned that these mild deflections will get an employer angry. When handled tactfully, that rarely happens. If you detect that the employer *is* getting angry, you could ask what range has been set for the position. If the employer provides the range, then indicate whether your needs will fall within that range.

If the employer is unwilling to give you the range, and you really are interested in the position, you might use a wide range by stating, "Probably $28,000 to $35,000 depending on the level of responsibility and benefits." If you make over $50,000 you might use a $10,000 range.

When The Interviewer Supplies A Salary Range

If the interviewer gives you a salary range for the position and asks whether the amount would be acceptable, you owe it to the interviewer to say yes or no. Some managers want to know immediately whether your salary needs can be met and may pose this question to you during the first ten minutes of the first interview. Their rationale is that they don't want to waste their time or yours. If the range is acceptable you may want to say something as simple as "The range seems adequate." You would not want to sound elated or concerned.

PLAN YOUR STRATEGY

The goal of all good negotiations is to allow both sides to gain most of what they want—this is the well-known win-win concept. During the first interview and immediately after, you will begin determining what you need to feel like a winner in this situation. You will learn a lot about the job, your prospective boss, and the culture of the company. If the job, boss, and company seem relatively undesirable, you might be unwilling to accept it for anything less than 30% more than you currently earn. With a much more desirable job, you might accept only a 5% pay increase. Before deciding whether to accept an offer, many factors will be considered; money will be only one of them. Take notes immediately after the interview, jotting down what you learned, observed, and felt, as well as issues that were raised and questions you would like to have answered.

Between the time you are invited back for a second interview and the time you actually attend the interview, you will continue to research the company to determine how desirable it is. You should also formulate questions that will help you decide whether you would accept an offer. If you have detected some undesirable aspects of the job, determine whether they could be altered, and if so, how.

EVERYTHING IS NEGOTIABLE

Keep in mind a key concept in negotiating—everything is negotiable, not just money. There is no guarantee you will get everything you want, but everything is fair game for discussion. The worst thing that can happen is that the employer will say no. Raising an issue, even one that ultimately gets rejected, can cause the employer to give in on another issue that otherwise would also have been rejected.

At the end of the first interview, you should ask about the intended process, including how many interviews are anticipated, and how soon they expect to fill the position. That way you'll know when to expect an offer. You'll also know when you need to be fully prepared to negotiate.

DEFINE WHAT IT WILL TAKE TO ACCEPT THE OFFER

Clients frequently tell me that they are going to turn down an offer, often before the offer is actually made. They point out problems with the job and assume that there is no way to make it work. Perhaps a salary range has been discussed and it won't be enough. Or there are job duties that are undesirable, or there would be too much travel. There are a hundred possible reasons why the job is not right. Often, however, with some creative negotiating, the individual might be able to get all, or nearly all, of what he wants.

When clients tell me they are going to turn down an offer, I usually ask them to determine what it would take to get them to accept the offer. Often the first reply is that the organization would never acquiesce to their requests. Although the organization may not budge, you'll never know until you ask. So ask. After all, you were about to turn down the offer. Take the time to figure what it would require to get you to accept the offer. Then ask for it. Don't demand, don't threaten, just explain that while you like many aspects of the job, there are reasons that will cause you to decline the offer unless certain changes can be made. If the only issue is money, tell them what it would take. Give them a chance to match it. If you've been getting five weeks of vacation a year with your present employer and the new company's policy states that you would only get two weeks until you've been there five years, ask for five weeks. Maybe they can make an exception, or maybe they can't. If they can't, at least you gave it your best shot.

Sometimes the problem with the offer is more complex. Perhaps there are several duties that you would rather not have to perform, or there may be some responsibilities that you would like to add. Maybe there are several things that would have to be changed. That's okay. Identify everything that is keeping you from accepting the offer. Then ask yourself whether you must get everything on your list. If there is some room for compromise, there is a greater chance of closing the deal.

Tact is critical if you hope to get what you want. Any hint that you are demanding changes will almost surely kill the deal. Instead, in your most genuine and tactful voice, tell the hiring manager that you would really like to work for her, but that it just would not work with the current offer. State the problem areas and then ask, "What can we do?" Since the two of you would like to work together, make her your ally. That shouldn't be hard since she selected you from among several candidates. This ally is critical to you since this is the person who will either make the decisions on your behalf or will sell your requests to higher authorities.

Stay open minded. Perhaps there are a couple issues that for various reasons the company just can't compromise on. Yet, on a couple other issues, they may exceed your expectations. A job offer is a total package, and rarely should you let one aspect of the job be a deal breaker.

BENEFITS ARE IMPORTANT

You won't know if you want the offer until you know the full range of benefits and perks. A health plan that pays 100% of all bills and has no deductible can save you a $1,000 or more per year. A company car might be worth $4,000 per year. Since many companies do not offer dental or orthodontic insurance, having such a policy may be worth another $1,000 per year. Tuition reimbursement could also save you thousands if you intend to pursue a degree.

As you look at the financial value of a job offer, you must consider its total value. Take into account salary, stock options, bonuses, profit sharing, insurance, tuition reimbursement, and determine the total value for *you.* In other words, tuition reimbursement may be nice, but it's of little use to you if you have no interest in entering another classroom. Likewise, if your kids are grown and married, orthodontic insurance will have little value for you.

A fairly complete list of benefits and perks includes: vacation pay; bonuses; stock options; profit sharing; health, dental, orthodontic, vision, disability, and life insurance; company car or payment for mileage; tuition reimbursement; expense account; professional memberships; country club or health club memberships; relocation expense; free parking; deferred compensation; pension funds; severance pay; outplacement assistance; physical exams; use of corporate plane or vacation property; estate and financial planning; tax and legal assistance.

WHAT ARE THOSE INTANGIBLES WORTH?

There are many intangibles to consider. Perhaps the last company you worked for did nothing illegal, but was always on the edge of doing things that were unethical. As a result, you didn't feel good about yourself and you felt no sense of pride when you told people where you worked. What would it be worth to you to work for a company with a great reputation?

Perhaps your present company watches you like a hawk. What would it be worth to you to work for a company that only hires highly responsible people and then trusts them to do whatever is necessary to get a task done?

These same questions could be posed regarding any of the factors that affect people in a work environment. People like working in organizations where people cooperate, where there is minimal office politics, where people get ahead on merit, where top management listens and keeps everyone informed, where employees receive recognition for doing good work, and where employees are treated fairly and with respect.

While it's hard to put a dollar value on these factors, most people would trade some money to work in a more suitable, positive work environment. Some would trade a lot, others only a little. But clearly, these factors must be taken into consideration when you determine the minimum salary you would accept to work for an organization.

YOU'RE WORTH WHAT THEY'RE WILLING TO PAY

While negotiating, keep in mind that neither you nor your prospective boss knows your true worth. Your worth is whatever someone is willing to pay you. Your challenge is to make the employer want you badly enough so he or she will offer you what you want.

You May Be Worth More Than You Think

When all is said and done, the most important aspect of interviewing is to make the employer want to hire you. Once that happens, good things will follow. The following story demonstrates this idea.

A young woman was interviewing for a position which was really going to make her stretch. She had convinced the employer of her potential, and he really liked her spunk. He asked her how much she wanted, and she responded by saying, "I think twenty-four would be fair." What she was really saying was that she wanted $24,000. The employer paused for a moment and said, "Fine, let's start you at twenty-four hundred. When can you begin?" Do you see what just transpired? She asked for $24,000 but the employer thought she meant $2,400 per month, which is $28,800. It was more than he had intended to pay, but she had created value in his mind, so he was willing to pay it without negotiating. This also demonstrates that she was worth more than she thought. She broke some of the rules of negotiating, but she ended up with far more than she had ever hoped for. The key to her success was that throughout the interview, she sold herself.

People Want What They Want

The psychology of salary negotiations is important to understand. A key psychological factor is that people want what they want. Once people decide they want something, they are virtually always willing to spend more to get it than they originally intended. In 1990 a Van Gogh painting called *Portrait of Dr. Gachet* sold for a record $82.5 million. Art appraisers had assumed it would sell for about $60 million, based on the sale price of a similar Van Gogh the year before, which set a record of $53.9 million. When the bidding got started, it quickly exceeded the $60-million level. The painting was finally sold to a wealthy Japanese businessman. No doubt he had hoped to spend *only* $60 million, but he really wanted the painting. As the bidding kept rising, he undoubtedly said to himself, "I don't care how much it costs, I'm going to have that painting."

Most of us don't go around buying expensive art, but we go through exactly the same process when we shop for a new car. Almost everyone ends up spending more than was originally intended.

So, even if your prospective boss says he or she simply can't go over a certain amount, don't accept that too quickly. Managers have budgets, and if they are willing to cut the budget somewhere else, it may free up some money.

Determine The Causes Of Roadblocks

If you reach a roadblock in your salary negotiations, try to determine the true cause. You might ask the employer, "What do you think is the main issue? Is it a problem with your budget, or will the wage-and-salary-administration folks feel that the job's structure doesn't warrant a higher salary?" By asking a question you will at least get a response. This will also give you something different to discuss for the next few minutes. Once you have a response, even if it's not the full truth, you can begin dealing with that issue. Get the person to agree that your worth is greater, and then help her come up with a creative way to find the money. If the human resources department is the problem, then suggest rewriting the job description to give you more responsibility. This would place you in a higher pay bracket. By helping to clarify the issue, you are also helping the manager decide how badly she wants you. She is psychologically committed and does not want to lose you. Furthermore, she's come this far in the process with you, and she does not want to lose you over a measly $2,000 or some other fairly minor sticking point.

To negotiate in the way I've just described requires confidence that you have something unique or valuable to offer. If you have identified your strengths, and if you are interviewing for a job that will fully utilize those strengths, you will have some unique attributes to offer. If, on the other hand, the employer was ready to flip a coin as to whether to give the job to you or candidate B, you are not in as strong a bargaining position. The employer may have reason to believe that candidate B would accept a lower figure than you. Although the employer wants to hire you, she may be unwilling to go to any great lengths to do so. During the interviewing, and then later during the negotiating, you must assess how much this person really wants you. At a certain point the person will say in essence, "That's as high as I can go, take it or leave it." When that point is reached the decision will be up to you.

The Value Of A Job Is Set By The Responsibility Level

Sometimes a job only has a certain value. While you might be capable of handling more responsibility than the job needs, the worth of the job is based upon the level of responsibility required. You may get the offer, but you will not be able to negotiate for top dollar unless you can get the employer to expand the duties and responsibilities.

You'll Gain Respect By Negotiating

Some people are afraid that by negotiating for salary they may offend the employer. If you negotiate fairly and reasonably, employers will actually respect you more. Almost all initial offers are less than what the employer is prepared to pay you. If you accept the initial offer, it may actually cause the employer to wonder why you were obtained so cheaply. Employers expect to negotiate, so accommodate them. For some it's even a game that they enjoy. Let them have some fun.

Ask For A Shorter Review Time

If you reach an impasse, asking for a shorter review time may break it. Typically, reviews come six months after joining the firm, and then annually thereafter. If you have the confidence that you can become a strong producer in three months, ask for a review at that point. If you are able to negotiate a sizable raise at that time, it will almost be as if you had started at that level.

When The Offer Is Just Right

If the initial amount offered you is perfectly acceptable, you have a quick decision to make. You could cordially accept the offer and thank the person for making a fair offer. That will make your boss feel good. Or, you could counter with an amount just 5% above the initial offer to see if there is room to negotiate.

Saving Face When You Have To Back Down

Sometimes an offer is made and the employer refuses to budge on the amount, or comes up only a token amount. During the negotiation you were fairly adamant that you wanted a significantly higher starting salary. You realize that you still want the job despite the large gap between offered and desired pay, but it seems awkward accepting what has been offered. Here's a solution: "Mr. Chang, I've always felt that the quality of the job is more important than the pay. This job is very attractive to me. In my mind there's no question that the job is worth $48,000 and I'm worth at least that amount. Let's go ahead and start at your $42,000 figure. It's my intention to quickly prove to you my worth. At my review, if I've demonstrated real value, I'll expect to be paid what I'm worth." At this point all Mr. Chang has to do is affirm that you will be paid based on your actual contribution. You're basically putting Chang on notice that he risks losing you if you are not compensated properly. You haven't actually said it, and you are not threatening Chang, but he's on notice, nonetheless.

You Need To Practice Negotiating

When it comes to negotiating, there is no substitute for actually practicing what you intend to say. In our society we are not used to haggling. The only haggling over price we do is when buying a car or attending a garage sale. For most of us, neither is an everyday occurrence. That's why practice is necessary just to become comfortable with the process of negotiating. Also, practice saying the amount you want. Let's say you want $44,000, although the most you've ever made is $38,000. If the first offer you get from an employer is $39,000, you'll need to counter with $49,000 just to have a chance to get your $44,000. If you haven't practiced saying that you want $49,000, that number will stick in your throat and you won't get it out.

Get The Employer To Redefine The Position

Because no one knows your strengths as well as you do, it's your responsibility to thoroughly present your capabilities and demonstrate the full range of your strengths. If your background exceeds the scope and salary of the position you're applying for, a smart manager may change the scope of the job without any prompting from you. Others will not be so perceptive, so the responsibility falls upon you to explain how the organization can maximize their investment in you by redefining the position. If you can show how they can get a higher return on their investment, you may be able to extract part of that return in the form of more salary.

BREAKING THROUGH AN IMPASSE

If it's important to you that you truly get what you're worth, you must be prepared to walk away from the bargaining table. You should be clear on the minimum you would accept. If, despite your best efforts, you can't get close to an acceptable salary, you'll be forced to restate your minimum requirements. If your prospective employer indicates those needs cannot be met, you'll shake hands and both express regret that it did not work out.

While you should be clear regarding the minimum you would accept, you must remember that you are not just talking dollars; there are also the benefits and the intangibles to consider. Only you can decide whether the combination meets your minimum needs. As both sides sense an approaching impasse, both parties will begin considering how they will feel if the deal does not go through. Reaching that stage often helps both sides get creative again to come up with a solution. You'll be saying to yourself, "I really do want to work for this person, and I think this company is going places. I don't want to miss out on this opportunity." The employer will be saying, "This is the person who can help me get my promotion. With her drive and past successes, I know she'll be effective. I've got to find a way to bring her on board."

As you sense an impasse approaching, you may choose to adjourn. It may work like this: "Mrs. Barkley, maybe the best thing to do is get back together tomorrow. I would really like working for you and I'm still excited about the opportunities here. From my standpoint, it would really help if you could add $2,000 to the starting pay." Barkley would probably then restate her position. Neither side is promising to budge, but sometimes a good night's sleep can put a new perspective on things.

NEGOTIATING THE SALARY

Salary negotiating is an art. Knowing how to respond and knowing when to be silent can make a difference in your paycheck.

When Silence is Golden

An effective negotiating technique is to respond to an offer by repeating the amount, or by repeating the high end of the range and then remaining silent, looking away as if you are pondering the offer. It is important to repeat the amount so that the employer will know that you fully heard and understood the offer. Since people hate silence, a common response is, "Well, I suppose for someone with your background we could start you at $X." You've already gotten a raise using very few words, and a strategic application of silence.

Let The Employer Know You Want The Job

Whether or not you managed to obtain a raise through your silence, you must now let the employer know that you really do want the job, but that the initial offer is not adequate. You will help prepare the employer to accept your request by expressing your desire for the job. It might be something like, "I appreciate the offer Mr. Gonzalez. I really believe the position will make excellent use of my strengths. But based on my research of what people with my background are receiving, I had really expected something close to $X."

Responding When The Employer Makes A Specific Offer

All of the discussion so far leads up to the point when an offer is actually made. Knowing what to say and how to respond is important to your success.

Note: As you read this next section, you will notice that in some of the conversations the dollar sign is missing. That's because in real conversations people often say, "I was thinking of thirty-seven thousand," rather than "I was thinking of thirty-seven thousand dollars."

Most employers know it is their responsibility to make an offer, so it may begin like this: "John, we'd like to start you out at $40,000 and then review your salary in six months." John must quickly decide whether he will negotiate, since he was expecting at least $42,000 and he wants $46,000. He is currently earning $39,000 and feels he is underpaid. In a case like this he might say: "Mr. Russell, I'm glad I turned out to be your top choice. Although money is not the only factor, it is important. In fact, it's the major reason I've chosen to leave my job. When I began this process, I made a decision to take a job at 20% above what I'm now earning. I really don't see a reason to change that decision. If there is any way you can adjust your budget, it would sure help. I never intended to accept anything below 46,000."

Although there is nothing that guarantees that John's worth to his new prospective company is 20% above what he is currently making, it is not unfair for John to want to make more. If he really wants 20% more, he will simply turn down all offers which are below what he wants. He can afford to wait since he currently has a job.

John could also use what I call the straight-forward approach when responding. It would go like this: "Mr. Russell, based on my potential I really feel I'm worth $48,000, but if you would make it $47,000, the decision would sure be a lot easier."

The creative approach should sometimes be tried. Remember, the offer was for $40,000. "Mr. Russell, based on the duties you've described, I agree that the job is probably worth no more than $42,000. I'm sure you would agree with me, however, that I'm capable of handling much more. And when I began this job search, I never intended to accept anything below $46,000. But perhaps if the responsibilities were increased you could justify $46,000." Notice what has been done. The offer was for $40,000, and the interviewee is basically agreeing, but then suggests that the job is worth $42,000. Even while agreeing, the interviewee adds a little to the salary, then asks if the responsibilities could be increased.

Another strategy is to use another job offer as leverage whenever possible. You may have received an offer where the salary is satisfactory, but the job is not what you really want. Then you may get another offer where the job is perfect, but the salary is low. You might want to say, "Mr. Stuyvesant, the job itself is perfect, and of course I would really enjoy working with you. The salary is below what I expected, and I already have an offer at 4,000 a year more than your offer. If you could adjust your budget, it would make my decision a lot easier."

Responding To "How Much Do You Want/How Much Are You Worth?"

When making an offer, most employers will specify a certain beginning salary. Some, however, will not, and they may ask, "How much do you want?" or "How much do you think you're worth?" If you get this type of offer, you will have to depend on what your research revealed. Your research should provide you with a good idea of what the typical range is for the position you want. If you believe the range is $52–57,000, you might say, "The starting salary is important to me, but not nearly as important as a job that fits me and allows me to make the kind of contribution I know I can make. I believe in three years I should be making at least $64,000." This is a good response. You are giving the impression of being very realistic and flexible. Actually, you have just put the interviewer in a corner. The interviewer may know that the best he or she can hope to do is get you an 8% increase each year. Therefore, to reach your $64,000 goal in three years the starting salary must be the $56,000 you actually wanted. Surprisingly, it is often easier for a supervisor to start you off high at the beginning than to obtain raises commensurate with your contributions later on.

If you believe the range is $52–57,000, you could present a range by saying, "Based on my experience and potential, an acceptable starting salary would be between 54 and 60,000, depending on my full range of responsibilities and other aspects of the benefits package." This is effective because it cannot be interpreted as saying you would accept an offer as low as $54,000. The idea is to state a range with the high end of your range slightly higher than what you assume their high end is, and your low range slightly higher than what you assume their low end to be. Or you might state a single figure about 5% above what you believe the top of their range is. If you think the top of the range is $57,000, you would look the employer in the eye and say, "I was thinking about 59,000." The employer will probably reject that amount. Don't let it bother you. Simply ask, "What's the *best* you can offer?" Because of your confidence and the potential you have demonstrated, the next figure will probably be very close to the top of their range.

Of course, the employer could respond, "We were thinking closer to 50." Perhaps you misjudged the range. For this company $50-52,000 may be the top of their range. Or you may not have completely sold the employer on your potential. Your response might be, "I feel I'm worth more than that. However, working for the right organization is really more important than the starting salary. I'd say 57,000 would be fair. The employer may still not go for it, or may come up to $52,000. If the employer counters with $52,000, you would counter with $55,000 and probably end up at $54,000. Not all negotiations, of course, end up with each counterproposal neatly meeting in the middle.

Wrapping It Up

How tough you negotiate depends on how strongly you feel about your worth. Once you have negotiated for the best salary possible, other factors must still be considered, particularly if the salary offer is below what you expected. If, for example, the employer offers a six-month salary review, ask for a three-month review. Other factors you will continue to negotiate at this point include: cost-of-living increases, moving expenses, tuition reimbursement, flex-time, an extra week of vacation, or anything else that is important to you.

In any negotiations, a final point is eventually reached. You know you've reached the end of negotiations when the two sides are close, yet neither side will go any further. At this point someone has to make the final compromise and say, "Let's call it a deal."

Salary negotiations are usually not long and drawn out. For entry-level to middle management positions the whole process may take less than two minutes.

Observe the following, typical negotiation:

Employer:	Bob, I'd like to have you join us. I'll start you out at $34,000 and then review your performance in six months.
Bob:	I appreciate the offer. As I'm sure you could tell, I'm really quite excited about the position. I'll be honest though; I had thought the job would be worth considerably more. I had figured on something closer to $42,000.
Employer:	(Pause) Bob, I know I'm not going to be able to match your figure, but I'll tell you what, let's start you at $36,000.
Bob:	That certainly helps. I really do want to accept the position and money is not the only issue. I feel that there are going to be excellent opportunities with this company. I still feel the job is worth 42, and I know I'm worth that much, but I would definitely consider 41.
Employer:	Bob, I'm sure you realize that any firm like ours has to place minimums and maximums on salaries at various levels to keep everything in the company balanced. I suppose I could offer you 38, but that's as high as I can go.
Bob:	Make it 39 and you've got yourself an employee.
Employer:	All right, you've got a deal at $38,500. Agreed?
Bob:	Agreed. Thirty-eight -five and a review in three months.
Employer:	Do you really think you can prove yourself in three months?
Bob:	I think so.
Employer:	Okay, thirty-eight-five and a review in three months. But I'm not promising a pay increase, you've got to earn it.
Bob:	I understand. I think you'll be pleased with my results.

At the executive level, however, negotiations may take a half hour or several days, as both sides propose and counterpropose. If one of the negotiation issues must be decided by someone else in the organization, it may take several days to conclude the negotiations.

The ability to negotiate for a higher salary is one of the most valuable skills you can develop. Once you understand the principles, the practice is up to you.

NOW YOU CAN DECIDE IF YOU WANT THE JOB

Once salary and benefits have been negotiated, you are almost ready to decide whether you will accept the position. You need time to consider the decision. Your emotions are strong at the moment, so you need an opportunity to step back and be objective. Just as the employer did not make the hiring decision after the first interview, you need time to consider everything. Employers realize that it is never an easy decision to accept a new position or to leave a current position. The employer had time to consider several people and to check references prior to making you the offer. The employer had a chance to sleep on it and make the decision with a proper frame of mind. You need the same opportunity.

Ask for time by saying something like, "I think the salary is going to be adequate and I think we're going to work very well together. How soon do you need a definite decision?" They should give you at least three days. If you have another offer pending, you might respond with, "Today is Thursday. How about if I confirm everything by next Wednesday?" If you're going to need more than a week you should be prepared to explain some of the reasons. If you have another job offer pending, but won't know anything definite for two weeks, you'll probably need to explain the situation. You might explain that if that job comes through, you feel you owe it to yourself to be able to weigh all factors. If you've established solid rapport with your prospective boss, the person won't like waiting for two weeks, but will understand. If the employer cannot wait that long, you may be forced to make a decision sooner than you would have liked. When you ask for the time to make the decision, do not say "I'll have to discuss it with my wife (husband)."

RESEARCH AFTER AN OFFER IS MADE

Once you've gotten the job offer, negotiated salary and benefits, and reached an agreement, you still need answers to your remaining questions. Some of the questions you did ask may not have been adequately answered, and there were other questions you did not ask at all because they seemed too sensitive. Now is the time to ask those questions. To the interviewer you might say: "Mrs. Torgeson, I'm glad you had the confidence in me to offer me the position. The salary is about right and I'm really looking forward to working with you. I do have just a few questions that I would like clarified so that I can make the right decision." Then proceed to ask every question you have, even those sensitive ones you did not ask earlier. As long as it is asked tactfully, almost any question regarding you, the job, or the organization is reasonable.

Having asked for time to decide, you now have two important tasks to complete: 1) Make a final, all-out effort to discover more about the company from inside sources; and 2) Contact those other organizations which have expressed interest in you.

Complete Your Employer Research

During the next several days learn everything you can even though you've basically decided to take the job. Perhaps you would turn it down only if another company made a better offer or if additional research uncovers serious problems concerning the organization. Many people regret their failure to do this final bit of research—I wouldn't want you to be one of them.

Throughout your research you learned a lot. During the interviews you learned a great deal more. After the offer was made you asked even more questions, including the sensitive ones you had postponed. The answers to those last questions probably cleared away all of your doubts. You may have been tempted to accept the job on the spot. Fortunately you didn't. On your way home from this interview, begin asking yourself if there are still any matters that need more clarification. Determine what sources might answer your questions. If you haven't talked to any competitors yet, this would be a good time. It's also the time to talk to employees and ex-employees of your prospective employer. Ask your contacts if they know anyone who works for or has worked for your target organization.

Things are not always as they appear. The boss who seems so understanding and likable in the interview may be completely different on the job. The company that seems so peaceful may be experiencing political infighting. Or the company that seems so stable may be ready for bankruptcy. Organizations often hide serious problems. It's now your responsibility to discover what those problems are.

Maintain a healthy skepticism. Talk the job over with your mate, a friend, or a career counselor—anyone who will be more objective about it than you are. It's amazing what a second party can see that you may be blind to.

Suppose the offer was made on Thursday and you agreed to give your final answer by Monday afternoon. Through several insiders you picked up some information plus a few rumors that need to be clarified. On Monday morning you might call your boss-to-be and ask for an appointment that afternoon: "Mr. Bradley, this is Paul Johnson. I've been doing a lot of thinking and I have essentially decided to accept the position. I still have a couple questions to ask you though, and it might be good just to meet with you for a few minutes this afternoon."

With most questions you will simply ask the question and then evaluate the response. If the answer is not complete enough, you may have to ask a follow-up question. When asking about any rumors, be tactful.

Get Additional Offers

After a job is offered, your second task is to contact those organizations that have interviewed you for definite openings. Your call might go like this:

> Ms. Esparza, this is Sandy Hogan. We talked last week about your scheduling coordinator position. You indicated it could be two weeks before I would be asked back for a second interview, but I thought I'd better call to explain my situation. I've just been offered a really good scheduling position with another company. But, based on our conversation, I would really rather work for you. What do you suggest I do?

If you are not being considered for the job, the employer will suggest you take the position already offered. If the employer is really interested, another interview may be quickly arranged. Do your best to get one or two additional offers. It may not work, but it is definitely worth the effort. It is extremely helpful to have two or more job offers to consider at one time.

If the job that hasn't been offered to you is really the one you want, this effort may cause the employer to speed up the decision-making process. What might have taken another week or two, may be reduced to two or three days if you really were the number one choice.

Chapter 29

RESEARCH THE ORGANIZATION

Researching an organization can yield big dividends during an interview. Research can reveal problems or challenges the organization is facing, and can enable you to select in advance appropriate experiences you should describe in the interview. At the minimum you should know what the organization's products and services are, how long it has been in business, and something about its growth and reputation. If you're working with recruiters or agency counselors, they should be able to supply you with valuable information. Even with that help, however, you should gather information on your own as well. Researching the organization will help you determine whether it is right for you. It will also enable you to answer questions more effectively. Employers commonly ask, "What do you know about us?" Harold, a graduating senior, once suffered through this question. In the very first question, a campus recruiter asked Harold, "What do you know about us?" Harold paused and squirmed. When the recruiter finally asked, "Did you read our recruiting literature?" Harold had to admit he had not, and the recruiter then coldly stated, "This interview is over." Although this was an extremely embarrassing experience, the recruiter actually did Harold a big favor—he never made that mistake again.

Sometimes it is even possible to learn about the interviewer. Check with your contacts to determine whether they or anyone they know is acquainted with the interviewer. Try to learn about the interviewer's education, biases, hot buttons, and general background. Then weave the information you gather into the interview. Do this carefully so you don't give the impression you are merely trying to make a good impression.

Julie learned from inside sources that her prospective boss was a sailing nut, but she didn't quite know how to weave her knowledge into the interview.

Knowledge is power. Knowledge also helps win job offers. In preparing for interviews, the two most important areas of knowledge are knowledge of the industries you are considering and knowledge of the organizations you will be interviewing with.

RESEARCH THE INDUSTRY

Begin by researching the industries you are interested in. Employers will often ask what you know about their industry or may ask why you want to enter that industry. Knowledge of the industry will help you answer the questions. It is also important to learn the vocabulary of the industry. Being able to understand and use appropriate terminology in essence makes you a member of that fraternity, even if you have never worked in it before.

Several sources provide valuable industry information. Begin with the *U.S. Industrial Outlook*, published by the U.S. Department of Commerce. It covers 350 manufacturing and service industries. It utilizes many types of information to describe the factors which will affect a particular industry in the next few years. From it, you can determine whether an industry is likely to grow or constrict.

Standard and Poor's Industry Surveys can also be helpful. Each survey contains an analysis of economic conditions, with growth projections.

Check the *Readers Guide To Periodical Literature, Business Periodicals Index, F & S Index,* or *Infotrac* to find magazine articles about an industry. A librarian can show you how to use each of these resources.

Articles about an industry can be especially useful. For example, the subject of multimedia is much in the news. A review of articles on the subject will give you a sense of the history of the field and the technology which is being developed. A well-placed comment or question about a development in the industry can quickly demonstrate both your knowledge of and interest in the field. Such articles will also describe key people in the industry and companies involved.

Several resources exist to help you locate appropriate trade journals and other useful periodicals. Each of the resources identifies thousands of magazines, newsletters, newspapers, and journals, or other periodicals you should read to better understand your industry. The guides list periodicals by subject. *Ulrich's International Periodicals Directory,* for example, lists 108,000 periodicals in 554 subject areas. Other resources frequently found in libraries include *Gale Directory of Publications, Standard Periodical Directory, Newsletters in Print,* and *Oxbridge Directory of Newsletters.*

Joining trade associations can also expand your industry knowledge. Determine whether there is an association that represents your industry. The *Encyclopedia of Associations* and *National Trade and Professional Associations* can provide this information. You'll also find local associations listed in the Yellow Pages under "Associations." Associations are usually formed to give an industry or profession more political clout, as well as to provide a forum for new ideas. They generally publish membership lists and newsletters, hold conventions and meetings, list job openings, and distribute free literature. Members of associations are usually quite helpful. With some trade associations you can attend meetings without becoming a member. Get to know people in the association, then determine if it will be helpful to you.

After researching appropriate industries your next step is to research specific employers.

RESEARCH THE ORGANIZATION

Knowledge of the employer is highly esteemed by interviewers, yet employer research is one of the most neglected aspects of a job search.

Reasons For Researching An Organization

There are four main reasons for researching employers:

1. **To determine whether the organization is right for you.** Try to discover all the pros and cons you can. Research may reveal a serious problem that might cause you to eliminate the organization, or it may reveal some outstanding opportunities that will further encourage and motivate you.

2. **To impress the interviewer.** You'll impress the interviewer by explaining in concise terms why you should be hired and by demonstrating that you are full of enthusiasm, experience, and potential. Because so few people bother to research a company, you'll stand out in a very positive way if you've done your homework and go armed with information. Weave your information into the conversation appropriately. Some employers will ask, "What do you know about us?" Most people will hem, haw, and fail this question miserably, but you will shine. Even when asked this question, however, don't overwhelm the interviewer with information or statistics. Give a thorough but concise response.

3. **To discover problems you can help solve.** Problems you have the ability to solve could come to light before or during an interview. If you discover them before the interview, you'll have time to prepare and perhaps even develop a proposal describing how your abilities and experience would uniquely serve their needs. Otherwise, listen for clues to such problems during the interview. An employer may come right out and describe problems, but will probably only allude to them. Careful listening can help you match your abilities or experience to the problem area. By all means emphasize those strengths that can help solve the organization's problems.

4. **To identify questions that must be clarified by the employer.** An annual report or a magazine article may have mentioned an exciting new product being developed by your target company. If the interviewer doesn't mention it, you may have to ask if you would have a role in developing, marketing, or selling it. If an inside source told you that a strike could cripple the company, you might ask about the effects of such a strike. If the company has lost money three years in a row, you might ask what the company is doing to reverse the losses.

RESOURCES FOR EMPLOYER RESEARCH

You will find many useful resources listed here to help you gather detailed information about your target organizations.

Researching Your Potential Employers

To research local companies, your first step is to visit the nearest major library. Many libraries will have such resources as clipping files, house organs, and annual reports. Others will have computers and their reference librarians will even show you how to access the Internet.

Standard Industrial Classification (SIC)

Many resources list organizations by their Standard Industrial Classification (SIC) code. The federal government has assigned codes to several hundred industries and the system is now used almost universally. Every business has one or more SIC codes. I'll discuss particular resources later, but for now remember that resources which arrange organizations by SIC will have a guide to help you identify the industries you are most interested in. Most libraries have the *Standard Industrial Classification Manual,* which provides a wealth of information concerning the SIC codes assigned to thousands of products and services.

Local Resources

People with no desire to leave their current geographical area will get better results with local, rather than national, resources. It would be impossible, of course, to list all local resources, but I can help you find them. The best place to start is in the business reference section of your library.

After you've scouted out the reference area, talk to the reference librarian and ask about resources. You'll find reference librarians very helpful. Some libraries will have a list of useful resources and directories.

Clipping files. Clipping files contain newspaper articles about local companies. Each company has a separate file. If you can't find a file for the company you're researching, it may be that the organization is so small that nothing has been written about it. Gathering information about organizations with ten or fewer employees can be difficult.

House organs. House organs, also known as in-house newsletters, can be particularly helpful. Published primarily for the benefit of employees, many companies also send these publications to customers, suppliers, and libraries for public relations purposes. Most contain a letter from the company president describing results from the recent past or plans for the future. Some provide clues about possible openings by including pictures of employees retiring or being promoted. Feature articles about special employees are also common.

On-line Services. Some newspapers allow you to access articles by way of a computer and modem. You find articles of interest by selecting key words by subject, name of an industry, or name of a company of interest. Articles that have these key words will appear on the screen. Those articles with desirable information can then be printed at the press of a key. Libraries often have the necessary computers and hookups to enable you to access the database of the local newspaper.

National Resources

Some of the national resources listed below cost over one hundred dollars per year and are found only in libraries with a major business section. Go to your nearest library first to find out what local and national directories they have. Eventually you may need to visit a larger library.

National resources are useful primarily for those who want to work for companies over 500 employees and are willing to relocate to do so. If you want to remain in your metropolitan area, or at least in your state, your local directories will almost always be more helpful than the national directories.

Annual reports. Publicly held companies are required by law to publish annual reports that contain detailed financial information. While very few people actually know how to make sense of the financial material contained in an annual report, there are other things to glean from an annual report. Invariably there is a letter from the president or chairman of the board summarizing the past year and making predictions for the next. Other sections describe subsidiaries, recent acquisitions, new products, and challenges faced.

Recruiting brochures. The placement offices of two and four year colleges will have many recruiting brochures. They usually describe the history and background of the company, the training you might receive, company benefits, and the desired backgrounds of employees.

The Career Guide — Dun's Employment Opportunities Directory. The guide describes several hundred companies which recruit on college campuses. It is primarily designed for recent college grads, but it can used by anyone. It describes the company, the college majors it recruits for, its training program, internships offered, and locations of facilities apart from the headquarters.

The College Placement Annual. The Annual contains national companies and lists the college degrees they desire most. Basic information about the company is provided. One section lists college majors and the companies which are seeking those majors.

America's Corporate Families. The listing describes 9,000 U.S. parent companies and 45,000 subsidiaries. Volume 2 lists U.S. subsidiaries and their foreign parents.

Directory of Corporate Affiliations. This directory lists 4,000 parent companies with addresses and phone numbers. Section 1 gives sales, number of employees, type of business, top officers, divisions, subsidiaries, and affiliates. Section 2 lists 45,000 divisions, subdivisions, and affiliates alphabetically and gives the parent company. This resource also has a geographical index.

Directory of American Firms Operating in Foreign Countries. Section 1 lists firms alphabetically and the countries each one operates in. Section 2 lists countries and tells which American firms operate in each.

Directory of Foreign Firms Operating in the U.S. This directory lists foreign firms operating in the United States and describes their products.

Moody's. Moody's Industrial Manual—Provides financial information, history, subsidiaries, products and services, sales, principal plants and properties, executives, number of employees. One to two pages are devoted to most companies. All of the Moody's Manuals concentrate on large companies.

Moody's OTC (Over the Counter)—Same format as above but covering smaller companies.

Moody's Municipal and Government Manual.
Moody's Bank and Finance Manual.
Moody's Public Utilities Manual.
Moody's Transportation Manual.

Indexes

You will want to use one or more indexes to locate articles in magazines or newspapers. First look up the company by name. If you don't find the listings you want, you could read articles about the industry that your target company falls in and possibly find a reference to your target company in that way. The indexes can also be used to research a topic, a product, a new technology, or an entire industry.

Encyclopedia of Business Information Sources. Lists trade associations, periodicals, directories, bibliographies, and an abstract index of recent articles. An outstanding resource.

Readers Guide to Periodical Literature. Lists articles found in over two hundred popular magazines, giving the periodical, date and title of article. This is the same green-covered resource you used in high school when you did research reports.

Business Periodicals Index. The *BPI* uses business periodicals which are generally not covered in the *Readers Guide to Periodical Literature.* Examples: *Human Resource Management* and *Automotive News.*

The Magazine Index. An automated system found in many libraries which indexes articles in about 400 general interest magazines. It is published by Information Access Company which in a similar format, also publishes *National Newspaper Index, Business Index,* and *Legal Resource Index.*

Infotrac. A computerized data base found in many libraries, it indexes 1,100 magazines, going back ten years. With the help of a librarian it takes under five minutes to learn how to use. Some libraries just have the magazine index, while others will also have the newspaper and business indexes as well. The business index indexes articles found in magazines which are not included in the magazine index. With it you can research industries, products, new technology, and companies. The business index provides information about the companies themselves, including address, products, number of employees, etc., and articles written about them. With each article you will get an abstract, which is a short version of the article, or the entire text of the article. Both the abstract or the entire text can then be printed out.

ABI Inform. Same concept as *Infotrac,* it abstracts 700 business journals.

F & S Index of Corporations and Industries. Lists articles on industries and companies, including mergers, acquisitions, new products, and emerging technology. Lists trade journals, addresses and their costs.

F & S Index Europe. Same format.

F & S Index International. Same format. Covers Canada, Latin America, Africa, and Asia.

Wall Street Journal Index. The first section is alphabetical by company; the second section is alphabetical by subject and peoples' names.

New York Times Index. Same format.
Chicago Tribune Index. Same format.
Los Angeles Times Index. Same format.
Washington Post Index. Same format.

Libraries which carry these indexes will probably also have the newspapers on microfilm.

Your Interviewer. Search the clipping file and house organs for articles about your interviewer. Before you go to a specific *Who's Who,* look up the name of your person in *Index to Who's Who Books,* which indexes 15 *Who's Who.* The information tends to be strictly biographical with date of birth, address, school graduated from, and offices held. Most of the information is supplied by the individuals themselves. The primary *Who's Who* include:

Who's Who In America.
Who's Who In The West.
Who's Who In The East.
Who's Who In Finance and Industry.
Who's Who Of American Women.

You will also find other specialized *Who's Who In . . .,* covering various subjects, such as human resources—*Who's Who In HR.*

Other resources that include biographical information include: *Dun & Bradstreet Reference Book of Corporate Managements*—Lists companies alphabetically, then lists executive with name, title, year born, summary of career, education. Also *Standard and Poor's*—Vol. 2, Register of Directors and Executives. Same information as Dun's, but executives are listed alphabetically by last name.

The Internet. Visit our web site at www.cmr-mvp.com to get links to key sites to help you research salaries, industries, and companies.

Gathering Information From People

As valuable as written resources are, information gathered from people is often the most helpful. Talk with people who work for or have worked for your target company, people with competitors or suppliers, and people who work for a customer of the target company. All of these people can add to your insights and information about a company.

You may be saying to yourself, "But I don't know anyone who works for my target companies." While this may be true, I can guarantee that someone among your friends and contacts does know someone who works for your target companies. If you want to *badly enough*, you can get direct information about almost any local organization.

Employees And Former Employees

Once you have your list of target organizations, call your contacts and ask them who they know in those organizations. If they don't know anyone, ask them to ask around for you. It's okay to ask for favors. After all, you'd do the same for them. Once you get a name, call the person to learn as much as you can about the organization. Be sure to mention the name of the person who referred you or your new contact may be rather cool and reserved. Also try to establish rapport before asking probing questions. For instance, you might start by asking the person his or her overall view of the company.

Competitors

Competitors are valuable sources of information, but they may have some obvious biases. When talking to competitors, talk to sales and management people. Employees at lower levels seldom keep up on competitors. For example, the purchasing manager of a competitor probably belongs to the same association as the purchasing manager in your target company; they may even know each other. Sales people are helpful because it's their business to know about competitors. As you're picking up information, determine whether the person is sincere. If the person shares both positives and negatives about your target organization, instead of just negatives, the information will probably prove useful.

Suppliers/Customers

Suppliers and customers may be harder to locate than competitors, but a few well-placed phone calls can reveal them. Most of your target organizations probably fall in a few industries. Call several companies that would be likely to purchase the products or services of your target organizations and ask if they buy from any of them. It's very possible that they buy from several of your target firms since an organization rarely buys everything from just one source. Each of these companies will give you a slightly different view of your target organizations. Invariably, two or three organizations will be consistently mentioned as having excellent products and providing outstanding service.

Inside Information

Insiders can give you a great deal of information that you won't find in any written resources. Be aware, however, that every insider, whether employee, former employee, competitor, customer, or supplier, is likely to have some biases about the organization. Be alert to such biases. Everything you hear represents only one viewpoint and needs to be treated as such. This is true of virtually any organization: some will love it, some will hate it. You'll need to determine whether the person you're talking with has an ax to grind (he may recently have lost out on a promotion), knows enough about the organization (she may really know only about her own department), or is even telling the truth. This is the fun part. You're a detective, evaluating motives and confirming stories.

Interviews are a very important part of employer research. During most interviews you'll learn a lot about the company and the department you would be working in. Make full use of the opportunity to ask questions. Ask about your growth potential, your duties, the interviewer's management style, and the future directions of the company.

Interviewing is a continuation of your research. Keep your detective cap on and discover all you can. Ask yourself if you would enjoy working for this person. Will you respect this boss? Do your management philosophies match? Will you like each other? These are some of the important questions that can be answered, in part, by the research you conduct during interviews.

Do some research before each interview, even if it's the third or fourth interview with the same company. This is particularly important if you feel really good about the job, your potential boss, and the company. Discover all you can. Answering questions effectively and asking the right questions could make the difference between being the number-one choice and the number-two choice.

Luck—the crossroads where preparation and opportunity meet.

Personality, Enthusiasm, And Attitude Make A Big Difference

• • •

Nothing great was ever achieved without enthusiasm.
Ralph Waldo Emerson

It may be that knowledge is power, but pulling
the switch is enthusiasm.
Anonymous

To really be able to persuade someone,
keep in mind that enthusiasm is
more effective than facts.
Anonymous

It's your attitude and not your aptitude
that determines your altitude.
Anonymous

Of all the things you wear,
your expression is the most important.
Janet Lane

Desire is the great equalizer.
Anonymous

There is little difference in people,
but that little difference makes a big difference.
The little difference is attitude. The big difference is
whether it is positive or negative.
Clement Stone

Chapter 30

WHAT YOU SHOULD KNOW ABOUT AN ORGANIZATION

Choosing the right occupation is easy compared to locating the right organization. There just aren't many really good organizations to work for. That's why employer research is so important. Going to work for a new company is always a risk. Your goal is to reduce those risks and find an organization that matches your needs. In the following nine pages I've described some of the factors you'll want to know about before accepting a position. Failure to consider these factors and to learn as much about the organization as possible, can lead to frustration and even grief. Suppose you're a person who needs a very stable work environment, yet you join a company which is being absorbed by a larger company? What if ethics are very important to you, yet your company misrepresents its ability to make delivery dates? You owe it to yourself to learn as much as possible about these factors. I've tried to stimulate your thinking so you can determine what is important for you.

Advancement

What is the potential for advancement? Some positions are dead ends. There is simply no place else to go. Ask where people in that position have moved to in the past. For advancement the best jobs are with fast growing organizations in fast growing industries. As the organization grows and new positions are created, everyone moves up. Determine whether promotions are given by seniority or ability.

Atmosphere

How does the place feel? Is it light and jovial or do you feel a heavy, serious atmosphere? Are people friendly or is there backbiting? You'll need to use your intuition and sensitivity for this one. Some clues might be a gruff receptionist or people passing in the hall without smiling or saying hi. Don't judge an entire organization by just observing it while waiting in the lobby. If you like what you see, look for supporting evidence that your brief glimpse was accurate. If you don't like what you see, gather further evidence to either confirm or change your initial impression.

Benefits

Does the health insurance cover 100% of hospital, doctor, check up, and prescription costs? Many only cover hospitalization and even then only 80%. Do you receive dental insurance and a life insurance policy? Do you receive disability insurance? Do you pay for any of your own coverage and must you pay extra for family members? Do you get three weeks of vacation after five years, as is common, or must you be there for ten years? Some organizations will allow you to accumulate sick leave and even pay you for a portion of that time after you retire or leave the organization. For executives there are additional benefits or perks, such as a reserved parking space, a company car, a decorating allowance for the office, stock options and a full year's salary if terminated. If it's important, you can inquire whether you could have an additional two weeks off each year at no pay.

Bonuses

Some organizations offer bonuses or profit sharing. Sometimes profit sharing is extended only to management. Bonuses range from twenty-five dollars at Christmas time to several thousand dollars. When formulas are used to determine the bonus it might be by the number of years with the company or a percentage of income.

Dress Code

Some organizations have dress codes, either stated or unstated. IBM male employees, with their dark suits and white shirts, were an example for decades before they loosened up a bit. If you might be bothered by working for an organization with a dress code, check it out. When you go for an interview observe the clothing to determine if there appears to be a formal or informal dress code.

Employee Suggestions

Do you like to offer suggestions and have them adopted? Part of your success will depend on the openness of your boss. During your interviews you'll want to assess this quality in your prospective boss. Some organizations have formal suggestion programs and give financial awards to people offering money saving suggestions. Boeing has a program where the cost savings are computed and the employee receives 10% of what will be saved during the first year, up to $5,000.

Environment, Physical

Are you happy in a cramped office with no windows, and drab walls, sitting at an old gray metal desk? If so, physical environment will hardly be an issue for you. You'll be satisfied almost anywhere. Some people need a much different environment. It could be open spaces, bright colors, lots of windows, fresh air, the absence of odors or loud noises, beautifully landscaped grounds, a pleasant eating facility, and quiet places to eat or talk outside.

Ethics And Integrity Of The Organization

You will want to determine ethics and integrity at several levels: top management, your immediate boss, your coworkers, and those who have direct contact with customers. First you need to be clear on your own ethics. Here are some of the things that often bother people: the organization does not keep promises, sells known defective products, bribes politicians and purchasing agents, postpones paying its bills as long as possible, tells customers the product has been fixed when it really hasn't, constantly looks for shortcuts which also decrease quality, backs out of commitments, misrepresents its products, doesn't back up its warranties adequately, abuses its employees, terminates employees unfairly, lies to customers, and overbills customers whenever possible. These are just a few examples.

Family Owned Company

Family owned companies seem to be some of the best or worst companies to work for. Dynamic family owned companies can make quick decisions, take risks that would be impossible for a publicly held company, and can be exciting, rewarding places to work. Stagnant family owned businesses which have been handed down through two or more generations can be very frustrating places to work. Some company owners are so autocratic and filled with "yes men" that they are almost impossible to work for. The real question is not whether the company is family owned, but how well managed it is.

Flexible/Rigid Structure

Is everything done by the book or is there flexibility? A flexible organization can change plans or policies when the situation requires it and cares more for results than tradition.

Goals of the Organization

What are the organization's goals? Is the organization trying to increase its market share, hire more minorities, develop new products each year, decrease its defective products, expand into new geographic areas, or decrease turnover? Knowing the goals of an organization or a department can be very valuable in determining whether you want to be a part of it.

Growth Potential

Where can you go with the organization? Advancement is part of growth potential but there are other ways to experience personal growth: attending company sponsored seminars, taking company paid college courses, being given new responsibilities, or working on projects that expose you to new ideas or experiences.

History Of The Company

Just knowing that the company lost money last year does not tell you a great deal. Overall the company may have a very good profit history. Where has the company been and where is it going? Has it been involved with mergers? Has it bought out other companies? How long has it been in business? Is it making the same types of products it started with? Have there been any major shakeups in the company? How did the company fare during the last recession?

Innovative

Innovative organizations seem to be more fun to work for. There's usually more challenge as they try new things, whether it's developing new products or implementing new management techniques.

Location

How far are you willing to commute? Does the organization have multiple local offices where you could be transferred to? Is it located in a safe or dangerous area?

Management Philosophy

McGregor developed the concept of Theory Y and Theory X companies. Each organization has a personality of its own which is usually determined by the management philosophy espoused by top management. Basically, Theory X companies believe that people don't like to work and must continually be pressured with threats, discipline, or monetary incentives. They must continually be watched and their production must be monitored. Managers tend to be autocratic and domineering. Rarely will they listen to criticism or implement ideas that originated in the lower ranks. Theory Y companies operate on the assumption that people have a psychological need to work, and that given the right environment, will rarely miss work, will work hard, and will produce high quality products. Managers tend to be democratic and use participative management to obtain greater results. Theory Y managers encourage cooperation and working out problems together.

Management Structure

The major distinction is between centralized or decentralized management. In centralized management all major decisions are made at the home office. With decentralized management a district office or a manufacturing plant is allowed to make all but the most major decisions without prior approval from home office. There are advantages and disadvantages to both methods.

Office Politics

Some companies are famous for their intrigues. Often the back-biting and fighting for position is actually encouraged by the president who purposely plays off one executive against the other. Such infighting is never beneficial to the employees or shareholders. Competition within an organization can be healthy, but it can easily cross over into backstabbing and empire building. Essentially you want to determine if the organization is experiencing infighting and dirty politics. Most will want to avoid those organizations and the only way to discover it is through insiders. Government agencies and non-profit organizations can be among the worst.

Progressive

Progressive firms are tying new things. If you have a hard time adapting to change, stay away from them. Progressive firms are at the forefront of hiring and promoting women and minorities, improving pollution controls, contributing some of their profits for the betterment of their community, demonstrating concern for employees, and trying methods such as participative management, management by objectives, flex-time, profit sharing, and total quality programs.

Parent Company/Subsidiaries

Small- to medium-size companies usually retain their name even after they've been bought out by a larger company. *Who Owns Whom* is an excellent resource to discover if a potential employer owns subsidiaries or is owned by another company. As part of long range planning, working for a subsidiary is one way to eventually move up with the parent company. If your potential company has just recently been acquired, it may face some real shakeups in the coming months.

Problems

Most companies have some skeletons in their closets. Your goal is to discover them before you start the job. Recently the vice president of a major company was hired away to become president of a somewhat smaller company, only to discover that he had been lied to about its financial strength. The company was near bankruptcy. An accountant was hired as controller of a company only to discover that funds had been misappropriated by company officers several years before. The three previous controllers, each of whom had stayed only about six months, had bailed out while they could. This controller unfortunately was still around when federal investigations began and his reputation was tarnished, although he had nothing to do with the scandal. Existing or potential problems might be takeovers or mergers, bankruptcy, scandals waiting to be discovered, old outdated products which will soon lead to decreased sales, union problems, or a lawsuit which could ruin the company.

Products/Services

Find out everything you can about a company's products. Annual reports are one of the best sources because they generally describe each subsidiary's products and also show pictures. By researching the products you can determine your interest. Can you relate to the product or services? Do you believe they have value?

Profits/Sales Volume

Knowing both the profits and sales volume of a company can be very enlightening. A highly profitable company can afford to take risks and try new things. A company which has lost money for several years has retrenched and usually cares more about survival than its employees.

Relocation

All national companies relocate managers from time to time but they have varying policies. With some you can refuse one or more relocations with no stigma. At others, turning down a relocation may mean no hope for future promotions. You'll want to know how soon a relocation might occur, how frequently they may occur, and where you might be sent. Most relocations involve promotions but not always. You also need to know what you can expect from your employer. Will they make it worthwhile?

If it's a promotion you should not only receive a raise but also an increased standard of living. When moving from Biloxi, Mississippi to New York, the difference in the cost of living is tremendous. More than one executive has found that the same house he just sold for $550,000 costs $750,000 in the new city. Find out what the company will do if you can't sell your home. The progressive firms will buy it from you at a fair market value and then sell it themselves. Learn as much as you can about relocation without having to ask your interviewer. Invariably this requires inside information. Until you've been offered the job, don't ask about relocation. Most employers will explain their policy, but if not, you definitely need to know before accepting the position.

Reputation

Every organization has a reputation. Local companies have local reputations and national companies have national reputations. Consumer product companies have reputations based primarily on their products. Your best source of information is insiders. For feature articles look in *Infotrac, Readers Guide to Periodical Literature,* and *Business Periodicals Index.*

Research

What percentage of sales is being plowed back into R&D? Dollars alone won't create new technologies, but it sure helps. Several years ago a cartoon showed a board of directors meeting, with the chairman pointing to a chart indicating a steady decline in sales and saying, "I don't understand it, we make the best buggy whip in the country."

The firm had obviously not been pumping any money into R&D. Only companies with a vision will invest a high percentage of their sales dollars into R&D. A shortsighted president, or one who doesn't expect to be around long, will concentrate on the short-term profit picture, to the detriment of future profitability. Learn where the company you're researching stands compared to others in the same industry.

Size

Large and small companies each have their advantages. Large companies may offer higher pay and more security but may cause you to become over specialized. Smaller companies typically offer greater opportunity to handle varied responsibilities and work on a project from start to finish. Companies under 20 employees account for only about 20% of all employment, but nearly 70% of the new jobs created in the last ten years. Don't be fooled by stereotypes or even your own experience. Don't say "I'll never work for another big company, you're just a number." Even big companies are divided into divisions, branches and departments. What you experienced may have been peculiar to *that* company, and would not be true of other large companies.

Stability

Stability and security go together. Large, more established firms tend to be stable. In times of recession they have good lines of credit to help survive the rough times. Stability can be measured in many ways: How regularly has the company made a profit? Has it always paid dividends? How many chief executive officers has the company had in the last 20 years? Have there been wild fluctuations in profits? Are employees loyal and do they work for the company for a long time? The number of CEO's a company has had tells a lot. Charles Revson, the owner of Revlon, was famous for canning CEO's every 2–3 years over personality clashes. Such changes can have a tremendous effect on long range planning and policies: one CEO believes in dress codes, the next one doesn't; one CEO insists on total corporate secrecy while the next tries to keep employees informed; one CEO hates unions with a passion while the next accepts them as a force to be reckoned with.

Training

Some companies are famous for their training programs. Merrill Lynch, for example, has trained many of the stock brokers in this country. Going to work for a company which provides thorough training can be especially helpful in your career. Employers will recognize you received solid training and this will make you more desirable. While valuable, don't assume that such formal training is the only factor to consider. Smaller companies may not be able to send you to the San Francisco headquarters for three weeks of training, but they may provide excellent on-the-job training.

Training that is intended to help you advance is valuable. This can take the form of tuition reimbursement at local colleges, sending employees to training centers, sending employees to local seminars, and bringing in outside consultants for trainings. Commitment to training is a good way to test a company's commitment to its employees and to its own future.

Tuition Reimbursement

It's nice to work for a firm that invests in its employees. Some companies will pay for tuition only if the course is directly related to the job, while others are more liberal. The amount can range from 50 100%, usually on the condition that you pass the course. Some companies strongly encourage their employees to use the program while others are rather reluctant.

Turnover

Greater than average turnover can signal serious problems with the job or the organization. Find out how many people have held your position in the last five years and where they are today. If five people have held the position and two were fired and three quit, I think you might have reservations about the job. Find out why they were fired and what caused the others to quit. Why weren't any of them promoted? Generally you would save your question until the second interview and then simply ask, "How many people have held this position in the last five years?" If the employer simply gives a number, without elaborating, follow up with, "Why did they leave?" It's a good sign if several have been promoted. If more than one person was fired, ask for the reason. You may determine that the factors causing the others to be fired, might get you fired as well.

Appendix A

IDENTIFYING YOUR TOP SKILLS

TRANSFERABLE SKILLS

Transferable skills are those skills that most people have at some skill level, and are useful in numerous occupations. The ability to build rapport, for example, is useful in many occupations, while the ability to program in COBOL is useful in only a few occupations and is therefore not a transferable skill. Selling transferable skills during interviews is particularly powerful. The skills you find in the following list of 261 transferable skills will enhance the transferable skills you identified in your accomplishments.

Transferable skills include finger dexterity, figuring out how things work, visualizing in three dimensions, and motivating people. Transferable skills develop early and can continue to improve throughout life. Many have traced their most valued transferable skills back to preteen years. Jan, a graphics artist, began drawing realistic animals at age six. Bill, an engineer, began designing and building model airplanes at age eight. Keith, an electronics technician, began fixing radios at age ten.

Work content skills, or people's specialized skills, are built upon transferable skills. Without the prerequisite transferable skills, a person will never develop competence with a work content skill. If a person lacks finger dexterity or eye-hand coordination (transferable skills), that person will not succeed in typing or surgery (work content skills).

Once you complete this exercise, you'll be clear on the transferable skills that you should emphasize in your interviews.

RATING YOURSELF ON TRANSFERABLE SKILLS

1. Rate yourself on all 261 transferable skills. Rate yourself quickly and spontaneously. Do not take time to analyze yourself.

2. Rate yourself using a scale of 1–10. A 10 is one of your absolutely top skills, while a 1 is a skill you have tried to use but failed miserably. You have used virtually all of these skills. Some you have used on jobs, while others were used in school, in hobbies, in volunteer activities, or in everyday living.

3. Rate yourself on all the individual skills and then come back and rate yourself on each of the 23 skill clusters. When giving yourself an overall rating, **do not average the scores.** Example:

9 Human Relations Skills

9 Sensitivity to others
8 Treating people fairly
10 Listening intently
9 Communicating warmth
7 Establishing rapport
6 Understanding human behavior
9 Empathy
10 Tactfulness
8 Cooperative team member
8 Avoiding stereotyping people
8 Feeling comfortable with different kinds of people

4. With a highlighter go through the list and highlight your top 50 skills and your top ten skill clusters. Once you have identified your top skills you can look for opportunities to sell them in interviews. For each skill recall one or two experiences where you used the skill and jot down a few words so you'll be able to recall which experience you were referring to. Practice describing the experiences so that during an interview you can tell vivid yet concise stories. In this way, whenever you want to sell a specific skill, you will have at least one example that proves you have that skill.

One effective interviewing technique is to mention a broad skill (such as a skill cluster title like planning skills) as one of your strengths and then mention 3–5 of the specific skills included in that cluster. In response to "What is your greatest strength?" you might say, "I would have to say it's my planning skills. I'm very good at planning projects and programs, anticipating problems before they occur, considering all the details of a project, and finishing projects on schedule. A good example of that would be . . ." All of the specific skills came right out of the skills list. Of course you could also pull in skills you had identified in your accomplishments as well. Feel free to reword the skills so they seem more natural to you as you talk about them.

TRANSFERABLE SKILLS

_____ Human Relations Skills

Sensitivity to others/Treating people fairly
Listening intently
Communicating warmth
Establishing rapport
Understanding human behavior
Empathy
Tactfulness
Cooperative team member
Avoiding stereotyping people
Feeling comfortable with different kinds of people
Fun person to work with
Dealing effectively with conflict

_____ Helping Skills

Helping people
Patient with difficult people
Responsive to people's feelings and needs
Counseling/Empowering/Encouraging people
Assisting people in making decisions
Enhancing people's self-esteem
Helping people help themselves
Encouraging others to expand and grow

_____ Training/Instructing Skills

Instilling the love of a subject
Perceptively answering questions
Explaining difficult ideas and concepts
Creating a stimulating learning environment

Enabling self-discovery
Encouraging creativity
Teaching at the person's or group's level
Developing training materials that enhance learning
Keeping classes interesting
Assessing learning styles of individuals and tailoring training
Quickly establishing rapport with a group
Maintaining productive group discussions

_____ Leadership Skills

A leader
Motivating/Inspiring people
People believe in you/trust you
Causing change
Making difficult decisions
Decisive in crisis situations
Sound judgment in emergencies
A person of vision
Getting others to share your vision
Recognizing the need for change and willing to undertake it
Sensing when to compromise and when to fight

_____ Managing Skills

Seeing the big picture
Completing projects on time
Setting priorities
Breaking through red tape
Managing projects
Negotiating and getting desired results

Making effective recommendations

Anticipating problems and issues and preparing alternatives

Taking the initiative when opportunity appears

Handling details well without losing sight of the big picture

Implementing new programs

Working effectively with superiors and people in other work units

Turning around negative situations

Obtaining allies

_____ Supervising Skills

Getting maximum output from people

Understanding human motivation

Developing a team that truly works together

Training and developing staff

Developing a smooth functioning organization

Supervising difficult people

Delegating work effectively

Consistently recruiting and hiring good promotable people

Increasing morale

Staying in touch/communicating with staff

Reducing turnover

_____ Persuading Skills

Influencing others' ideas and attitudes

Mediating between groups

Obtaining consensus among diverse groups

Effectively selling ideas to top people

Really listening to people and sensing their true needs

Selling products/services

Selling ideas to others

Selling yourself

Closing a deal

Helping people see the benefits of a course of action

_____ Speaking Skills

Holding the attention of a group

"Reading" a group

Thinking quickly on your feet

Using humor

Handling questions well

Getting a group to relate to you

Making convincing arguments

Providing clear explanations of complex topics

Presenting ideas in a logical integrated way

_____ Numerical Skills

Solid ability with basic arithmetic

Multiplying numbers in your head

Gaining lots of valuable information from graphs, tables, and charts

Quickly spotting numerical errors

Sensing when an answer or number could not logically be correct

Storing large amounts of numerical data in your head

Making decisions based on numerical data

Making rough calculations/estimates in your mind

Analyzing statistical data

_____ Financial Skills

Developing a budget

Staying within a budget

Finding bargains

Estimating costs

Eye for a profit

Recognizing money making opportunities

Managing money/making money grow

Setting financial priorities

Developing cost cutting solutions

Understanding economic principles

_____ Office Skills

Making arrangements
Scheduling
Expediting
Concentrating on details
Efficient with paperwork
Using the telephone to get things done
Knowing how to get information
Organizing an office
Organizing records
Creating systems for data storage/ retrieval
Memory for detail
Thorough understanding of regulations and procedures
Cutting through red tape to achieve a goal
Expert at using the system to resolve a problem
Learning office procedures quickly
Proofreading, correcting

_____ Body Skills

Finger dexterity
Hand dexterity
Eye-hand coordination
Physical coordination
Quick reflexes/reactions
Walking long distances
Strong arms/legs/back
Lifting/carrying
Physical endurance
Steady hands
Depth perception
Sense of rhythm
Working quickly with hands and fingers
Sense of taste/smell
Sense of hearing
Sensitive touch
Able to see/spot things others miss
Enduring pain or discomfort

_____ Mechanical and Tool Skills

Improvising with a machine or tool
Assembling/building/installing
Precision work
Operating power tools
Using hand tools
Operating machinery/equipment
Fixing and repairing
Troubleshooting/diagnosing problems
Figuring out how things work
Understanding manuals/diagrams
Mechanical ability

_____ Idea Skills

Imaginative
Conceiving and generating ideas and concepts
Improvising
Innovative/Creative
Conceptualizing
Synthesizing ideas and creating something new
Seeing the big picture
Recognizing new applications for ideas or things
Open to new ideas from others
Able to look beyond the way things have been done in the past
Finding ways to improve things

_____ Writing Skills

Overall writing ability
Writing clear concise sentences
Grammatically correct writing
Strong, versatile vocabulary
Developing a logical, well organized theme
Vividly describing feelings, people, senses, and things
Developing logical and persuasive points
Summarizing and condensing written material
Editing/strengthening someone's writing
Humorous writing
Simplifying scientific and technical material
Making "dry" subjects interesting
Writing letters/memos/reports

Writing position papers/research reports
Writing news articles
Writing speeches
Writing manuals
Writing proposals for funding
Writing poetry/song lyrics
Writing fiction/satire
Writing slogans/advertising

_____ Planning Skills

Planning programs or projects
Setting attainable goals
Determining priorities
Forecasting/Predicting
Scheduling effectively
Time management
Accurately assessing available resources
Anticipating problems before they develop
Finishing projects on time
Developing innovative methods and techniques
Considering all the details of a project

_____ Troubleshooting Skills

Anticipating problems
Solving problems/Untangling messes
Bringing order out of a chaotic situation
Determining root causes
Recognizing and resolving problems while they're still minor
Able to come in and take control of a situation
Selecting the most effective solution
Improvising under stress
Staying calm in emergencies
People have confidence that now you're here, things will be taken care of

_____ Organizing Skills

Organizing/Planning events
Organizing offices
Organizing systems
Organizing people to take action
Organizing data/information
Making sure people are in the right place at the right time

_____ Researching/Investigating Skills

Working on research projects
Researching in a library
Knowing how to find information
Investigating
Following up on leads
Organizing large amounts of data and information
Keeping an open mind
Summarizing findings
Relentlessly seeking an answer
Gathering information from people
Producing surveys or questionnaires
Detecting cause and effect relationships
Using statistical data
Weaving threads of evidence together
Developing hypotheses

_____ Analyzing Skills

Interpreting/evaluating data
Evaluating reports and recommendations
Analyzing trends
Accurately predicting what will occur based on facts, trends, and intuition
Designing systems to collect or analyze information
Weighing pros and cons of an issue
Simplifying complex ideas
Seeing both sides of an issue
Clarifying problems
Diagnosing needs/problems
Constantly looking for a better way
Identifying more efficient ways of doing things
Getting to the heart of an issue

_____ Artistic Skills

Artistic
Sense of color combinations
Drawing/Painting scenes/people
Envisioning the finished product/
sensing how it will all come
together
Sense of proportion and space
Envisioning in three dimensions
Spatial perception
Designing visual aids
Calligraphy/Lettering
Capturing a feeling, mood, or idea
through photography, drawing,
sculpting, cartoons, music, etc.
Developing visually pleasing
things (charts, reports, manu-
als, etc.)
Sensing what will work and look
right

_____ Performing Skills

Poised and confident before
groups
Showmanship
Responsive to audience moods
Making people laugh
Getting an audience involved with
you
Getting an audience to relate to
you
Getting an audience enthusiastic
or excited
Eliciting strong emotions from an
audience
Entertaining an audience
Playing musical instruments
Dancing/Acting/Singing

WORK CONTENT SKILLS AND INTERVIEWS

Work content skills are skills that people get paid for using. During interviews you must sell your work content skills. To prepare for interviews you should list all of the work content skills you believe may be useful to you in the types of jobs you are seeking. Practice describing your experience with each skill and sell it to its fullest. Do not exaggerate, but definitely do not undersell yourself.

Work content skills are the specialized skills and knowledge developed throughout life. They are primarily learned in vocational schools or colleges, though apprenticeships, by watching experts, by practicing, or by self-study. A surgeon memorizes parts of the body, learns to recognize symptoms, watches operations, and then practices surgical procedures. A mechanic memorizes the parts of an engine, learns how to diagnose problems, and practices overhauling the engine.

Work content skills are the least transferable of the three types of skills (personality, transferable, work content). A car mechanic's knowledge of automobile engines would provide little benefit if he or she were required to repair a jet engine. However, should the mechanic choose to study jet engine mechanics, his/her manual dexterity and ability to figure out how mechanical devices work (transferable skills), and his/her inquisitiveness and resourcefulness (personality skills) would all be great assets.

During interviews it is often necessary to sell exposure to a particular skill. In other words, you may never have actually done the activity that the employer is looking for, but you have observed others do it, you have read about it or studied it, or you have assisted someone who has done it. Having done a specific task is best, but having exposure will put some weight on your side of the scale. On the other hand, saying you've never done it but you'd be glad to learn, will do little. See page 47 on exposure and page 83 on avoiding saying "I've never done it."

You never know when a skill could have a real payoff for you. It might come down to you and one other person for a particular job. Through the interview process you may recognize a need for one of your skills which is not typically utilized in that position. By mentioning to the employer how that skill could come in handy at times, it could just tip the balance in your favor. If you don't take time to assess those skills now, you may not think of them later.

Guidelines For Identifying Work Content Skills

1. There are over 100,000 work content skills. Because of the vast number it is necessary for you to identify as many of your own work content skills as possible.

2. Knowledge itself is a work content skill. Examples include, knowledge of the causes of the Civil War, knowing all the bones and muscles in the body, knowing all the cloud formations and what they mean regarding weather, understanding electricity, and visually recognizing one hundred strains of bacteria. To identify knowledge-based work content skills, recall courses you've taken and books you've studied, then recall the subject matter. Don't worry if you can't remember the details, that's to be expected. To list a knowledge-based work content skill does not require that you can presently explain all of the details. The fact that you knew the material at one time is reason enough to list it. Keep in mind, it's always easier to learn a subject the second time than it was the first.

3. Your hobbies and free time activities are a rich source of work content skills. People have turned hobbies into lucrative jobs. To list a work content skill requires only that you have done it, not that you are an expert. Skill clusters that you might use would include Mechanical, Tools/Equipment, Carpentry/Repairs, House work, Kitchen, Yard/Garden, Home, Office, Sports, Arts/Crafts.

4. Begin by developing a list of all the skill clusters you will be using. Every part-time or summer job you ever had should have a

cluster. The cluster titles might simply be, Bucking Hay, Burger King, Waitressing, Mowing Lawns, Retail Clerk. Then list skill clusters that result from your education. If you are a college graduate you should list your major and your minor as separate skill clusters. Then recall some other subjects in which you took several courses. I majored in history and minored in political science, so I would use both of those clusters. I took two courses in economics plus I continue to read a lot about economics, so that would be another cluster. I took an art appreciation course, which I enjoyed, but I have done little reading about art since taking that class in 1971. Because of that I would not create an art appreciation cluster.

Next list your hobbies. If you are a fairly serious photographer, create a photography cluster. People often hesitate to list hobbies because they feel they are not good enough. Just because you are not a graduate of a major photography school, and haven't had a photograph printed on the cover of *Life Magazine*, doesn't mean you should not have a photography skill cluster. If you have read books and magazines on photography, have two or three lenses, and put genuine effort into obtaining high quality photos, you should have a photography cluster. I think you get the idea. I have used photography just as an example. If you work around the home you should have such clusters as Tools/ Equipment, Carpentry, Plumbing, Electrical, Automotive, etc.

5. For each cluster list as many skills as you can by listing whatever pops into your mind. Don't eliminate anything because you feel you are not skilled enough in it or feel that you could never get a job doing that. Make a game out of this exercise and identify at least 150 work content skills.

Work quickly when identifying the skills learned in summer jobs or part-time jobs, particularly if you held the job more than ten years ago. I wrote the skill cluster for bucking hay. It took less than two minutes because there just wasn't much to remember. There was no need to wrack my brain coming up with more than five items.

6. Avoid being too general. For example, it would not be adequate for a contractor to simply list carpentry as a work content skill. It should be broken down into its components such as: building concrete forms; laying foundations; building walls; installing doors, windows, and cabinets; constructing roof trusses; and installing sheet rock. The list would also include any types of machines, equipment, or tools that have been used.

7. When looking at a past job or hobby, try to list all of the things you learned in that job. One way to identify skills is to visualize yourself doing that job or hobby. What are the things you do and what areas of knowledge do you use? Remember, knowledge is a work content skill.

List those things as quickly as they come to mind. Do not filter anything out just because you feel you are not that skilled at it. Don't worry about that because later you will have an opportunity to go through your list and identify those skills you are good enough in to get paid for.

Another way to identify skills is to ask yourself what causes someone who is really talented to stand apart from the rest. That will get you thinking about those special abilities and areas of knowledge.

8. Treat this as a game. The game is to come up with as many skills as possible. Upon finishing this exercise, many people are amazed that they know how to do so many things. List every conceivable work content skill. Some seem mundane or minor, but that's okay, list all the small ones with the big ones. It can be enjoyable considering all the things you know how to do.

9. Place a check by those skills which may be useful in future jobs you may apply for.

10. Place an X by those skills you are skilled at enough to be paid to do.

WORK CONTENT SKILLS

The following work content skills have been provided to give you a clearer idea of the types of skills which should be labeled work content skills. Feel free to use the cluster titles or the skills themselves, but this list is only intended to give you ideas.

Note the claims adjusting skill cluster below. This example is included to show what a really complete skill cluster might look like. This person did a thorough analysis of what he did on the job, but notice that it is not a list of duties, it is a list of skills.

You should also realize that these skill clusters were supplied by many different people.

Claims Adjusting
Estimating cost of repairing cars, boats, homes
Read the crash book guides to know how many hours to remove and replace bumpers, fenders, and other parts
Know all the tools used by body shop mechanics
Know exactly how body panels will be straightened and how much time it should take
Know how paint is matched

Know all the preparatory steps to painting
Negotiating with body shop managers
Explaining to insureds and claimants why a part does not need to be replaced
Being fair but getting repairs done at the lowest cost possible
Knowing how to threaten a body shop manager that I will pull the car and take it to a different shop if he won't get reasonable

Know when to total a car and how to accurately assess its value

Finding witnesses of accidents

Getting good statements from insureds, claimants, and witnesses

Knowing how to settle small injuries quickly and inexpensively to avoid financial exposure

Knowing how much an injury is worth

Being fair with injured claimants and getting them to trust me and not hire an attorney

Really getting the facts about an accident

Studying the facts so can be in a strong bargaining position when negotiating with attorneys

Know when to call the bluff of an attorney

Settle even big cases by negotiating fairly but effectively with claimants without attorneys

Write well-written reports for the file

Arts and Crafts

Macramé

Knitting

Crochet

Weaving

Latch hook rug making

Sewing simple and complex patterns

Silkscreening

Stained glass, soldering

Making clay

Pottery making and firing

Candle making

Understanding how colors work together

Knowing psychological effects of color

Charcoal sketching

Painting—oil, water, tempera, landscapes, portraits, modern art

Making dolls

Drawing cartoons

Tools/Equipment

Hammer, screwdriver, pliers, hand saw

Crescent wrench, grinder, glass cutter

Compressor, generator

Airless paint sprayers

Socket set, wire cutters

Soldering iron

Electric drill, hand drill

Table saw

Router, jointer, planer

Drill press

Chain saw

Level

Skill saw

Forklift

Hand truck

Winch

Backhoe

10-speed two ton truck

Office

MS DOS/ Windows commands

Answer phones on a 20-line system

Programmable calculator

Send and receive e-mail

Microfiche reader-printer

Troubleshoot fax machines

Troubleshoot photocopiers

Microsoft Word, Word Perfect

Excel

Lotus 123

    Creating spreadsheets

    Using macros

Statistics

(knowledge gained from courses)

Probability

Chi-square analysis

Simple regression analysis

Sample selection processes

Confidence intervals

Prepare frequency distributions

Median, mean, mode

Normal curve

Standard deviation

Standard scores, Z scores
Correlation—Pearson, product-
  moment
Random sample
Null hypothesis
Type I, Type II errors
F distribution
ANOVA

Bookkeeping
General ledger
Accounts payable ledger
Accounts receivable ledger
Write checks
Balance checking account
Check posting
Making deposits
Trial balance report
Keep full set of books
Credit analysis
Collections
Shipping invoices
Receivable invoices
Credit invoices
Debit Invoices
Medical insurance forms

Bucking Hay
Driving trucks
Hooking up loader
Using bale hooks
Techniques of stacking bales
Tying bales down

Burger King
Taking customers' orders
Getting customers to say yes to
  fries and cheese on burger
Giving change
Preparing french fries
Making sundaes

Carpentry/Repairs
Hammer a nail straight
Put together shelves and book-
  cases
Roofing
Framing
Installing sheetrock
Taping and mudding sheetrock
Installing siding
Installing gutters
Cutting glass and installing win-
  dows
Installing doors and locks
Installing insulation
Plumbing for a new sink
Installing drain pipes around the
  house
Building a fence
Built a deck—designed, framed,
  built stairs
Installed wiring
Installed dimming switch, light
  sockets
Refinished oak floor
Building concrete forms
Pouring concrete
Finish concrete work

Mechanical
Change oil and tires
Put on tire chains
Charge battery and use jumper
  cables
Use timing light
Tune engine
Lubricate chassis
Welding
Replace brake shoes
Rebuild engine
Align front end
Fixed grandfather clock
Repaired small electric motor
Fixed a copy machine—bad circuit

Selling

Really listening to customers
Identifying needs and problems of customers
Getting customers to tell me the real objections
Establishing rapport with potential customers
Developing strong product knowledge
Keeping up-to-date on new products
Always know what the competition is doing
Serving as a consultant to customers
Researching accounts before calling on them
Able to get through to decision makers
Put together thorough bids and proposals
Very complete with paperwork
Able to sense buying signals
Know how to close and get the sale

Ceramics

Clay characteristics
Glaze formulas
Firing techniques
  Raku
  High firing
  Bisque firing
  Glaze firing
  Low firing
  Luster firing
Kiln loading
Wheel throwing—centering, opening, lifting, plates, bowls, cups
Handle pulling
Slab building
Texture techniques—ribbing, ruffing, burnishing
Glaze application—dripping, stripping, painting, spraying
Trimming
Drying
Mold use
Wedging

BIBLIOGRAPHY OF EXCELLENT INTERVIEWING RESOURCES

For reviews on these and other books visit www.cmr-mvp.com

101 Dynamite Answers To Interview Questions: Sell Your Strengths, Caryl and Ron Krannich, Impact Publications, 1999

Get Hired! Winning Strategies to Ace The Interview, Paul Green, Bard Press, 1996

Tom Jackson's Interview Express, Tom Jackson and Bill Buckingham, Times Books, 1993

Interview Power (video), Tom Washington, NationalVideo Profiles, 1995

Knock 'Em Dead 2000, Martin Yate, Adams Media Corp., 2000

Negotiating Your Salary: How To Make $1000 a Minute, Jack Chapman, Ten Speed Press, 1996

60 Seconds & You're Hired, Robin Ryan, Robin Ryan, Inc., 1994

Sweaty Palms: The Neglected Art Of Being Interviewed, Anthony Medley, Ten Speed Press, 1992

The Complete Job Search Handbook, Howard Figler, Owl Books, 1999

INDEX

SERVICES PROVIDED BY CMR

Skills Identification

It's great if you can find someone who will help you identify the skills, qualities, and characteristics within your accomplishments. When that's not possible, we at Career Management Resources can help. Each member of our staff has helped identify the skills contained in hundreds of accomplishments. A benefit of having a professional help you is that we can identify more skills within each accomplishment and word them in such a way that they have more impact.

Generally it takes 2–4 hours to identify the skills in ten accomplishments. We charge $95 per hour. You can hire us for as few or as many hours as you like. Send us your hand written or word processed accomplishments with a three inch margin on the left and one accomplishment per page. Legible handwriting is acceptable, but it really is best for you and for us if each accomplishment is printed out on a laser or ink jet printer.

Send us your accomplishments and phone numbers with the best times to reach you weekdays and weekends. We will then call you to arrange a time to review your accomplishments with you. If you have questions, call us at 425/454-6982.

OTHER RESOURCES BY TOM WASHINGTON

Interview Power ($29.95)

Interview Power (the video), National Video Profiles, 1995. Written by Tom Washington, this video takes key concepts from *Interview Power: Selling Yourself Face To Face* and uses video to *show* the viewer how to interview effectively. *Interview Power* demonstrates how to impact the interviewer with stories and anecdotes. You have the opportunity to see and hear how to best perform in an interview. This 70-minute video will enable you to get job offers that previously might have gone to your competitors. Purchase *Interview Power* and get a 30-day, money-back guarantee.

What others are saying about *Interview Power:*

Interview Power is a state-of-the-art presentation and guide for today's job seeker. This video is packed with useful information. The wealth of teaching examples are guaranteed to improve the presentation of even the most confident and prepared interviewee.
Larry Gaffin, President, Center For Life Decisions

Anyone using these techniques will increase their self-confidence and effectiveness in selling themselves at an interview. The systematic approach given in this video provides the best method I've seen for fully preparing for successful interviewing.
John Knapp, Senior Human Resources Administrator, Olin Aerospace Co.

Excellent basic video with many tips and techniques for job interviewing.
David Roy, Director, Christian Employment Network

Every question you're likely to get about "Why should we hire you?" is covered with practical examples. It sets you up for no-surprise interviews.
Jack Chapman, author of *Negotiating Your Salary: How To Make $1000 a Minute*

The Psych Yourself Up Audio Tape ($9.95)

The Psych Yourself Up Audio Tape is designed to be listened to just prior to leaving for an interview, or on your way to an interview while driving or riding a bus. It reminds you of all the positive things you will do in your interview and does so in a motivating and calming way. It can give you just the edge you need to fully sell yourself. Author/Reader: Tom Washington. Read the text of the audio by visiting our web site at www.cmr-mvp.com.

Resume Power ($14.95)

Resume Power: Selling Yourself On Paper has been among the best selling resume guides each year since first published in 1985 (currently in its fourth revised edition). It contains practical guidance for preparing a truly powerful resume. *Resume Power* is an easy-to-understand, step-by-step guide to writing an effective, interview-getting resume. Quick to read and packed with information, *Resume Power* answers virtually every resume question you may have, and gives practical examples that show you how to write and design the best resume possible.

If you want more job offers, *Resume Power* gives you time-tested advice that will help you achieve your goals. *Resume Power* is the most thorough and complete resume guide available. No other book comes close to offering so many useful tips and insights—all to help you write a great resume. (*Resume Power* is available at all finer bookstores)

What Others Are Saying About *Resume Power*

Very few resume books are good. *Resume Power* is one of those few. The author discusses each section of the resume in detail, answering all the typical questions.
Journal of College Placement

Resume Power is thorough and understandable. No gibberish here; it's loaded with practical examples.
The Home Row, **Newsletter for self-employed professional secretaries**

Exceptionally well organized and well written, *Resume Power* is a must for job seekers.
Michael Grubiak, Assistant Dean of Students, Highline Community College

Your book *Resume Power* is the best thing that has ever happened to me. Wow! It has given me so much more confidence.
  R.A. Rough and Ready, California

I just want you to know how fantastically successful your book was to me in my search for employment. A total of fifteen resumes were sent out in a two week period. I got four interviews. I accepted a position where I can better my career.
  J.Y. Fullerton, California

Order Today

Interview Power (VHS video, 70 minutes) @ $29.95   _____
The Psych Yourself Up Audio Tape @ $9.95   _____
Resume Power @ $14.95   _____
Shipping and handling add $3.95 for first item,
     $1.50 for each additional item   _____
Washington residents add 8.6% sales tax   _____
Grand total (U.S. dollars only)   _____

Payment   ❏ Check or Money Order   ❏ Visa   ❏ MasterCard

Account # _____Expiration Date _____

Name (print) _____

Street Address _____

City _____ State _____ Zip _____

Phone (_____) _____

Mail your order to:
  Career Management Resources
  1750 112th N.E. #C-224
  Bellevue, WA 98004

All products have a 30-day money-back guarantee.